Family, Gender, and Law in a Globalizing
Middle East and South Asia

Gender and Globalization
Susan S. Wadley, *Series Editor*

Family, Gender, and Law in a Globalizing Middle East and South Asia

◆ ◆ ◆

Edited by **Kenneth M. Cuno**
and **Manisha Desai**

Syracuse University Press

For a listing of books published and distributed by Syracuse University Press,
visit our Web site at SyracuseUniversityPress.syr.edu.

ISBN: 978-0-8156-3235-1

LIBRARY OF CONGRESS CATALOGING-IN-PUBLICATION DATA
Family, gender, and law in a globalizing Middle East and South Asia / edited by
Kenneth M. Cuno and Manisha Desai. — 1st ed.
     p. cm. — (Gender and globalization)
   Includes bibliographical references and index.
   ISBN 978-0-8156-3235-1 (cloth : alk. paper)
  1. Domestic relations—Middle East.   2. Domestic relations—South Asia.
3. Women—Legal status, laws, etc.—Middle East.   4. Women—Legal status, laws,
etc.—South Asia.   I. Cuno, Kenneth M., 1950–   II. Desai, Manisha.
   KMC156.F36 2009
   346.5401'5—dc22   2009039475

Contents

Table

Acknowledgments

The chapters in this volume were presented in preliminary versions at the international symposium "Family, Gender, and Law in a Globalizing Middle East and South Asia" held at the University of Illinois at Urbana-Champaign on October 7–9, 2004. The symposium was organized by the university's Center for South Asian and Middle Eastern Studies and cosponsored by the Program in Women and Gender in Global Perspectives.

We gratefully acknowledge major funding for the symposium by the Office of the Chancellor of the University of Illinois and the College of Liberal Arts and Sciences, and support from numerous other campus centers, programs and departments. We would also like to thank Marilyn Booth, Thomas Ginsburg, Suad Joseph, Winnifred Poster, Aisha Sobh, and Gail Summerfield for their participation, contributions, and comments during the symposium.

Contributors

FLAVIA AGNES is a women's rights advocate and feminist legal scholar based in Mumbai, India. She is the director of Majlis, a legal advocacy center for women.

ZEHRA F. KABASAKAL ARAT is professor of political science and women's studies at Purchase College of the State University of New York. Her research focuses on human rights, women's rights, and democracy, and her latest publications include *Human Rights Worldwide* (2006) and *Human Rights in Turkey* (2007). She is the founding president of the Human Rights Section of the American Political Science Association and chair of the Human Rights Research Committee of the International Political Science Association.

JUAN COLE is Richard P. Mitchell Collegiate Professor of History at the University of Michigan. He is past president of the Middle East Studies Association of North America and has appeared widely in the print and mass media as a commentator on Middle Eastern and South Asian affairs. His most recent books include *Sacred Space and Holy War* (2002), *Napoleon's Egypt* (2007), and *Engaging the Muslim World* (2009).

KENNETH M. CUNO is associate professor of history at the University of Illinois at Urbana-Champaign. He is writing a history of marriage and family formation in modern Egypt, and his most recent publication is "Divorce and the Fate of the Family in Modern Egypt," in *Family in the Middle East: Ideational Change in Egypt, Iran, and Tunisia*, edited by Kathryn Yount and Hoda Rashad (2008).

MANISHA DESAI is director of the Women's Studies Program at the University of Connecticut. Her research interests include transnational feminism, gender and globalization, and contemporary Indian society. Her latest publication is *Gender and the Politics of Possibilities: Rethinking Globalization* (2009). She is a former president of Sociologists for Women in Society.

SHELLEY FELDMAN is professor of development sociology and director of Feminist, Gender, and Sexuality Studies at Cornell University, and a visiting professor in sociology at Binghamton University. Her ongoing research includes projects on moral regulation, social and spatial restructuring, state formation, and militarization. She is currently the president of the American Institute of Bangladesh Studies and a former director of the South Asia and the Gender and Global Change programs at Cornell. Her publications include *Unequal Burden: Economic Crises, Persistent Poverty, and Women's Work* (1992) and *Informal Work and Social Change* (1998) as well as "Exploring Theories of Patriarchy: A Perspective from Contemporary Bangladesh" (2001) and "Intersecting and Contesting Positions: World Systems, Postcolonial, and Feminist Theory" (2001).

FRANCES S. HASSO is associate professor of sociology and affiliated faculty member in the Institute for Gender, Sexuality, and Feminist Studies at Oberlin College. She has published numerous articles and is the author of *Resistance, Repression, and Gender Politics in Occupied Palestine and Jordan* (2005).

HOMA HOODFAR is professor of anthropology at Concordia University in Montreal, Canada. She has conducted field research on development and social change in Egypt, Iran, and Afghanistan with an emphasis on gender, household, women, religion, and politics in the MENA region as well as Muslim women in diaspora communities. Among her publications are "Women, Religion, and the 'Afghan Education Movement' in Iran" (2007), *The Muslim Veil in North America: Issues and Debates* (2003, with Sajida Alvi and Sheila McDonough), and *Between Marriage and the Market: Intimate Politics and Survival in Cairo* (1997).

FRANCES RADAY is director of the Concord Research Institute for Integration of International Law in Israel at the College of Management and Elias Lieberman Chair in Labour Law at the Hebrew University of Jerusalem (Emerita). She is honorary professor at University College London and has been awarded an honorary doctorate at the University of Copenhagen. Professor Raday has held an appointment as Expert Member of the UN Committee for the Elimination of Discrimination Against Women. As a human rights litigator, Frances Raday was the founding chair of the Legal Centre of the Israel Women's Network. She has appeared as counsel before the High Court of Justice in Israel in precedent-setting labor law, human rights, and discrimination cases. She presently chairs the Law Society's Committee for Advancement of Women.

ZAKIA SALIME is assistant professor in the Sociology and Women's and Gender Studies Departments at Rutgers University. Her publications and research interests include gender, race, empire, the political economy of the "war on terror," development policies in postcolonial contexts, Islamic movements, and the Middle East. Her forthcoming book, tentatively titled "Between Feminism and Islam," looks at the interactions of the feminist and Islamist women's movements in Morocco.

ANITA M. WEISS, professor and department head of the International Studies Program at the University of Oregon, received her Ph.D. in sociology from the University of California at Berkeley. She has published extensively on social development, gender issues, and political Islam in Pakistan. Her current research project is *Interpreting Islam, Modernity, and Women's Rights in Pakistan,* which analyzes how distinct constituencies in Pakistan are grappling with articulating their views on women's rights. She is a member of the editorial boards of *Citizenship Studies* and *Globalizations,* is on the editorial advisory board of Kumarian Press, and currently serves as the treasurer of the American Institute of Pakistan Studies.

LYNN WELCHMAN is professor of law at the School of Law, SOAS, University of London, where she specializes in law and society in the Middle East and North Africa. Previously, she worked with the nongovernmental human rights movement, mostly in Palestine but also elsewhere in the region and internationally.

Introduction

The essays in this collection examine issues of family and gender in relation to law—especially family law—in eleven states of the Middle East and South Asia. The result, we hope, is a comparative picture of how family life and family law (which cannot be separated from gender) have been contested, constructed, and reconstructed in these two regions in the contemporary era.

The linkages between the regions we today call the Middle East and South Asia[1] have been ongoing for more than two millennia. The two regions have been linked by trade; religious and cultural movements; imperial projects from the Greek, Arab, Turko-Afghan, and Mughal to British and French; and today movements of labor, cultural products, and capital. Despite the long and complex nature of these interactions, few scholarly works examine these regions together (for exceptions, see Fawaz and Bayly 2002; and Kandiyoti 1991b).

Our own location in South Asian and Middle Eastern studies facilitated our thinking about these regions together. Comparisons between the Middle East and South Asia today are potentially fruitful, as both regions have multiethnic and multireligious societies in which colonialism, religious laws, modern nation-state building, and women's movements and other political actors have shaped modern family codes. Family law[2] often is a selective codification of religious law, differing for citizens of different

1. We recognize that both these place-names are colonial terms that are highly problematic, but we use them because they are part of both scholarly and popular discourse.

2. Family laws or personal laws pertain to marriage, divorce, child custody, and inheritance, among other issues.

faiths. One consequence is a pattern of contradictory activism by women and other religious and civil actors promoting either a universal civil code, often in conformity with international norms such as those expressed in the Convention on the Elimination of All Forms of Discrimination Against Women (CEDAW, 1979), or, alternatively, a restrictive application of religious laws. A third approach adopted by some Muslim activists, notably in Egypt, accepts the notion of religiously based family law but promotes certain reforms as more consistent with Islam than the existing law, which is said to be based on custom (Singerman 2005).

Given the quite similar debates around family laws in the two regions and the paucity of comparative literature, we organized the symposium "Family, Gender, and Law in a Globalizing Middle East and South Asia," which met in October 2004 at the University of Illinois. The chapters in this volume, to varying degrees, make the following arguments. First, although each chapter focuses on a specific national context, the forces that shape family laws, family, and gender roles have been forged in larger global contexts, an earlier colonial one and the contemporary transnational one. Second, colonial-era family law reform often meant the introduction of European patriarchal norms and the reworking of local ones, usually to the detriment of women's status. Third, local actors, mostly elite men and some women, using nationalist, secular, and religious frames, actively participated in negotiating these changes. Fourth, these new hybrid patriarchies and practices became the basis of family law in the independent nation-states in the region. And finally, family laws continue to be contested by many actors.

In both regions there is an ambivalent view of the modern ideal Western family—a nuclear family based on romantic love—and a tendency to reject some aspects of it in favor of a "traditional" ideal, such as the extended family based on arranged marriage and endogamy. At the same time, "traditional" gender roles have been renegotiated and "traditional" family structures have been redefined owing to increasing female education and participation in the workforce. In debates and struggles over "family," women's bodies and behaviors are often the sites of conflict, and the goal is to shape state law. In what follows we discuss these arguments under four themes: colonial modernity and its contradictions, nationalism and family law, contemporary contestations of family law, and renegotiating gender roles and family.

Colonial Modernity and Its Contradictions

For several decades now, feminist scholars have shown that while colonial powers and administrators saw themselves as bringing "enlightenment" to the "backward" status of colonized women, in reality they both imported their own patriarchal norms and modernized local patriarchies, selecting, homogenizing, and rigidifying diverse local customs and practices. These efforts often led to a decline in women's status (see, for example, Sangari and Vaid 1989). Although this analysis has mostly emerged from work on South Asia, it is also being adopted by scholars in the Middle East.

Feminists, again based on colonialism in South Asia, have also argued that in the colonial period "the woman's question," often conflated with social reform in general, was really a site for colonial and elite local men to argue about their privileges and control over women and property rather than about women's status (Mani 1989). Or, as Gayatri Spivak succinctly questioned, "Can the subaltern speak?" The papers in this volume answer yes they can and do in multiple registers.

As Kenneth Cuno and Flavia Agnes show in chapters 1 and 2, respectively, the Europeanization of local patriarchies was not a unilateral process but one in which local actors, whether elite reformers or ordinary litigants, participated in contesting and negotiating this process. Cuno and Agnes examine the process of codification of family law under semi-colonial or colonial rule in Egypt and India, respectively. In both situations a previously flexible system became more rigid as a result of conformity with European (British and French) standards of legal procedure and judicial organization. Though British administrators and local cultural conservatives agreed that family law should continue to operate according to Islamic and Hindu principles and practices, the more rigid "modern" codes and the manner in which they were applied significantly reshaped the legal terrain on which ordinary Egyptians and Indians found themselves as litigants. In both situations, also, the changes worked to the detriment of the position of women, reinforcing patriarchy within the family. It is especially ironic that these changes occurred at about the same time as the first stirrings of women's movements and nationalism in both Egypt and India. But as we argue below, neither nationalism nor elite women's feminism guarantees the "liberation" of women.

Nationalism and Family Law

Jayawardena (1986) argued in her pathbreaking work on women's movements and nationalism in the third world that women's status and family law often served as bargaining points for the secular versus revivalist factions of nationalist movements, and despite the presence of both elite and poor women's mobilizations, independent nation-states did not always support women's equality in the public sphere, much less in family law. Since then others, such as Charrad (2001), Kandiyoti (1991b) Kaplan, Alarcón, and Moallem (1999), Ranchod Nilsson and Tétreault (2000), and West (1997), have all shown that "modern" nation-states in most postcolonial countries did not "emancipate" women from legal inequality or social inequalities more generally.

In particular, some of these scholars have shown that women's rights in family law have been a casualty of the tension between secularism and freedom of religion. The chapters in Part 2 discuss how multireligious nation-states address this tension. They discuss how religion, custom, and the state are factors in the reproduction of patriarchal norms in family law in three countries that have defined themselves as "modern" and "secular." Israel, discussed by Frances Raday, and India, discussed by Manisha Desai, are comparable insofar as being secular republics officially committed to equal rights for all citizens. Yet neither republic has a Uniform Civil Code governing family law. Rather, family law is governed by multiple religious laws administered according to the interpretations of the leading clerics in each community. The result is a dichotomy between the egalitarian principles proclaimed by the state and to a large extent realized in the public sphere and the enforcement of gender inequality under religious law in the private, familial sphere.

The Turkish Republic, discussed by Zehra Arat, is likewise an officially secular republic but with a Uniform Civil Code adapted in the 1920s from the Swiss civil code. But the abandonment of religious law for European-derived family law meant exchanging one set of gender inequalities for another, in both civil and penal law, albeit reduced in recent decades, under pressure from the European Union.

Contemporary Contestations of Family Law

As discussed in the previous two sections, family laws have been contested in the two regions at least since colonial times. But what differentiates the contemporary contestations are the new forces at play. In particular, the authors in this section identify three new forces: the new global gender-equality regime and transnational feminism, the electoral victories of Islamist parties, and the aftermath of the war in Iraq and the "war on terror."

The "global gender equality regime" (Kardam 2004) of women's rights norms, laws, mechanisms, and structures for monitoring and reporting progress at the governmental level emerged out of the conferences of the International Women's Decade held in Mexico City (1975), Copenhagen (1980), Nairobi (1985), and Beijing (1995). But the impetus for the UN decade and changes in law in various countries itself was a result of complicated negotiations between elite women leaders in government, at the UN, and middle-class and grassroots-based transnational activists from many countries as well as the changing status of women, particularly middle-class women, in countries around the world (Moghadam 2005).

The rise of the global equality regime coincided first with the rise to power of Islamist parties in several countries in both regions. This along with the subsequent invasion by the United States of Afghanistan and Iraq and the "war on terror" that ensued are the other forces that have shaped the contemporary contestations of family law in the region, as discussed in the four case studies in this section.

Juan Cole follows the conflict over the fate of personal status law in post-Baathist Iraq. Lynn Welchman examines recent struggles over the revision of Jordanian personal status law and the simultaneous struggle to create for the first time a unified personal status law in post-Oslo Palestine. Zakia Salime discusses the long-running contest over Morocco's personal status law, the *moudawana*, from independence to the recent revision of the law in 2003, and Anita Weiss analyzes the conflict between Pakistan's federal government and the Islamist-controlled

North West Frontier Province (NWFP) government over the latter's determination to "implement Islam" in law. In all four states and the Palestinian territories, as Welchman puts it, "constructions of 'the family' are . . . key in representations of national identity," although this has taken different forms.

Constructions of the family in Jordan and Morocco are connected with patriarchal constructions of the two monarchies, and their family law was influenced by the rulers' strategy of appealing to tribal identities and hence loyalties. In contrast, Republican and Baathist Iraq adopted state feminist policies aimed at diluting tribal authority and the influence of the clergy, though there were reverses after 1991 due to a weakened Saddam Hussein's need to appease tribal values. Similar to postcommunist Eastern Europe, in post-Baathist Iraq women's gains in legal rights, welfare, and opportunity are likely to be rolled back under the new regime. In Pakistan the Islamist coalition in charge of the NWFP government has drawn on local Pashtun tribal traditions in defining what is "Islamic."

While local feminists have been important in promoting reform, conservatives in every case have tried to portray their efforts as a struggle against global forces that are undermining the national culture. Despite such structural similarities, these contested processes of (re)construction of family law have thus far produced contrasting results because of contrasting political contingencies. Such contrasting consequences are also evident in the negotiations of contemporary gender roles in the region, discussed in the last part of the book.

Renegotiating Gender Roles and Family

The fourth part comprises three studies of "women's roles and the family renegotiated and redefined." Here Shelley Feldman examines the role of local, customary, and informal institutions in Bangladesh in adjudicating family issues and policing women's behavior. In a way analogous to the situation in Pakistan described by Weiss, the decentralization of government opens a space at the local level for religious conservatives to impose regulations that contradict the human rights policy of the national government, as expressed in its acceptance of CEDAW and related international conventions.

Frances Hasso examines a recent trend in the formation of conjugal relationships in Egypt and the United Arab Emirates, namely, the increasing resort to so-called *'urfi* (customary) and *misyar* (traveler) marriages, beginning in the 1990s. Women's rights are at risk in *'urfi* marriage due to its clandestine nature, whereas in a *misyar* marriage women agree to forgo cohabitation and financial support. Though socially disapproved of and, initially at least, not officially recognized, the sheer extent to which these forms of marriage are practiced has resulted in a degree of official recognition. As with the local councils in Bangladesh discussed by Feldman, Hasso's study reminds us that law codes in themselves are not necessarily an indicator of the lived experience of people and that developments in social practice can exert pressure from below to change formal law.

Homa Hoodfar's study of Afghan refugees in Iran illuminates both the refugees' experience and the discourses on women and the family in postrevolutionary Iran. In Iran the refugees encountered a family culture much less patriarchal than their own, one in which women's education and professional work are highly valued. Moreover, it is an unquestionably "Islamic" culture, enabling Afghan women and men to accept its norms. Though examining quite different situations, Hoodfar, Hasso, and Salime emphasize the importance of transnational movements of people (refugees, migrants, and networking activists, respectively) and hence of ideas and practices in the renegotiation and redefinition of family relationships.

◆ ◆ ◆

Together these case studies contribute to the growing critical feminist scholarship on family, gender, and law. In some instances they echo earlier work. For example, several essays confirm that colonial and local patriarchies have been complicit in articulating family laws and norms of behavior that have tended to undermine women's status and freedom. Others show how ordinary women and men as well as activists have contested unjust laws and norms and continue to do so along with other political actors. These complex and nuanced essays undermine the often monolithic images of women in these regions, in both academic and popular presses.

In other cases, the essays break new ground. For example, they contribute fresh insights to the theoretical and methodological discussion about the complex relationship of the global to the local by showing that this terrain has been in construction for many centuries and the local is not just the site where "global" forces play out but rather various local actors engage the global forces for their own ends and in the process shape them as well. Finally, the focus on Middle East and South Asia decenters "the West" and sheds light on important debates in feminism, law, gender roles, and family arrangements in these regions that can inform the study of these issues in "the West."

PART ONE •

Colonial Modernity and Family Law Codes

1. Disobedient Wives and Neglectful Husbands

Marital Relations and the First Phase
of Family Law Reform in Egypt

KENNETH M. CUNO

After thirty years of marriage, al-Sayyida, the daughter of Ali Jirjis, became a "disobedient" wife. Her case was recorded in the register of the provincial Sharia court of al-Daqahliyya, which was located in the town of al-Mansura, in Egypt's eastern Delta, in February 1909. Although her act of disobedience was not described, presumably she had left the marital home that she shared with her husband, al-Mursi al-Adib, which was the standard according to which a wife could be found legally to be "disobedient."

Al-Sayyida's act of defiance may have been triggered by concern over al-Mursi's financial support for her and their small son, Abbas. He may have ceased his support or threatened to do so. She may have feared he might divorce her, a realistic fear since divorce was not unusual (Cuno 2008). Women were disadvantaged by divorce, especially women with young children.

In court the couple affirmed their marriage. Then al-Mursi affirmed that he owed al-Sayyida and Abbas two piasters per day in maintenance, plus forty piasters every six months for al-Sayyida's clothing, and that he should provide her with proper housing. Al-Sayyida requested that the judge order Ali to provide those things, and al-Mursi asked the judge to order al-Sayyida to return to "obedience." The judge obliged both requests (Daqahliyya Legal Proceedings 1909, 8–9).

3

The case of al-Sayyida and al-Mursi highlights the mutual obligations of husbands and wives as defined in Islamic law. Moreover, cases such as this one show how ordinary Egyptians responded to changes in the legal environment in which marital relations were adjudicated (and hence negotiated) during the late nineteenth and early twentieth centuries.

The nineteenth and early twentieth centuries saw the global diffusion of European legal norms, including the idea of the law code. European-style and -derived law codes and courts were imposed in various parts of the globe under direct colonial rule, but they were also adopted by defensively reforming regimes in states that escaped formal colonization, such as Japan, China, Thailand, and the Ottoman Empire, including its autonomous Egyptian province.

The latter states adopted legal reforms to satisfy a European "standard of civilization" and in the hope of eliminating unequal treaties imposed by the Western powers and participating as equals in the international community (Horowitz 2004). In conformity with this pattern, Egypt adopted codes of commercial, criminal, and property law based on European norms. By the last quarter of the nineteenth century the jurisdiction of the Sharia (Islamic law) courts was largely limited to personal status law, which comprises most aspects of family law.

Although personal status law was not codified until after the First World War, its application was affected significantly by procedural codes governing the Sharia courts that were adopted in 1856, 1880, and 1897. These codes were part of the larger European-inspired movement of law reform through codification. Presented as merely organizing *(tartib)* the courts and their procedures, in actuality they significantly changed the way in which the law was applied, and thereby changed the rules according to which marital relations were adjudicated.

This chapter will discuss two aspects of marital life that were affected by those changes during the interval between the procedural code of 1897 and the first code of personal status law in 1920: the husband's duty to support his wife and children financially and the wife's duty of obedience to her husband. A sample of the Sharia court records of that period shows how ordinary women and men responded to the new rules, devising strategies to use them to their best advantage. These rules were particularly disadvantageous to women, yet women's use of the legal system to protect their rights shows that they were not mere victims, neither silent nor constrained. The experiences of litigants and the jurists who heard their cases influenced the subsequent reform process in the 1920s, in which some of the disadvantages to women introduced earlier in the procedural legislation were corrected.

Most studies of the reform of Egyptian personal status law focus on the phase of legislative activity that began in the 1920s, in which codes of positive law governing marriage and divorce were first enacted, or else on the more recent phase of reform that began in the late 1970s. Scholarly neglect of the nineteenth-century procedural reforms and their effects has made it possible to imagine that the legal disadvantages faced by married Muslim women at the turn of the twentieth century were entirely a legacy of the past. Yet as this chapter will show, some of those disadvantages were generated by the law-reform process itself.

Traditional Jurisprudence and the New Sharia Court Regulations

Marriage in traditional (that is, precocified) Islamic jurisprudence was a strongly patriarchal institution in which husbands and wives had certain well-defined though unequal rights and responsibilities, and in which the husband was assigned a superior role. A man's ability to marry multiple wives and his right to unilateral divorce by repudiation *(talaq)* are perhaps the best known of the many asymmetries in the marital relationship. However, the focus here is on the mutual obligations of spouses.

Marriage was and is a contractual relationship. Thus, in traditional Islamic jurisprudence the rights of the spouses were contingent on fulfillment of their obligations toward one another. In marrying, a man incurred a number of obligations toward his wife, the most important of which were financial. First, and before consummation of the marriage, he had to make an advance payment of part of the agreed-upon dower to his bride. The

1. I refer to "Islamic jurisprudence" rather than "Islamic law" to emphasize that it comprised a diverse and ongoing discussion among legal scholars. I distinguish "traditional" jurisprudence, which was a process, from the Sharia-based law codes enacted in most Muslim countries during the past century and a half.

advance or prompt portion of the dower was traditionally one-third of the whole, the delayed portion being due upon dissolution of the marriage. Second, and as was evident in the judge's order to al-Mursi, a husband had to provide adequate support or maintenance *(nafaqa)* for his wife's needs, along with clothing *(kiswa)* and proper lodging *(maskan shar'i)*, and he had a similar obligation to provide child support. The level of maintenance he owed was contingent on his wealth, not the wealth or income of his wife, which she was free to manage without his interference.

A wife's principal obligation was "obedience" *(ta'a)* to her husband. In addition to the obvious meaning of that word, in traditional jurisprudence an obedient wife would remain in the marital home, which was referred to variously as "his [the husband's] house," "the house (or home) of his obedience," or simply "the house of obedience" *(bayt al-ta'a)*. It was an act of "disobedience" *(nushuz)* for her to leave it without his permission or a legal justification (Ibn Abidin 1905–1908, 2:664–65; Al-Sawi 1995, 4:483; Al-Dhahabi 1997, 4:15).[2]

Those terms, at least, were the legal formulation. Their application in real life varied according to the economic and social status of the household. Most women contributed to their households' incomes, assisting in field work and tending livestock in the rural areas and working as market vendors, artisans, and domestics in the towns (Tucker 1985, 64–66). The juridical concept of a "disobedient" wife who left the marital home referred not to her mundane comings and goings for work, errands, or visits, provided her husband did not object, but rather to abandonment of the marital home. The higher the socioeconomic status of the family (or of its pretensions), the greater were the restrictions placed on the movement

---

2. These sources represent the late traditional jurisprudence of the Hanafi, Maliki, and Shafi'i schools applied in Ottoman Egypt. The fourth, Hanbali, school had relatively less presence, and there was no Shi'i population. Ibn Abidin's (1784–1836) book is a supercommentary on Ala al-Din al-Haskafi's (1616–1677) commentary on a study of Hanafi jurisprudence by Shams al-Din al-Tamartashi (1533–1595). Al-Sawi's (1761–1825) book is a commentary on Ahmad al-Dardir's (1715–1786) shorter explication of his own study of Maliki jurisprudence. Al-Dhahabi's (d. 1863) book is a supercommentary on Abd Allah al-Sharqawi's (1737–1812) commentary on Zakariya al-Ansari's (1423–1520) explication of his own study of Shafi'i jurisprudence.

of its women in public space. Yet that limitation had more to do with class respectability than with obedience, in the juridical definition. As was noted earlier, there was a more or less standard scenario in which a jurist determined a wife to be "disobedient." According to it she would leave the marital home, returning to her father's house, and refuse her husband's demand that she return to "the house of obedience."

The case of al-Sayyida and al-Mursi discussed above shows that the obligations of husbands and wives were not theoretical but subject to litigation and enforcement. Women could ask a judge to specify the maintenance their husbands owed them and to order them to provide it. Men with "disobedient" wives could ask a judge to order them to return to "the house of obedience." However, failure to fulfill one's obligations to a spouse resulted in forfeiting one's own rights. That is, a woman was not required to move into her husband's house if he failed to pay the prompt dower, nor was she required to remain in the home if he failed to maintain her. Similarly, a disobedient wife sacrificed her right to maintenance (Tucker 1998, 63–65).

The jurists of the four schools (*madhhabs*) of Sunni jurisprudence agreed on the foregoing general principles, but differed on some additional points. While accepting one another as orthodox, over centuries the jurists of the four schools had applied somewhat distinct methods in interpreting the sources and occasionally arrived at different results. For example, the majority of Egyptians adhered to the Shafi'i and Maliki schools, both of which regarded a neglectful husband's duty of maintenance as a debt that began to accumulate against him from the day he failed to provide it. Additionally, both the Shafi'i and Maliki schools allowed judges to grant women a divorce if they could prove desertion or nonmaintenance on the part of their husbands (Esposito and DeLong-Bas 2001, 34; Al-Sawi 1995, 4:483; Al-Dhahabi 1997, 4:15, 166). However, the Ottoman Empire officially adhered to the Hanafi school. In the Hanafi view, maintenance became a collectible debt only from the time of the husband's legal affirmation of it or a judge's prescription of it (Ibn Abidin 1905–1908, 2:676). The Hanafi school also severely restricted women's access to divorce, not accepting desertion or nonmaintenance as a cause (Esposito and DeLong-Bas 2001, 33–34)

Traditional Ottoman policy accommodated the diversity of the juridical schools in its provinces. The judges appointed in the Sharia courts were Hanafis, but deputy judges were appointed from the other schools of jurisprudence adhered to by the population, whose rulings were as valid as the decrees of the chief judge. Egyptians chose to appear before the judge or deputy judge of a certain school of jurisprudence because of their identification with it or because of the advantages that it offered in the case at hand. For example, Maliki jurisprudence predominates in Morocco, and Moroccans living in Cairo preferred to appear before a Maliki deputy judge. Hanafi jurisprudence was the most permissive in matters of trade and investment, and Hanbali jurisprudence offered advantages when it came to endowments *(waqfs)*. The Maliki school was the most permissive when it came to women's access to divorce (Sonbol 1996a, 237–38; Esposito and DeLong-Bas 2001, 34).

This flexibility in the traditional judicial system was lost with state centralization and the codification of law. In the area of family law four important changes were introduced by the codes of 1856, 1880, and 1897. First, the traditional system of reliance on notary witnesses *('udul)* was abandoned in favor of the use of documents. Second, and concurrently, the Sharia courts were assigned the role of notarizing contracts, judgments, and so on, so as to establish a proper documentary record. Third, Sharia court judges were instructed to rule only in accordance with the predominant view in the Hanafi school of jurisprudence. Fourth, there was stricter provision for enforcement of certain of the courts' decisions, including orders of a wife's obedience, as a result of which the term "house of obedience" acquired a more ominous connotation.

Similar to other codes issued in the mid-nineteenth century,[3] the 1856 law emphasized the use of documents as legal proof. It instructed the courts to provide records of judgments to those individuals in whose favor they ruled, while maintaining internal records of these judgments. Judges were instructed to accept records of a sale or gift of property that

3. The land codes of 1847 and 1858 required transactions to be recorded in properly notarized documents in order to be accepted in court (Cuno 1992, 192–94).

were properly notarized in a court, or inscribed in privately kept records, without recourse to witnesses. The proper way to describe property in these documents was also spelled out ("Ordinance of Judges" 1856, §8–10). The 1880 law went further, stating that a judgment confirming or deny- ing a right should be notarized at the request of a litigant and instructing judges that no document notarized in a court should fail to be accepted as valid ("Ordinance of the Sharia Courts" 1880, §13–14). The law of 1897 went a step even further, instructing judges not to hear any claim regard- ing marriage or divorce, or any plea to establish either after the death of a spouse, that was not supported by documentary evidence free of suspi- cion of forgery ("Ordinance Organizing the Sharia Courts" 1897, §31).

This was not as radical a change as it might seem. There was a long tradition of using documents in the courts, though under the old system documents were verified by notary witnesses. Contracts made the tradi- tional way could still be validated after 1897 by the testimony of the wit- nesses, which was recorded and notarized in the court. However, spouses could not defend their marital rights without proper documentation.

The transition to reliance on documents was accompanied by the organization of a cadre of local registrars of marriages and divorces in the villages and urban quarters, known nowadays as the *ma'dhuns*. Even before 1856 religious dignitaries in the villages acted as judges in mun- dane issues like the notarization of marriage contracts, divorces, and inheritance, since the courts of first instance were urban (Cuno 1992, 81, 87, 141). The 1856 law provided for the deputizing of "a learned man" in each village or two to oversee and record marriage contracts, divorces, and related legal affairs ("Ordinance of Judges" 1856, §12). The term *ma'dhun* was first used in the 1880 law, which instructed these registrars to provide each bride and groom with copies of their contract, keeping a third copy in his register, and to send the court monthly accounts of the marriages (and divorces) they recorded and the fees they collected ("Ordinance of the Sharia Courts" 1880, §159–78).

Marriage and divorce registers compiled by the registrars of Dami- etta, Rosetta, and Alexandria from the 1880s through the early 1900s are preserved in the Egyptian National Archives and testify to the use of this system by ordinary Egyptians.[4] The registrars were accessible, and their rates were not overly expensive.[5] In a high divorce-rate system, registration ensured the protection of spouses' rights in the courts. The 1880 law marks the beginning of systematic civil registration of marriages and divorces, which enabled Qasim Amin to present nearly a decade of data on marriage and divorce in Cairo in his book *The Liberation of Women* (1899, 98). Amin's book, which stirred up a major controversy, is best known for criticizing the veiling and seclusion of women, but that matter was part of a broader agenda of reform of women's role in the family and society that he advocated. Civil registration provided data to support his claim that divorce was too frequent (Cuno 2008).

The instruction to the courts to apply only Hanafi jurisprudence also occurred in the 1880 law ("Ordinance of the Sharia Courts" 1880, §10). This too was not new, as a similar instruction had been issued from Istanbul in 1839 and applied in Egypt, though it was not always followed to the letter (J. Anderson 1951, 36–37; Al-Abbasi 1883–1886, 2:153–54). Its reiteration in the 1880 law seems also to have been in keeping with Ottoman imperial policy (Deringil 1998, 48). The renewed policy seems to have been more strictly enforced, with dire implications for married women, whose maintenance became less secure and whose access to divorce was severely reduced.

The notorious rule permitting a "disobedient" wife to be compelled to return to her husband's home, the "house of obedience," did not derive from traditional jurisprudence. Rather, it was an innovation in the 1897 law. The relevant section stated in part, "The enforcement of a judgment [ordering] a wife's obedience (*al-hukm bi-ta'at al-zawja*), [or] keeping a child in the custody of a close relation (*mahram*), [or] separating two spouses, and the like, having to do with personal status (*al-ahwal al-shakhsiyya*) shall be compulsory (*qahran*) even if it leads to the use of force and entry

---

4. These registers were received by the Egyptian National Archives and cataloged in the mid-1990s, and one expects that similar registers from other locales may be found and made available to researchers in the future.

5. The fee for recording marriage contracts and other decisions relating to marital life was five piasters ("Notice of Fees" 1880), whereas the courts calculated the consumption needs of someone in the urban middle stratum as coming to two piasters daily.

into houses" ("Ordinance Organizing the Sharia Courts" 1897, §93). Since we are lacking explanatory minutes and memoranda, the intention of the men drafting the law is not clear, though the wording suggests their concern to enforce court decisions that were defied in some cases. At any rate, the police were now authorized to use force and even to enter houses to enforce these decisions.

In traditional Islamic jurisprudence the strongest legal sanction faced by a "disobedient" wife was the loss of financial maintenance. For example, in 1849 a man went to court and obtained an order of obedience against his wife, but she refused to comply. Then the man asked the judge to find her disobedient and to release him from the obligation of providing her with maintenance. The judge found her disobedient and undeserving of maintenance as long as she persisted in her disobedience (Al-Abbasi 1883–1886, 1:379). It is clear from this example and similar cases that before 1879 a husband's last resort in dealing with a "disobedient" wife was to withhold maintenance. The 1897 law contained a radical innovation, permitting "disobedient" wives to be compelled to return to their husbands.

The following sections discuss the responses of women and men to the new legal environment created as a result of the reform of Sharia court procedures, mainly through a reading of one court register, the Daqahliyya Legal Proceedings register no. 44, which contains 288 lawsuits recorded from January 7, 1899, through January 2, 1900. Reflecting the narrowed jurisdiction of the Sharia courts in the late nineteenth century, nearly every case in this register deals with family affairs.

Establishing a Right to Maintenance

Beginning no later than 1880, the Sharia courts' exclusive application of Hanafi jurisprudence put the wives of neglectful husbands at a greater disadvantage than before, for the maintenance they were due did not automatically become a collectible debt without legal action, namely, a husband's affirmation or a judge's prescription. Moreover, the 1897 law forbade judges from hearing suits regarding claims of marriage or divorce that were not supported by documents notarized in a Sharia court.

Women responded to this situation by going to court to secure judgments prescribing the maintenance they were due from their husbands.

By far the most frequent type of case entered in register no. 44 consisted of lawsuits brought by women to establish a legal record of their husbands' financial responsibility to them and their children. These women were not divorced but in ongoing marriages. Their husbands' financial responsibilities were well established in the legal and popular culture. In addition to the dower, they included quotidian maintenance *(nafaqa)*, clothing *(kiswa)*, or a clothing allowance, and the provision of proper lodging *(maskan shar'i)*, plus child support. The 89 cases of this type represent a little less than a third of all the cases entered in the register. Women had used the courts for this purpose previously, but less frequently, to judge from similar cases appearing in the Daqahliyya and Mansura legal proceedings registers before 1899. Thus, it appears that women were responding to the new requirement that their claims be based on notarized documents.

Unlike in the case of al-Sayyida and al-Mursi discussed earlier, in these cases there is no suggestion of the wife's "disobedience." But as in their case it is often unclear whether the lawsuit was caused by a husband's negligence or merely a prudent move by his wife to establish a legal record of his obligations, making them a collectible debt if neglected. For example, in January 1899 Sadiqa, the daughter of Muhammad al-Bahri, sued Ali Muhammad Siraj al-Katib ("the secretary"), of al-Mansura, testifying that they were married and had a one-year-old son. She demanded that he provide proper lodging and maintenance for herself and her son. Ali acknowledged her testimony to be true and agreed to provide the residence and maintenance (Daqahliyya Legal Proceedings 1899, 1). Sadiqa did not claim that Ali had failed to meet his obligations, but a complaint of his negligence prior to his affirmation of the maintenance and housing he owed her would have done her no good. The purpose of the suit was to obtain a legal judgment establishing the amounts due to her and her son for lodging and maintenance, whereupon they became debts if her husband neglected them. Cases such as this one typically concluded with the judge ordering the husband to provide specific sums for his wife's and children's clothing and maintenance, which were entered into the record.

In June 1899 a somewhat similar case was recorded, involving Muhammad Muhammad Kashif, the sheikh of his own agricultural settlement ('izba), part of the village of Shubra Hur, and his wife, Hanifa, the daughter of Ibrahim. Hanifa sought to establish a legal record of the maintenance Muhammad owed her and their three daughters. Monthly, the amount came to six *kaylas*[6] of grain, half in wheat and half in maize, plus fifty piasters, one-third for her and the remaining two-thirds for their children. For clothing he owed them eight piasters per year, and he also owed Hanifa proper lodging. Finally, she stated that the delayed portion of her dower came to six hundred piasters. Muhammad affirmed her statements, and Hanifa requested that the court record it for notarial purposes. However, the judge refused the request as legally unsound, since there was no dispute and nothing irregular about the details in the testimony (ibid., 38–39). The judge's ruling indicates the necessity of a lawsuit in order to secure a legal judgment of the maintenance due wives and children. Hanifa's mistake was her failure to use that strategy.

A month later Sayyida, the daughter of Ahmad al-Sandubi, represented by her brother Muhammad Afandi al-Sandubi, sued her husband, Ibrahim Layla al-'Attar ("the pharmacist"). She demanded that her husband provide her and her children proper lodging, maintenance, and clothing and that these items be legally recorded. The children, she testified, were five-year-old Bakhiyya; Muhammad, about three years old; and Hafida, an infant. Ibrahim acknowledged his wife and children and said he was able to provide proper lodging. However, he claimed to be poor and unable to pay more than one and a half piasters per day in maintenance. Since his financial status was in question, the case was delayed while the judge deputized two notables of the town to look into his affairs and to determine whether he was wealthy, of middling status, or poor. They concluded that he belonged to the middling class and should pay a daily maintenance of four piasters, half of which was for the children, and for clothing seventy-five piasters every six months, one-third of it for the children. The judge ordered him to do so (ibid., 47–48).

The amount of maintenance due from a husband was, in Islamic jurisprudence, contingent on his wealth. This case illustrates the way in

---

6. A *kayla* is one-twelfth of an *ardebb,* or about fifteen and a third liters.

which that principle was put into effect. Most of the husbands mentioned in these cases were from the middling class of artisans and tradesmen, along with a handful of wageworkers and professionals. In addition to the secretary or scribe and the pharmacist in the first and third cases above, we find husbands designated laborer, weigher, tobacco merchant, carter, stoker, work supervisor, silk merchant, builder, water seller, cloth merchant, seller, porter, and coffeehouse owner. The daily maintenance owed by most of these husbands to their wives was in the range of one to two piasters, and in light of the case of Ibrahim Layla al-'Attar above, that would indicate middling status.

The predominance of families of middling economic status in these cases and the relative absence of upper-class and lower-income families are striking. The relative absence of the poor might be attributed to the court fees. Although people who established their poverty were supposed to be exempted from the fees ("Notice of Fees" 1880), it is not clear how well that system worked. Lower-income women may have had less incentive to obtain a court finding of the maintenance they were due from their husbands, since many worked for an income and may have been self-supporting more often than women of the middle stratum. Women who worked as market vendors, seamstresses, or domestics might have been less inclined to go to court to secure maintenance from a neglectful or absent husband. Possibly another disincentive for working-class women was the Hanafi rule denying them a right to maintenance if they worked outside of the home against their husband's wishes (Ibn Abidin 1905–1908, 2:665).

Members of the upper class were loath to display their problems in public by resorting to the court (Badran 1995, 127). In upper-class families divorce, and hence the threat of it, seems to have been less common. Upper-class women who divorced could count on the financial support of their natal families, if necessary, and they also had resources of their own.

Securing the Rights of Divorcées

The second most frequent kind of lawsuit in register no. 44 involved divorcées suing their ex-husbands to achieve a legal record of the delayed dower and the temporary maintenance that they were due, for payment of these sums, or both.[7] In some cases the delayed dower was paid in court, or the divorce itself occurred in court, in order to establish a documentary record. There were sixty-two such cases, or between a fifth and a fourth of the total.

One of these cases was the only one in the register involving the urban upper class. Al-Sitt Banba, the daughter of Muhammad Bey 'Arafa, had been divorced by her husband, Mahmud Afandi Husni, an official in the provincial government (Daqahliyya Legal Proceedings 1899, 11). Her upper-class status is indicated by the respectful title "lady" (*sitt*), her Turkish name, her father's rank of bey, and her ex-husband's government post. In response to her suit her ex-husband affirmed that he had divorced her and that he would pay her fifty piasters monthly as temporary maintenance, another fifty piasters monthly to cover the cost of a wet nurse and nanny for their two daughters ages two and five, and one hundred piasters monthly for the girls' food and clothing (ibid., 11). Similarly, Ayusha, the daughter of Ali Abu Jabana, sued her husband, Hasan Mahmud, stating that he had pronounced a single revocable divorce thirty days earlier and that he owed her a delayed dower of one and a half pounds sterling plus maintenance. He acknowledged it and agreed to pay a daily maintenance of one and a quarter piasters. Whether the marriage was resumed afterward is uncertain, but if so it did not last long, for a marginal note records her remarriage in 1902 (ibid., 1).

As with the lawsuits to notarize the maintenance due in ongoing marriages, these divorce-related suits were not contested by the male defendants. Thus, although undoubtedly there was a lot of negotiation out of court, these suits appear to have been motivated by the women's need to establish a legal record of the obligations their ex-husbands owed them and their children. The *ma'dhuns'* divorce register testified to the delayed dower owed, but usually it did not specify the sums due for temporary maintenance and child support (Damietta Divorce Register 1897–1898). A judge's decision was needed to fix the sums due and to make them collectible debts.

---

7. Upon divorcing his wife a man is obliged to pay her the remaining or delayed portion of her dower, usually two-thirds of the total, and to provide her temporary maintenance during the mandatory waiting period (*'idda*), in which she is forbidden to remarry.

Predictably, not all ex-husbands lived up to their financial obligations. In just under a tenth of the cases (twenty-five) divorced women sued their ex-husbands for unpaid child support, occasionally along with payment of the temporary maintenance.

The "House of Obedience" in Application

A little more than a year after the 1897 law made it possible for men to seek the forcible return of "disobedient" wives, about one-sixth of the entries (forty-five) notarized the reconciliation *(sulh)* of a married couple, in which case the husband's obligation to provide maintenance, clothing, proper lodging, and child support was usually detailed, establishing a legal record of these obligations, as in the first category of cases. A closely related type of case, representing about 5 percent of the entries in this register, involved a man suing to demand his wife's obedience *(ta'a)*.

Obedience suits were not a new phenomenon, as illustrated by the example cited earlier. Presumably, men pursued these suits to be released from the obligation of supporting disobedient wives as much as or more than they did in the hope of securing their return to the marital home. The 1897 law changed things by enabling orders of obedience to be enforced, but in other respects the law remained as it was before. A woman's duty of obedience was still contingent on her husband's maintenance, and the court records reflect that fact. The case of al-Sayyida and al-Mursi, with all of its ambiguities, is a good example: in order to get an order of obedience, al-Mursi had to specify the maintenance he owed al-Sayyida, so that it became a collectible debt. In another illustrative case from January 1899 the butcher Mahmud Abu al-Su'ud sued his wife, Bahiyya, the daughter of Musa Sharshira, to enforce her obedience. Bahiyya was able to prove that Mahmud had not paid the advance portion of her dower in full, contrary to his claim, and the judge threw the case out (Daqahliyya Legal Proceedings 1899, 4–5).

◆ ◆ ◆

The history of law reform in the Muslim Middle East is usually framed as a progressive process of modernization. Family law in most of these countries continues to be based on the Sharia, and past as well as ongoing reform efforts in this area tend to be seen as a struggle to bring an ancient and outmoded law into conformity with modern norms either by finding the appropriate bases in Islamic sources or by ignoring them altogether. In particular, the legal disadvantages of women are perceived to be a legacy of Islamic law or of traditional culture. It is rarely appreciated that the law-reform process itself might have disadvantaged women.[8]

This chapter has highlighted two aspects of the nearly forgotten first phase of Egyptian family law reform in the late nineteenth century that put married women at a greater disadvantage than they had been beforehand. The rule requiring judges to apply only Hanafi jurisprudence meant that the maintenance due a married woman and her children was not automatically considered a collectible debt if her husband neglected to provide it and that lack of maintenance and desertion were not grounds for seeking a divorce. The law of 1897 provided for the enforcement of orders of obedience, making it possible for women to be confined in the marital home against their will.

This chapter also highlighted the agency of everyday litigants, particularly women, in responding to these changes in the application of the law. Following the 1897 law's stipulation that only suits based on notarized documents would be heard, significantly more women used the Daqahliyya court to notarize the amounts they were due for maintenance and clothing, as well as their right to proper housing, plus child support. There was a similar increase in the number of suits raised by divorced women to secure their financial rights. Similarly, orders of obedience were accompanied by stipulations of the husband's obligations.

The experiences of litigants and the jurists who heard their cases influenced the subsequent reform process, beginning with a committee of religious scholars formed in 1915 to recommend changes in the personal status law. The committee's work led to enactment of Law no. 25 of 1920, which drew on Maliki jurisprudence to make maintenance a collectible debt from the time of its nonpayment, and likewise the temporary maintenance due a divorcée. Women were also enabled to obtain a divorce for nonmaintenance or desertion, or the absence of a husband, including those husbands sentenced to prison (Abu Zahra 1950, 9–10). The

8. Amira El Azhary Sonbol's recent work is an exception to this trend (1996a).

work of a subsequent committee, also drawing on non-Hanafi sources, led to Law no. 25 of 1929, permitting women to seek a divorce on the additional ground of harm suffered in the marital relationship (ibid., 12–14). Notwithstanding gains in other areas, to a large extent these two laws restored legal options that had been available to women previously, before the courts were instructed to rely exclusively on Hanafi jurisprudence.

The "house of obedience," that is, men's ability to call on the police to enforce orders of obedience against their wives, had a much longer life. In the first two decades after 1897 it does not seem to have been perceived as the social evil that it would be in subsequent reformist discourse. In his 1899 report on the reform of the Sharia courts Grand Mufti Muhammad Abduh criticized the haphazard enforcement of orders of obedience and other court decisions by the administrative authorities, asserting that no more than 1 percent of any of them were enforced. Men used various maneuvers to evade court orders attaching their wages to pay maintenance, he wrote, and divorcées were often prevented from visiting children in the custody of their ex-husbands. If the police returned a "disobedient" wife to her husband, there was nothing to stop her from leaving again the following day (1900, 67–71). Although Abduh's discussion suggests that he viewed the misbehavior of men as a bigger problem than the disobedience of wives, he clearly was not troubled by the idea of enforced obedience.

Opposition to the "house of obedience" began to be voiced in the 1920s by feminist activists and reformers (Al-Nowaihi 1979, 116; Badran 1995, 131–32). The enforcement of orders of obedience was eventually curtailed by an administrative order in 1967, and it was abolished by Law no. 44 in 1979, which initiated the current phase of family law reform (Hill 1979, 83, 89; Shaham 1997, 73).

2. Patriarchy, Sexuality, and Property

*The Impact of Colonial State Policies
on Gender Relations in India*

FLAVIA AGNES

The nineteenth century is considered the century of social reform movements focused on violence against women in India. In response to these campaigns, significant pieces of legislation were enacted by the colonial state. Significant among these laws are the Sati Regulation Act of 1829, the Widow Remarriage Act of 1856, and the Age of Consent Acts of 1860 and 1891. These laws came to be projected as the colonial state's commitment toward protecting women and loosening the patriarchal hold over them by the conservative Hindu society. The campaigns focusing on the "barbaric" customs of the natives, such as burning of a child widow on the funeral pyre of her husband (suttee) or the marriages of infant girls to adult men that resulted in extreme sexual violence upon them, provided the colonial state a moral justification for ruling India as a harbinger of enlightenment. Through these legislative interventions, the colonists argued, the Hindu society could rid itself of its "barbarism" and enter an era of "civilization." They assumed that by incorporating the concepts of modernity into native jurisprudence, the status of women in India would be elevated.

But several postcolonial feminist historians have challenged this claim (Sangari and Vaid 1989; Chakravarthy 1989; Mani 1989; Kumar 1993; Nair 1996). In the same vein, I argue that merely by tracing a few legislative interventions it cannot be surmised that the colonial state enhanced women's rights. The working of the colonial state cannot be measured merely through legislative enactments but needs to be assessed through other markers such as judicial pronouncements, land regulations, and the economic restructuring of precolonial agrarian communities. The colonial interventions served to usher in a new patriarchal legal order that legitimized several traditional antiwomen practices and recast them into a new modernity through a complex interface of contest and collusion between colonial and local indigenous patriarchies.

This essay traces some important markers that vested economic power in the hands of individual men and consequently weakened women's position within the family and community. This weakening in turn boosted men's control and authority over women and gave a new lease to indigenous patriarchies. The power of individual men was consolidated and received a boost as title holders of land tenements in the new economic order as opposed to the earlier notion of community or joint ownerships and inalienability of land. Women's traditional economic rights over their *stridhana* (women's separate property) were weakened through judicial pronouncements that derived their ideology of women's rights over property from the English legal regime that denied all rights over property to married women. Alongside the material changes, the ideology of the patriarchal nuclear family gained acceptability with notions of Victorian morality woven into the modern family structure. The husband was vested with a new authority to enforce his conjugal rights over his wife. A claim of the wife to a meager maintenance dole could be denied by hurling allegations of unchastity against her.

The implications of the reconstitution of patriarchies in the colonial period bear significantly upon the present. The legal order and administrative norms that were introduced by the colonial state have continued in the postindependence period and resonate in contemporary Indian family law. Even while claiming to be a protector of women's rights, the family law regime has constantly pitted the economic rights of women against sexual purity in present-day matrimonial litigation. This essay sketches these developments and their implications for women's rights in India in contemporary times.

Conjugality, Property, and the State: The Rukhmabai Case

Of particular importance to the motif of women's resistance is the struggle of a young woman, Rukhmabai, who defied tradition and the colonial legal dictates by refusing to be bound to a marriage contracted when she was barely eleven. The social drama that unfolded around her legal case has been described as a unique event in colonial India by some historians (S. Chandra 1998). Her legal battle can easily be termed one of the "glorious events played out in the theatre of a great court" (Agnes 2004). Questioning what was assumed to be natural, she offered a subversive model of assertion by women of their desires, as individuals, in a terrain dominated by family, community, and imperial notions of justice and governance.

The social drama was triggered when Dadaji Bhikaji filed a case against Rukhmabai in the Bombay High Court in 1884. It reached its peak in 1885, when Justice Pinhey, in a historic verdict, declined to pass a decree of restitution of conjugal rights in favor of the husband. In a bold and fearless verdict, he declared that since conjugality had not been instituted, the question of granting the relief of "restoring conjugality" did not apply in this case. The judge proclaimed:

> It is a misnomer to call this "a suit for the restitution of conjugal rights." Restitution of conjugal rights can only apply to a situation when a married couple, after cohabitation, separate and live apart. Here, the husband has asked the court to compel the wife to go to his house, so that he may complete his contract with her by consummating the marriage. It seems to me that it would be a barbarous, cruel and revolting thing to do, to compel a young lady under those circumstances to go to a man whom she dislikes, in order that he may cohabit with her against her will. No law or practice justifies such an order. I am not obliged to grant the plaintiff the relief which he seeks, and to compel this young lady of twenty-two to go to the house of her husband in order that he may consummate the marriage arranged for her during her helpless infancy. . . . The practice of allowing suits for the restitution of conjugal rights originated in England under peculiar circumstances, and was transplanted from England into

India. It has no foundation in Hindu law. . . . For many years after I came to India such suits were not allowed. It is only of late years the practice of allowing such suits has been introduced into this country from England (I think only since the amalgamation of the old Supreme and Sadar Courts in the present High Courts which has brought English lawyers more into contact with the mofussil). It is, in my opinion, a matter for regret that the remedy of restitution of conjugal rights was ever introduced into this country. (*Dadaji Bhikaji v. Rukhmabai* 1885)

Ironically, the revivalists interpreted this judgment as an interference in the sacrosanct arena of Hindu conjugality by the British courts (and a breach of the assurance of noninterference).[1] For the reformers, the intervention of the English courts was an armor in their campaign against the upper-caste Hindu custom of child marriage. The litigation, the judgment, and the controversy that followed were all laden with ironies. The husband's case was trumpeted by the revivalists, and it was with their support that he had approached the English courts rather than the caste *panchayat* for the remedy of restoring his Hindu conjugality.[2] Within the customary law, the relief of restoring conjugality was nonexistent, and the husband could not obtain any relief in this sphere. Also, the parties belonged to the lower caste among whom the custom recognized the right of the wife to dissolve her marriage. And most important, Justice Pinhey had declined the relief on the ground that it was an outdated medieval Christian remedy under the English law and further that the Hindu law did not recognize such a barbaric custom!

But in the highly politicized climate these subtle legal points were lost. And within this politically surcharged atmosphere, the husband filed an appeal. The colonial courts succumbed to the political pressure. In 1886 the division bench presided over by Chief Justice Sir Charles Sargent and

---

1. "Revivalists" is the term used for the conservative Hindus during the late nineteenth century who wanted to bring in reforms within Hindu society by reviving the ancient Hindu traditions of the Vedic (5000 BC) and post-Vedic (that is, *smriti*, 200 BC–AD 500) period. The Hindus who wanted to bring in modernist reforms were termed "reformists."

2. A *panchayat* is a local (nonstate) dispute-resolution forum that was widely prevalent during the precolonial era and is still in existence in rural areas and among lower castes. The word indicates community representatives or community elders.

Justice Bayley rejected the argument that there was no authority for a decree for "institution" of conjugal rights under Hindu law and decreed: "The gist of the action for restitution of conjugal rights is that married persons are bound to live together. Whether the withdrawal is before or after consummation, there has been a violation of conjugal duty which entitles the injured party to the relief prayed." The court ruled in favor of the husband and granted him the decree of "restitution of conjugal rights" (*Dadaji Bhikaji v. Rukhmabai* 1886, 301).

But how was this decree to be enforced? The civil courts did not have the power to bodily reinstate conjugality, a power that the European ecclesiastical (church) courts had. Hence, the only way the decree could be enforced was through civil imprisonment and attachment of property. In a moment of pride and glory for Indian women for centuries to come, Rukhmabai declared that she would willingly undergo imprisonment rather than let a man she detested enforce conjugality! If the court was compelled to execute its own order, it would indeed have been a matter of blemish for the colonial rulers, who had justified their rule on the premise of ushering in modernity and defending women's rights. The prisons at the time were primitive places lacking provisions to imprison a woman, let alone a woman of Rukhmabai's stature. Fortunately for all concerned, the matter was finally "settled" by payment of compensation by Rukhmabai to her husband.

Rukhmabai's struggle is relevant not only for its times but even for the contemporary international women's rights discourse. The motif of Rukhmabai's defiance of both the verdict of the alien English judges and the patriarchal dictates couched in national pride, in defense of her right over her personhood, at a time when English women were waging a battle for their right to own separate property as wives, would indeed serve to shift the rigid and fixed binaries of first-world feminists and third-world victims (Agnes 1999).

Interspersing of Sexuality and Property:
The Widow Remarriage Act

The Widow Remarriage Act of 1856 was enacted amid two sets of contesting claims: the revivalists' proclaiming that the bill, if enacted, would affect a vital part of the Hindu scriptures and widows marrying under it would be regarded as social outcasts and the reformers' claiming that the custom prohibiting widow remarriage was a modern innovation that was unknown in ancient Vedic times (Basu 2001, 69). These contentions were overlaid by another reality, caste hierarchies. The prohibition of widow remarriage was seen as a badge of respectability. Castes that did not allow it ranked higher in social estimation. This hierarchization was carried to the extent that castes were sometimes divided into two sections, one following and the other forbidding the practice.

Although this act is hailed as one of the first attempts to bring in legislative reforms in the realm of family law, in actual terms the act had little impact on improving the status of Hindu widows. At one level, there were competing claims regarding the scriptural prohibition to widow remarriage. At the other, it did not improve the economic rights of a Hindu widow. On the contrary, upon remarriage, it deprived her of her right to retain her late husband's property. Since the widows from the lower strata already had a customary right of remarriage, the enactment did not bestow any new rights on women from the lower strata of the Hindu community.

Through cases reported in law journals of this period, I will examine how the act unfolded upon women from the lower castes. From the brief sketch, it is evident that any woman remarrying under this act lost her right to her late husband's property. Even if one can concede that it would be logical to apply these constraints to women who acquired a right of remarriage owing to this statute, it is difficult to reconcile with the perverse logic through which even women who had a preexisting right of remarriage under the custom of their caste were deprived of their property.

The statute needs to be contextualized in comparison with the legal status of English women who obtained the right to divorce, and subsequent remarriage, only in 1857 and under very stringent grounds of a husband's adultery coupled with another matrimonial offense of cruelty or desertion. And the battle for the absolute and unhindered right of married English women to hold property was waged in 1870 and went on for another half century. The disabilities suffered by married women with respect to separate ownership of property were finally laid to rest in 1935.[3] Despite this fact, the rationale for denying Hindu widows their right to retain their property was based on judicial interpretations of Hindu law!

As per the British jurists, a woman could hold property only owing to the legal fiction under Hindu law that upon marriage she became a part of her husband's body. According to this view, a woman's personhood was sublimated into her husband's. A widow could be granted a right to inherit her husband's property only on the presumption that she was the surviving part of her husband's being. Upon remarriage, a widow ceased to be a part of her former husband's body, and hence she lost her right to hold his property. This prohibition against remarriage had no scriptural foundation. In any case, women from the lower castes were out of the purview of scriptural doctrines and had a customary right of remarriage. These interpretations of the principles of Hindu law governed judicial notions from 1860, when the new courts were set up, until the enactment of the Hindu Succession Act in 1956 that finally discarded this principle.

Regional and caste-based diversity in the property rights of women did not seem to have any bearing on this rigid notion, and the courts continued to apply these principles even to lower-caste women who were not governed by these principles. For instance, in the Maraveer caste, widows could remarry even prior to the 1856 enactment. But in 1877, while deciding the case of a woman from this community, the Madras High Court held, "The principle upon which a widow inherits is that she is the surviving half of her husband. So it cannot apply where she remarries. The law cannot permit the widow who has remarried to retain the inheritance. As per the principles embodied in Steele's Hindu Law and Custom, the custom in the shudras[4] is that a widow on remarriage gives up all properties of her former husband's relations except what has been given her by her own parents" (*Murugayi v. Viramakali* 1877, 226).

---

3. With the enactment of the Law Reform (Married Women and Tortfeasors) Act of 1935 the distinction between the rights of married and single women was finally abolished.

4. *Shudras* are the lowest caste in the hierarchy, just above the *dalits* (oppressed), who as untouchables are outside the caste system.

The court relied on a quote that is attributed to Brihispati (one of the early lawgivers): "Of him whose wife is not dead half his body survives. How should any one else take the property while half his body lives?" (ibid.). This metaphor became a legal maxim in all subsequent judgments. The Madras High Court in 1884 applied this rule in the case of a woman from the Lingait Gounda community that followed the custom of remarriage prior to the act (*Kaduthi v. Madu* 1884, 321).

In the Deccan region widow remarriages in the name of *pat* or *natra* marriages were performed among several castes.[5] But following the trend of the Madras High Court, in 1898 an Indian judge of the Bombay High Court, Justice Ranade, held, "So far as this Presidency is concerned it is obvious from the information collected in Steele's Law and Custom of Indian Castes in Deccan among whom *pat* marriages were allowed or forbidden. But when a widow performs *pat* her husband's relatives succeeded to her husband's estate. There is not a single caste mentioned in which any custom to the contrary prevails" (*Vithu v. Govind* 1898, 321 FB).

The recording of customs within the Bombay Presidency, hastily and haphazardly done by Steele during the early phase of the presidency and published in 1827, seems to have provided the basis for denying women from the lower castes their customary right to property in litigation several decades later. Rather than relying on a living tradition of the people, the courts adopted the rules of sexual morality from the chronicles of an official administrator.

A dissenting and more rational view was expressed by the Allahabad High Court in the year 1933. Since the act was a beneficial legislation, the court ruled that it cannot be interpreted so as to impose further disabilities upon women who were not burdened with such disabilities prior to the enactment. The court held: "A custom of remarriage does not necessarily carry with it, a further custom of forfeiture upon marriage. Anybody who claims there has been forfeiture by reason of remarriage, must

5. *Pat* and *natra* are local indigenous terms used among lower castes to denote the remarriage of a divorcée or widow. What is denoted here is that these remarriages are not Brahmanic forms of marriages where *saptapadi* (seven steps around the sacred fire) is performed. The terms denote informal marriage alliances that have legitimacy.

prove affirmatively that such forfeiture is an incident of the custom under which the remarriage took place" (*Bhola Umar v. Kausilla* 1933, 247).

But, ironically, this decision was not followed by the high courts of Bombay, Madras, Calcutta, or Hyderabad even in the postindependence period. These courts continued to apply the principle of forfeiture to an increasing section of lower-caste women. Since the right was so well established among many lower castes, despite a century of negative interpretations, the claims of widows continued to be litigated even in the postindependence period. Many women lost, but not without a struggle. Cases were initiated in lower courts and were followed to the high courts and from then on to the Privy Council (and hence were reported in law journals). Individual women lost out to the combined strength of local patriarchies and a gender bias inherent in the imperial legal system. Some decisions of the postindependence period are mentioned below.

In 1952 the Calcutta High Court applied the rule of forfeiture to a woman from the Bairagi community who remarried under the custom of the caste (*Lalit Mohan v. Shyamapada Das* 1952, 771). In 1954 the Bombay High Court reversed the decision of the subordinate courts and applied the rule to a woman from Kolhapur district, which was a princely state until independence (hence the Widow Remarriage Act had not been applied there), and upon remarriage widows could retain the property of their former husbands. Ruling against the premise that as per the custom of the caste the rule of forfeiture upon remarriage did not apply, the court declared, "The foundation that widow is the surviving half of her husband does not disappear merely because certain communities recognise a custom of remarriage of widows. It would indeed be a startling proposition to say that even though she takes the property of her deceased husband by inheritance as his surviving half, she is entitled to take away that property with her to her new husband on remarriage when she can no more be regarded as the surviving half of her first husband" (*Rama Appa v. Sakhu Dattu* 1954, 315).

Hyderabad was another princely state that came under the new dominion. In 1952 a full bench of the Hyderabad High Court, by a majority view, overruled several of its earlier decisions that granted women the right of retention of property, despite a strong dissenting note from the section of the judiciary that vociferously argued that Manu, the primary lawgiver of ancient (Brahmanic) Hindu law, did not lay down rules for the *shudras* and was concerned only with the three higher castes, and hence his views could not govern *shudra* women (*Basappa v. Parvatamma* 1952).

The significant factor here is that these decisions of the postindependence period with the constitutional mandate of equality were not even following the established rules of the community. They were setting new precedents for these communities through which women's right to property was being eroded, at a point in history when the debate about the reform in Hindu law and women's rights of inheritance was raging in the country.

Through an active collusion between patriarchal premises of the state and the manipulation of male relatives, women of the lower community were deprived of their rights over property. It is indeed ironic that just two years after the Bombay High Court unsettled the established rights of women in Kolhapur district, the Hindu Succession Act came to be enacted after a prolonged and acrimonious debate. One of the salient features of the act was the abolition of the concept of "limited estate," besides awarding widows an absolute right over property inherited upon the death of their husbands.

During the period 1860–1930 the rights of widows in general were adversely affected through the judicial interpretation of the concept of *stridhana* (women's separate property). A new legal principle was gradually introduced through court decisions that whether the property is inherited by a woman through her male relatives (father, son, husband) or through her female relatives (mother, mother's mother, daughter), it was not her *stridhana*, and it would devolve on the heirs of her deceased husband. The widow lost the right to will or give away her *stridhana*, and it acquired the character of a limited estate. Upon the widow's death, the property reverted back to the husband's male relatives. The introduction of this concept of "reversioners," which is basically a legal principle under English law, bestowed upon the male relatives the right to challenge all property dealings by Hindu widows (Agnes 1999, 46–52).

The establishment of a legal system based on the procedures and rules of the English courts and a clear hierarchy of courts was meant to make the arbitration forums certain and definite. The legal structure was seen by the administrators as an important forte of its civilizing mission. The British interpretations of the ancient texts became binding and made the law certain, rigid, and uniform. This clear marker of modernity was welcomed by the newly evolving English-educated middle class of Bengal and provided the British a moral justification for ruling India as harbingers of enlightenment (Kumar 1993). Through the British's interventions the Hindu society could rid itself of its "barbarism" and enter an era of "civilization." An image of the cruel and superstitious natives who needed Christian salvation was deliberately constructed by the evangelists.

An interesting strategy used by women during litigation, it appears, was to claim *shudra* status and thereby application of customary law. Conversely, male relatives, in order to defend their rights, claimed Hindu status. If courts bestowed a Hindu status upon the communities, women's rights would be curtailed. Most of these situations were borderline cases where the pendulum swung from one end to the other. But when the issue was finally decided by the Privy Council or the respective high court, as the case may be, the religious status of the community (and thereby the fate of its widows) would be sealed for all future litigations. Since the standard of proof required to prove the existence of a custom was very high, a wide range of customs that diverged from Anglo-Hindu law were eliminated.

Lucy Carroll (1989) cites a case that was initiated by members of a tribal family claiming that on remarriage one of their widows had forfeited her right to the property that she had owned. The case was won through a minimal show of evidence that certain Hindu practices had been adopted by some branches of the tribe (the Rajbansis). The court held this fact as sufficient evidence to bring the entire tribe under the scope of the act. Carroll states that the act provided mercenary reasons for non-Hindus to "Hinduize" their customs. Contrary to popular belief, many of the customs that were crushed were ones in favor of women. J. D. M. Derrett comments that in this manner, Anglo-Hindu law, with its *dharmashastra* background, spread more widely than ever before. The only customs that were saved from the crushing effects of the British courts were the customs of the agricultural classes in the Punjab and matrilineal practices of the Malabar region (1957, 78).

Land Settlements and Subversion of Women's Property Rights

The British interventions also carved out a space for men's individual property rights from a system based on community or joint ownership. Changes in property ownership through "permanent settlements" developed a landowning class, and conversely this shift served to undermine the claims of women. Although it is true for all of British India, in this section the specific focus is the Punjab region and the matrilineal practices of Kerala. The customs that Derrett mentions need to be reexamined in light of more recent feminist scholarship. To understand the imperial policies and subversion of women's property rights in the Punjab, I find the works of Prem Chowdhry (1989, 1994) and the more recent publication of Veena Talwar Oldenburg (2002) particularly useful.

Chowdhry (1989) contends that the mere practice of widow remarriage or bride price cannot be construed as a marker of a higher status for women within the communities practicing these customs. For instance, rural Haryana, one of the most backward and underdeveloped regions of the Punjab under the British, exhibited a peculiar contradiction in relation to its women. On the one hand, the region reflected accepted indexes of a high status for women, namely, bride price, widow remarriage, polyandry, and relatively greater economic participation of women in agricultural activities, and, on the other hand, it reflected indexes of women's backwardness, such as a very low female sex ratio,[6] a total neglect of and prejudice against female education, and the complete absence of women from any positions of power and decision making.

The importance of a wife in the agrarian economy made marriage an acknowledged economic necessity among the Jats and other agriculturist

6. The sex ratio for Haryana continues to be far below the national ratio, which in itself is adverse. Per the 1991 census Haryana recorded a mere 865 females per 1,000 males as opposed to the national statistics of 927 females per 1,000 males. According to the 2001 census the national statistics improved slightly to 933, while Haryana recorded a further decline at 861 females per 1,000 males.

castes in the region, including Brahmins. The customs of bride price and widow remarriage have to be contextualized within this need (ibid., 312). The term for widow remarriage was *karewa,* a custom that sanctioned the remarriage of a widow with the deceased husband's younger or elder brother or an agnate cousin. Chowdhry argues that the *karewa* form of marriage served to control a woman's sexuality in order to control her property. Even the limited right of an unmarried widow to retain her husband's property was seen as a menace, and the *karewa* form of marriage served to dispossess her of her rights (ibid., 315). The widow could alienate the property for her own maintenance, for her daughter's wedding, or for payment of revenue, reasons termed as "strict necessity." That the women were able to manipulate these provisions to a certain extent to their advantage can be gauged from the constant appeals made to the Deputy Commission protesting against widows who had alienated their property "without consent." This self-assertion by widows in taking control of the economic resources after their husbands' deaths must have assumed such a proportion that for a variety of reasons, government action against it became essential.

She further mentions that J. M. Douie, compiler of *The Punjab Land Administration Manual* (1931), advised the revenue officials that a widow's attempt to partition the land should be disallowed. A widow's right to control land had been legalized under the Land Revenue Act because after the husband's death, she was held responsible for the payment of government revenue dues. However, since such advice could not have held much weight legally, the only solution to the fast-growing claims to partition was, according to official instruction, to be sought in a firm anchoring of the widow in remarriage. This setup, in the manual instruction, "could be the only satisfactory arrangement against which she had no appeal" (271).

Such advice was an inevitable outcome of the colonial policy followed in the Punjab because of its economic, political, and military importance. From the beginning, the imperial government had adopted the preservation of the village community as a settled policy for the Punjab. The general argument of British officials was that the mass of the agricultural population of this province did not follow either the Hindu or the Muslim

law. Therefore, a recording of tribal custom was done by settlement officers who at each settlement had compiled the local customs, known as
rivaj-i-am, in consultation with the village headman of each principal
landowning tribe in the district; these headmen were from the most influential families in each village.

Consequently, the customs of the landowning class in regard to civil
matters such as succession, alienation, marriage, tenure of land, adoption,
and the like came to be settled primarily by the Punjab customary law
that then became the first rule of decision. Thus defined, the customary
law of the land, backed by the full force of the colonial administrators,
safeguarded the landed property from a woman's possession. Not allowing women to inherit property was a view that struck a sympathetic, even
enthusiastic, chord among many British officials. The British perception of
these customs, which they also made legally binding, is significant.

A curious parallel observation about the situation of women prevailing "back home" as compared to the circumstances in the Punjab dis-
closes the ambivalent attitude of British officials toward women: "The
proportion of females to males in England and Wales rises continuously
from childhood to old age, indicative of the excessive care lavished on
women in England qua women, and not merely qua child bearer. Social
reformers may well stand aghast at the neglect of and the contempt for
female life shown by all religious groups in the Punjab, but no less extensive, and, possibly fraught with serious consequences to the future of the
race, is the excessive pampering of females in England" (*Census of India,
1921* 1924, 234). For *karewa,* they held, "Most officers conversant with this
tract of country had entertained in the existence *sub rosa* of a system of
polyandry. This institution is probably the first stage in development of
a savage people after they have emerged from a mere animal condition
of promiscuity. It is the concomitant of female infanticide. . . . The family
is the first organization when all wealth including the wife are owned in
common" (*Punjab District Gazetteer* 1911, 88).

In the Punjab the fundamental political interest of the British tran-
scended their less well-defined concern for social progress. This low
level of civilization as signified by *karewa* had to be retained because
the British concern lay in strengthening the hold of the existing peasant

society over land; its breakup was inevitable if the widow was allowed to have her way.

The apprehension regarding the danger of social disequilibrium to Haryana was sharper because this region, with its insecure agricultural conditions, had provided the best recruiting ground for the British Indian Army. The *karewa* custom contributed significantly to the unceasing heavy recruitment, despite the insecurity of life and the equally heavy rate of mortality. Simultaneously, the agricultural interests of the recruits' families could not be allowed to be jeopardized by the ever-growing number of widows' claims. This situation could prove to be very costly to the imperial government and unsettle not only its military recruitment but also the social equilibrium upon which its rule in the state was founded. Moreover, even economically, such a demand, if conceded, would have only added to the fragmentation and subdivision of holdings and, consequently, to the fast-growing number of smaller uneconomic holdings in this region, as elsewhere in the Punjab, which were posing a direct threat to the agricultural prosperity of the province and hence to the collection of revenue.

Chowdhry concludes that widow remarriage—a seemingly progressive feature—continued to be applauded by the British administration. The practice, however, as it was encouraged to exist, merely reinforced the social ethos that safeguarded the land in the family, clan, and community. The British administrators' own attitudes regarding female inheritance were closely identified with the primary concern of the colonial government, which did not want to disturb the patriarchal equilibrium within the rural society of the Punjab (Chowdhry 1989, 320).

This causal connection between imperial policies and subordination of women's rights is explored further by Oldenburg, who argues that land-reform policies and the creation of a masculine culture deprived women of their rights and made them vulnerable to family violence. She traces the collusion of the imperial state and Punjabi men who reconfigured patriarchal values and manly ideals in nineteenth-century Punjab. The two became enmeshed in an unsurprising alliance against the customary right of women. Pressing for a need to look beyond the statute book to comprehend a central paradox of colonial policy in India that persists in postcolonial India, she contends, "Although the legislative record is indeed impressive and includes the outlawing of several customs that underscored the bias against women, there was in the colonial period a profound loss of women's economic power and social worth. This was a direct consequence of the radical creation of property rights in land" (2002, 2).

Oldenburg argues that modern capitalist ideas in their attenuated form seeped unevenly through the mesh of colonial needs and priorities and infiltrated Punjabi society via two major colonial initiatives—the *ryotwari* system and the codification of "customary" law (ibid., 100). Land was declared a marketable commodity capable of private and determinate ownership so that a fixed and settled land revenue in cash could be recovered on every plot of land in two annual installments on two fixed dates. Annual assessments that had been customary in preceding native regimes were abruptly discontinued because they were found to be cumbersome and expensive and provided an opportunity for corruption.

The British, in striving to put the administration on a rational, efficient, and economic footing, ordained that their revenue settlements for various districts would stay in effect for two or three decades without regard to the situation that prevailed in any given year, be it drought, famine, or plenty. This mandate was the policy in a nutshell and rationalized, in the British view, the jumble of competing shares, varied annual collections, bargaining matches, and corruption that had plagued the revenue collection of the Sindh regime.

The second initiative was the codification of "custom" as adjudicable law in the Punjab countryside (ibid., 101). These two processes worked in tandem and illuminated how the equation of gender and power came to be skewed further. By tracking the enormous change that took place when the world of peasants of the Punjab became decidedly more masculine and as land, hitherto a community-held resource, became private property, we can recapture the moment women's voices and customs were erased as men's rights and voices were recorded with singular clarity. The shared control formerly accorded to all those individuals who worked the land came to be replaced by the arbitrary privileging of tillers as owners of the soil. Women—who sowed, weeded, hoed, harvested, and threshed and milled grain and vegetables; looked after dairy cattle; collected fuel; and processed produce and prepared it as food—who had been implicit coparceners in precolonial landholding arrangements, found themselves tenuous legal dependents of men, with their access to economic resources subordinated increasingly to the control and will of the husbands. Oldenburg comments with a note of sarcasm:

> The British had not granted their own women rights to property, so it was highly unlikely that they would shed their prejudice while introducing this "progressive" notion of private property to the Punjab. (And progress meant assimilation to modern European norms.) They granted these rights exclusively to men so that they could collect their taxes from male proprietors who could be taken to court or sent to jail if they defaulted. Clearly women, already hindered by the custom of seclusion and veiling, could not conveniently interact with the legal machinery of the new rulers so their husband and male kin quietly subsumed their rights. A robust patriarchal mentality was reinforced in this collusion. (ibid.)

According to Oldenburg, what made these initiatives doubly powerful was the fact that they were deployed simultaneously. At the same time that land titles were formalized and revenue settlements made for each district, revenue officials (earlier called settlement officers) went further by collecting, organizing, and constituting oral informal *rivaj* (literally, "custom") from male heads of each "tribe" or "caste." The officers themselves redefined these categories and reworked the information into a formal set of laws capable of being adjudicated in the new court system. The Punjab acquired a fully codified set of customary law that was laid out in a manual. By 1880 the revised recession of these laws was completed. They were to operate in lieu of the Muslim and Hindu personal laws (ibid., 102).

The registration of ownership of land was the first phase, the foundation stone, of making the agrarian economy masculine, Oldenburg comments. The next step taken in each district of the Punjab was the attempt to translate social and customary practices into legal codes. The new regime insisted on consulting only the male heads of a village, caste, or household in order to inscribe the *rivaj-i-am* (the customs of everyday life situated in a place or region, particularizing them in the attributes of a caste or tribe). New meanings invaded the husks of many familiar words. The complex and plastic universe of oral, implicit, flexible, and informally transmitted customary practices, interpreted as much by women as by men, that ordered everyday life and relationships was systematically elicited from only males and reduced for administrative effect into a written, fixed, judicable, actionable, and enforceable corpus of laws. The timing of the project was, perhaps, as critical as the project itself. That customary laws were to be collected and written down for the first time when the record of who owned the land had just been noted, with the power and the danger of individual ownership unleashed, informed much of what the respondents, all male landowners, would call custom.

Women's share in production of the land became meaningless, but traces of what their rights might have been are discernible in these codes. They provide a faint approximation of the rights women had in a society where land was a common resource with varying levels of entitlements. According to Oldenburg, the process emptied the female category of older subtler meanings—of shares of birthright—and other safeguards of the indigenous patriarchal tradition (ibid., 133–34).

Linking landownership to male preference, she continues, "Sons were the key to survival and prosperity in the relentlessly agrarian Punjab under the British. Acquiring land during auctions or sales, finding a job in the lower rungs of the imperial bureaucracy or the army, or finding a niche as a retainer in the expanding market were the new plums to fight over. The newly enhanced worth of sons with such prospects can be reflected in the confidence of some families in demanding a consideration for a marriage alliance" (ibid., 16).

Conjugality, Morality, and Maintenance

The links between sexuality and property claims continue to the present day. It is indeed interesting to explore how this relationship between notions of morality and women's economic rights is foregrounded in contemporary matrimonial litigation.

Within Indian family law, women's economic claims arising out of a marriage contract are confined to recurring monthly maintenance.

Although these amounts owed can be claimed under the personal laws of the parties, most destitute and poverty-stricken women opt to claim them under the summary proceedings available under the Criminal Procedure Code (1973). This provision is beneficial social legislation to prevent vagrancy and delinquency.

This otherwise innocuous section came alive through the *Shah Bano* controversy in 1985 and is retained in public memory because of the furor it caused at the time.[7] But the notions of sexual morality with which this section is governed have not received due attention in contemporary feminist legal discourse. The mischief is caused by clauses 4 and 5 of S.125 of the Criminal Procedure Code (1973), which stipulate:

> (4) No woman shall be entitled to receive an allowance if she is living in adultery.
>
> (5) On proof that any wife whose favor an order has been made under this section is living in adultery . . . the magistrate shall cancel the order.

These stipulations provide the armor for husbands to entangle women in vicious and dilatory litigation over a pittance of maintenance. A careful scrutiny of reported cases in any law journal would reveal the extent to which allegations of sexual promiscuity are made to subvert women's claims. To give an example, *Divorce and Matrimonial Cases* (2001), a journal widely used by lawyers practicing matrimonial law, reports around forty-five cases under the title "Maintenance." In almost half of these cases, sexuality and morality were the core issues that were contested. A significant point is the winding and prolonged litigation that the women had to undergo, despite the provision being summary. After the first round of litigation in the lower courts, these cases were appealed in the higher courts, which is why they merited reporting in the law journal. Hence, they reflect only the tip of the iceberg. In each of these cases the women

7. The case created a major political controversy and caused a backlash from the minority Muslim community for its adverse comments regarding Islam and resulted in a new enactment that deprived the divorced Muslim woman of the right to avail herself of the provisions under S.125 of the Criminal Procedure Code.

were assaulted and driven out. Most of these cases also contained allegations of dowry harassment. But none of these women had filed a criminal complaint under S.498A of the Indian Penal Code. All they did was file an application for maintenance, and it is then that the husbands lashed out with allegations of sexual promiscuity.

The layered and multiple contexts through which sexual morality surfaces, as per the norms of patriarchy, serve only one end: to challenge the legitimacy of women's claims. It is a clear case of "heads I win, tails you lose." The allegations ranged from adultery on the part of the wife and disputing paternity of a child to a subsisting previous marriage of the wife, a husband's subsisting first marriage, and concubinage and a husband's subsequent marriage. But issues of sexuality, morality, and polygamy, whichever way they emerge, can always be turned against a woman's claims of maintenance. For instance, it really does not matter whether a woman's previous marriage or a husband's previous marriage is in dispute. So long as sexuality is pitted against maintenance claims, it is the woman who has to pay the price.

Scanning through the judgments, one can see a positive trend emerging, where the courts have upheld the women's claims and disallowed the husbands' contentions. But despite this turnaround, S.125, clauses 4 and 5, provides the scope for husbands to entangle deserted women from the lower strata in prolonged, cumbersome, and costly litigation. And negative rulings, though less frequent, still prevail.

A judgment of the Allahabad High Court is quoted here to convey the extent of humiliation a woman goes through during such litigation:

> If the man and woman choose to live together and indulge into sex no such marriage status can be conferred automatically by their so living upon such a woman. She is not entitled to the legal status of a wife in the eyes of law and society. Law and society treat such women either as concubine or a mistress. . . . The two may agree to live together to satisfy their animal needs. But such a union is never called a marriage. A woman leading such a life cannot be bestowed with the sacrosanct honor of wife. No marital obligations accrue to such a woman against

her husband. Such a wife must be termed as an adulteress. (*Malti v. State of Uttar Pradesh I* 2001, 104)

This section is included to highlight the fact that even in contemporary court proceedings, the courts continue to frame women's rights in archaic and sexist language. Notions of women's sexual purity have framed Indian family law reform from the colonial period to the present.

PART TWO · ·

Religion, Custom, the State, and Patriarchy

3. The Monotheisms, Patriarchy, and the Constitutional Right to Human Dignity in Israel

FRANCES RADAY

The place of religion in the Israeli legal system is derived from a complex historical and political reality. Israel was created as a homeland for the Jewish people after two thousand years of persecution as a religious and racial minority dispersed throughout the world. In this respect, Israel was established as a Jewish state, and this fact is reflected in constitutional documents that mandate Israel to be a Jewish and democratic state. In regard to the Jewish population, there has been a constant clash of ideologies as to the nature of the "Jewishness" of the Jewish state, whether its identity was and is religious of necessity or whether it is secular, based on historical, cultural, and political aspects of Judaism (Rubinstein 1991, 164–83, 197–99). It has been said that mainstream modern political Zionism has a clear preference for a secular definition of the Jewish character of the state (England 1987, 194–95).[1] Nevertheless, the association between national-cultural and religious identification cannot be ignored. The group identity of the founding Jewish population had been formed through generations of minority existence in hostile social and political environments under which, in accordance with the prevailing political norms, Jewish identity became indistinguishable from religious identity (ibid., 187–88). In seeking to give content to the "Jewishness" of the state,

---

1. For discussion of the right of the Jewish and Palestinian peoples to self-determination, see Raday 2003d.

obviously the well-tried and -documented religious definition was the most easily available.[2]

Israel inherited from the British Mandate the Ottoman Millett system, which granted autonomy over matters of personal status, including marriage, divorce, maintenance, inheritance, and the custody of children, to the religious courts of the Jewish, Muslim, and Christian communities in Palestine.[3] The national-cultural identities of all three communities were perceived in prestate Palestine as being an extension of their religious definition. After the founding of the state, the religious autonomy retained by the Muslim and Christian minorities has continued to be regarded, from the perspective of these communities, as a central element of their national-cultural autonomy, representing, in a wider sense, a form of community autonomy. Interference in the autonomous jurisdiction of the religious courts would be likely to bring the government into conflict with the Muslim or Christian religious leadership.

These brief glimpses into the historical development reveal the ongoing political expediency of retaining the status quo (the existing mode of regulation) of state and religion. Forces for change have to contend with a formidable array of vested political considerations, religious institutional interests, and cultural preconceptions in favor of maintaining the status quo. Furthermore, Israel's coalition politics has almost consistently given power to the Jewish religious political parties as the pivot between contending secular parties, which has created an effective veto against change.

Thus, in Israel, there is institutional promotion of religion, not only for the Jewish majority but also for the Muslim and Christian minorities. Indeed, Israel is the only country in which personal status is determined exclusively by the religious law of the three monotheistic communities— Jewish, Muslim, and Christian—as applied by their own religious courts.

2. Furthermore, for the Orthodox religious sector, according to the traditional Jewish conception, "the function of state-government is the enforcement upon the population of divine law as established by the legitimate religious authorities" (England 1987, 188).

3. King's Order in Privy Council, Articles 47, 51; Law and Administration Ordinance 1948, Sec. I.1. See Shawa 1991, 69–85.

The religious courts—rabbinical, Sharia, and canonical—have exclusive jurisdiction over license and prohibition in marriage and divorce and, in some circumstances, also exercise jurisdiction over associated issues regarding matrimonial property, maintenance, and custody.

In this essay I shall explore the impact of the value dichotomy between religion and women's human rights in Israel.[4] I will show how this dichotomy has affected the formulation of constitutional principles, legislative norms, and judicial policy.

Constitutional Principles: Between Human Dignity and Equality?

Israel's Declaration of Independence was one of the first such declarations or constitutive documents to include sex as a group classification within a guarantee of equality in social and political rights. However, the Declaration of Independence was not subsequently ensconced in a constitution. In 1951 the Women's Equal Rights Law was passed, providing for women's right to equality in all laws and regulations, but it was an ordinary statute and, although it provided a framework of equality, did not have constitutional status. Neither the Declaration of Independence nor the 1951 law bestowed constitutional authority on the courts to cancel subsequent primary legislation, enacted by the Knesset, Israel's parliament, as unconstitutional. They were interpretative tools to be employed by the courts in applying legislative provisions and in reviewing the exercise of administrative powers and, as such, enabled the High Court of Justice to adjudicate some significant rights to equality for women.

As regards the dichotomy between religious norms and women's human rights, Section 5 of the Women's Equal Rights Law expressly excluded from the scope of the law and, hence, excluded from the reach of protection of women's right to equality all issues of "prohibition and license to marry and divorce." The significance of this provision was preservation of religious patriarchy. The law in effect exempts the religious courts from being bound to the principle of equality for women and thus frees them to exercise their exclusive jurisdiction to adjudicate on the

---

4. I have discussed the theoretical and comparative aspects of this dichotomy in Raday 2003a.

basis of the patriarchal family order mandated by the three monotheistic religions. Indeed, it is self-evident that the legislature was fully aware that it was endorsing a patriarchal concept of women's role in the family; had it not been so, the provision of an exemption for marriage and divorce law would have been unnecessary.

Since 1951 there have been many initiatives by members of the Knesset to introduce a constitutional bill of rights. However, they have almost all been marked by an unwillingness to insist on the right of women to equality in marriage and divorce. The only constitutional proposals that have uncompromisingly insisted on full equality for women in the personal law are those bills proposed by Member of Knesset (MK) Shulamit Aloni, but her attempts have consistently met a solid wall of parliamentary opposition.

In 1992 the Knesset found a way to circumvent the opposition of the religious parties to a constitutional principle of equality by introducing a partial constitutional bill of rights, the Basic Law: Human Dignity and Liberty, which guaranteed, among other rights, the right to human dignity. The Basic Law: Human Dignity and Liberty provides that the human rights under the law must not be infringed except by a law that is in accordance with the values of the State of Israel as a Jewish and democratic state, which is for a justified purpose and is not disproportionate for the achievement of that purpose. The inclusion of human dignity as a constitutional right was acceptable to the Jewish religious parties, who undoubtedly regarded it as the very essence of Jewish law and not as a threat to religious values. Human dignity (*kvod haadam*) is indeed a basic ethical value whose source can be attributed, in some of its aspects, to the biblical recognition of the human being as being created in the image of God, or *bezelem* (in the Hebrew Bible). However, the concept of human dignity has very different connotations in the modern human rights discourse from its biblical predecessor. Among other distinguishing conceptual implications, the biblical concept of human dignity is consonant with patriarchy. The Bible sees human dignity as consonant with the exhortation that "the dignity of the King's daughter lies within." This passage is commonly understood to mean that women's proper place is in the private and not the public sphere. In contrast, human dignity in human rights law inherently incorporates the right to equality and prohibition of group discrimination, including on grounds of sex. Accordingly, a number of Supreme Court judges have held that equality for women is incorporated in the constitutional right to human dignity.[5] The response of the religious parties and much of the Orthodox religious public to this development is one of consternation and anger.

In 2000 MK Yael Dayan found a way to elaborate on the basic right to equality for women without confronting the religious lobby's opposition to applying that right to the area of marriage and divorce. She introduced a wide-reaching progressive concept of equality through an amendment to the Women's Equal Rights Law, which transforms that law without altering its original Section 5, which remains untouched on the statute books. This approach had, at least, the rhetorical advantage of not having the Knesset reiterate in the year 2000 the deference to religious patriarchy that it had adopted in 1951. However, the amended Women's Equal Rights Law is only a basic and not a constitutional law and so still does not introduce an express constitutional right to equality. Furthermore, it does not cancel the preexisting exclusion of marriage and divorce from the purview of women's right to equality.

In spite of the various attempts to mitigate the damage, the absence of an express right to equality in Israel's framework and constitutional legislation remains a serious human rights flaw. Even more important, the saga of the struggle over the principle of equality for women in Israel's constitutional history stands as incontrovertible evidence of the fact that women's equality is regarded as a threat by Orthodox religious factions.

Legislation: Personal Law, Reproductive Rights, and Sexual Violence

The religious political parties have had a significant impact on the legislative agenda on matters of personal law, reproductive rights, and violence against women. This impact has been patriarchal, denying women

---

5. See Justice Barak, *Recanat v. the National Labour Court*, Tak-Al 2000(4), 587 (in Hebrew); Justice Dorner, *Miller v. Minister of Defense* (1995), 49(4) P.D. 94; and Justice Maza, *IWN v. Minister of Transportation* (1994), 48(5) P.D. 501.

equality and autonomy. It has, however, also been in some cases paternalistic, protecting women against various forms of abuse and violence. I shall examine the way in which religious values have influenced personal law, reproductive rights, and the law on sexual violence.

Personal Law

The Knesset has, as said, conferred exclusive jurisdiction over matters of personal status to the religious courts; thus, for Jews, Muslims, and Christians prohibition and license in marriage and divorce are exclusively adjudicated by the religious courts of their various communities. Membership in a community is determined in accordance with birth identity or a legal conversion to another religion. Hence, secular women fall within the jurisdiction of the religious court of their community, as do religious women. All three monotheisms impose patriarchal norms on the matrimonial relationship, each in its own way mandating male authority in the family. The exclusive jurisdiction of the religious courts over personal status law also effectively excludes women from judicial decision making on matters of marriage and divorce, as there are no women rabbis, *qadis,* or priests in the various religious courts. The result is imposition of a patriarchal regime of family-law norms on all Israeli women, both religious and secular.

Under Jewish law, the *halakha,* women are subject to male power in the family.[6] Although it can be said that, for the era in which it was promulgated, the *halakha* exhibited a considerably advanced sensitivity to the need

6. Under *halakha* women are not regarded as fully qualified to give evidence in court and cannot be appointed as rabbis or judges (Deut. 17:6; Maimonides, *Laws of Evidence,* 9:2, *Laws of the Study of Torah,* 1:13). For a recent exposition of the *halakhic* position, see "Extracts from the Petition in the *Shakdiel* Case," *Newsletter of the Association for Civil Rights in Israel,* May 31, 1987, where Rabbi Halevi Steinberg is quoted as giving the most recent authoritative summation of the *halakha* on the issue: "To all functions only a man should be appointed. Hence a woman does not have the capacity to be a judge." The reference is of course to judges in rabbinical courts, as Jewish law is not binding in the Israeli legal system except in the rabbinical courts, which exercise jurisdiction on personal status matters of Jews.

to protect women against male exploitation,[7] in modern terms it blatantly subordinates women to men in marriage. The basic concept of the marriage ceremony is "purchase" of the woman by the husband, who takes her as his wife in a unilateral ceremony. Divorce is not a judicial act and may be achieved only in accordance with the husband's wishes, that is, until the husband declares that he is willing to divorce her, there is no way a woman can be released from the bonds of marriage, even by injunction of the rabbinical court.[8] At most, the rabbinical court may give an order compelling the husband to divorce the wife, and he may be imprisoned until he agrees to do so; this mandate is very rarely decreed. Later introduction, in the eleventh century, of a requirement of the wife's consent to divorce did not result in a symmetrical impediment to divorce and remarriage for men and women.[9] Women refusing a divorce cannot remarry and, if they bear a child from a union with another man before the divorce is given, face the severe problem of *mamzerut* for that child, a form of bastardy applicable only to the children of adultery by a woman.[10] By contrast, for men whose wives refuse to agree to a divorce, the husband may, in accordance with *halakha*, acquire a rabbinical license to remarry, and, if so, the marriage will not be considered bigamy under the Penal Law (Shochatman 1995). Such cases do in fact exist. Furthermore, the husband faces no problem of *mamzerut* if, while still married, he parents a child with another woman.

For the Muslim community, different forms of patriarchal rules are imposed by Sharia law. Polygamy is permitted. All the Muslim communities allow polygamy, but it is widely practiced only in the Bedouin community. The other religions—Judaism, Christianity, and Druze—do not permit polygamy. Polygamy is prohibited under the bigamy provisions

7. For example, *halakha* protects women against exploitation of their property during marriage or loss of it upon divorce (*Ketubot,* 78a–30b), and rape within marriage is prohibited (Maimonides, *Personal Laws,* 15:17; *Shulhan Arukh,* "Orah Haim," 25:2; Rakover 1980, 295–317).

8. Deut. 24:1; *Gittin* 85a–b.

9. Ban of Rabbenu Gershom, eleventh century.

10. *Mamzerim* (bastards) cannot marry within the Jewish community (Deut. 23:3; *Shulhan Arukh,* Even HaEzer).

of the Penal Code, which, of course, runs contrary to the provisions of Islam and limits the authority of the Sharia courts. Under Muslim law, men may unilaterally divorce their wives. This power severely disadvantages women, who cannot seek to negotiate any rights on dissolution of the marriage. Unilateral divorce may take place without a public religious ceremony or judicial process. The Women's Equal Rights Law, however, requires that the divorce be authorized by a court that has divorce jurisdiction. This measure theoretically protects women against the husband's right of repudiation, but, since the jurisdiction to authorize the divorce is the Sharia court, the procedural requirement does not necessarily offer Muslim women any substantive protection, as the court may itself authorize repudiation as an acceptable mode of divorce. The Muslim law on guardianship and custody also impacts Muslim women severely: when a woman who is divorced or widowed remarries, the right to custody of her children goes to the paternal line, either to the father himself or, if he is deceased, to the father's family.

The Christian community includes thirteen denominations, each with its own decentralized churches, priests, and canonical authorities. Catholic and Orthodox doctrine and symbolism are articulated in terms of female subordination and cultic incapability. Women have not been appointed to the priesthood. In almost all the Christian denominations, women take an oath of obedience in the marriage ceremony. Furthermore, the stand of the Catholic Church against abortion severely harms women's reproductive autonomy.

Women in Jewish, Muslim, and some Christian denominations are, in addition to the problems discussed above, also subject to discrimination in maintenance, matrimonial property, and inheritance laws (Raday, Shalev, and Liban-Kobi 1995; Raday 2003a). Thus, women under the three monotheisms are subject to various patriarchal norms. These norms divide into ones that regulate personal status—prohibition and license in marriage and divorce—and ones that relate to matters of custody, maintenance, matrimonial property, and inheritance.

The religious courts have exclusive jurisdiction over personal status but not over the related matters. Although the religious courts have exclusive jurisdiction only over the issue of marriage and divorce, the impact of this jurisdiction in practice extends to matters of custody, division of matrimonial property, and inheritance. The extended impact results in part from the provisions of the legislation, which vests jurisdiction in the religious courts over matters related to divorce proceedings filed in court, if jurisdiction has not already vested in a civil court. It also results from the indirect impact of the divorce jurisdiction, which facilitates the exercise of pressure on the person seeking a divorce to waive his or her civil rights in order to acquire a religious divorce. In view of the patriarchal nature of the system, it is usually women who will be the victims of such pressure. Finally, the religious courts exercise jurisdiction when the parties agree to it, and there is usually agreement as to the jurisdiction of the religious courts in the more traditionalist sectors of the community. Clearly, in traditionalist patriarchal communities, the agreement of women to forgo their rights is part of the problem and not part of the solution. The result of this jurisdiction by consent is that, for the most part, ultra-Orthodox Jewish women (approximately 12 percent of the Jewish population) and traditionalist Muslim women (more than 50 percent of the Muslim population) may be subject to discrimination in their rights to custody, maintenance, matrimonial property, and inheritance.

Alongside this patriarchal religious personal law, there is a full range of civil legislation that provides an egalitarian and progressive basis for adjudication on matters of custody, maintenance, and matrimonial property. Over these matters the Family Affairs Courts have jurisdiction. However, women are often hampered in their enjoyment of the equality under the civil law as a result of the pressure and blackmail to which they can be subjected by husbands who threaten to refuse to give a *gett* (divorce). Many secular young couples attempt to avoid the religious regime of marriage and divorce by marrying in private marriage ceremonies not recognized by the state as legal marriages. There is wide acceptance of this kind of marriage in the secular society, and, indeed, the law bestows many of the fiscal rights of married couples to couples who are publicly known partners.

Reproductive Rights

Legislative regulation of reproductive freedoms has been influenced by pressure of the religious lobby to ensure conformity with Jewish law.

This regulation has produced a set of norms that do not meet feminist requirements for women's autonomy over their reproductive functions but nevertheless allow some room for protection of women's reproductive needs. Abortion is legal on certain approved grounds: age (under sixteen or over forty), a prohibited or extramarital relationship or incest, a physical or mental defect of the fetus, and danger to the woman's life or her physical or mental health.[11] Under Jewish law abortion is permissible only when the continuation of the pregnancy threatens the mother. In the late 1970s the religious parties successfully lobbied to repeal a social-circumstances ground for abortion, which had allowed abortion because of difficult family or social circumstances. It is notable that the lobbying of Jewish religious parties against abortion has been less violent than the influence of Christian religious parties in North America, which may be because under Jewish law life begins at birth and not at conception, and, hence, the mother's life and safety are given preference over the life of the fetus.

A law was passed in 1996 allowing surrogacy agreements.[12] This legislation may be in part attributed to the very strong emphasis placed on parenthood in Jewish religion and culture. Legal surrogacy was, however, restricted to surrogacy by unmarried women in order to avoid the possibility that the child would be the product of the adulterous pregnancy of a married woman, which under Jewish law would make the child a *mamzer* not eligible to enter into a Jewish marriage. This requirement, of course, created a double problem in the execution of the law— first, regarding the surrogate herself, who as an unmarried woman is likely to be in a highly vulnerable position, has probably not previously experienced pregnancy and birth, and will therefore be even less able than women who have experienced motherhood to make an informed decision about surrogacy, and second, regarding those persons seeking surrogate mothers, who are less likely to find them in the limited market of single women.

11. Penal Law sec. 316.

12. Agreements to Carry a Foetus Law (Authorisation of Agreement and Status of the Newborn).

Sexual Violence

As regards sexual violence against women, the influence of Jewish religious law on legislation has been benign. The Jewish religious parties supported legislative bills imposing prohibitions and requiring preventive measures in the sphere of violence against women, including amendments to the substantive and evidentiary laws of rape; the conferral of jurisdiction on the courts to give protection orders, removing a violent person from the family home, and prohibition of marital rape. Jewish law clearly prohibits sexual relations in marriage without the consent of the wife, and on this basis of Jewish law principles the Supreme Court had held, even prior to the legislation, that, contrary to the criminal law provisions inherited from the British Mandate, marital rape is prohibited.[13] Two of the judges had been unsure whether this prohibition applied to non-Jews, whose personal law did not prohibit marital rape, and only the minority judge, a woman, said that it must, as a matter of human dignity, apply to all. The legislation subsequently clarified in 1988 that the prohibition on marital rape applies to all persons in Israel.

Contrast with Purely Secular Legislation

There is empirical confirmation of the fact that it is religious values and not other traditionalist cultural determinants that are the primary barrier to equality for women in Israel: legislation on matters not connected with the religious jurisdiction over the personal law and not offensive to religious sensibilities has been developed in a highly progressive way since the late 1980s.[14] There has been progressive legislation on feminist

---

13. *State of Israel v. Cohen* (1980), 35(3) P.D. 281; 35(1) P.D. 371.

14. The reforms of the late 1980s came more than a decade later than the commencement of similar reform in Western democracies. The delay in the initiation of legislative reform to guarantee equal opportunity for women can be attributed to two factors. First, the founding premises of Israel in socialist Zionism made it natural to provide accommodation for women's needs—especially the rights of "working mothers." Thus, from the 1950s, women were entitled to maternity-leave compensation paid by the National Insurance, protection against dismissal during pregnancy, and affordable child-care facilities, all of which combined to allow women to integrate work and family life. It took time before the

and gender issues regarding matters that do not conflict with Jewish law concepts, and such legislation was indeed supported by the religious parties. Thus, the Knesset has promulgated an egalitarian family-law regime as regards inheritance, division of matrimonial property, and custody. It has passed laws on equal retirement age; equal employment opportunity, with remedies for all forms of employment discrimination in the public and private sectors and conversion of child-care rights from maternal to parental rights; rights to equality in division of matrimonial property; affirmative action in public-sector employment; and an obligation to compensate equal pay for work of equal value. It has introduced criminal prohibition of sexual harassment, which extends beyond the workplace to other dependent relationships, in education, health care and the military, and also to nondependent relationships where there are repeated acts of harassment. It has passed legislation to ensure women's right to fill any role they are capable of performing in the army.

Supreme Court Decisions

Although the principles of equality for women under the Declaration of Independence and the Women's Equal Rights Law were not endowed with constitutional force and although the 1992 Basic Law: Human Dignity and Liberty does not expressly include the principle of equality, the courts have regarded gender equality as a basic principle of the legal system, and some judges have regarded it as part and parcel of the constitutional right to human dignity. The courts have thus had to contend with the clash between religious norms and the concept of equality. This clash has a different impact as regards the private sphere (the family) and the public sphere (economic and political life). In family law the legislative imposition of religious jurisdiction and norms has exercised a significant

stereotype of the working mother was perceived as a barrier to women's advancement. Second, there was a myth of gender equality from the early years of the state, which derived from the participation of women in the pioneer organizations, army service, politics, and professions. However, the myth was deconstructed in the 1970s to '80s when it became apparent that presence was not power and that women were subject to disadvantage in Israel as elsewhere.

restraint over the development of gender-equality jurisprudence. In the public sphere the reach of the religious restraint is more limited, and an impressive body of gender-equality jurisprudence has been developed. However, even here, the dichotomy between religious and secular norms is apparent in the court's deliberations on petitions that impinge upon religious sensitivities.

The Private Sphere: Family and Religious Values

The exclusion of marriage and divorce from women's constitutional right to equality, established in the Women's Equal Rights Law, has been clearly regarded by the courts as beyond challenge. Hence, the court has not interfered in the exclusive statutory jurisdiction of the religious courts over these issues and their application of religious law to them. Even more, the Supreme Court has not taken it upon itself to develop indirect incentives to lessen women's disadvantage under the *halakhic* rules of marriage and divorce. Thus, the Supreme Court has refused to sanction the use of punitive maintenance payments given by rabbinical courts against husbands who were unreasonably withholding a *gett*.[15]

The Supreme Court has regarded itself as not having jurisdiction to intervene in the discriminatory *halakhic* system of divorce law. When a woman filed a petition to overturn the ruling of the Grand Rabbinical Court, which had refused to oblige her husband, who had been separated from her for more than six years, to give her a divorce, the High Court of Justice ruled unanimously to dismiss.[16] The High Court of Justice ruled that it could not intervene in the Grand Rabbinical Court's holding. Justice Cheshin remarked that the situation of a slave was preferable to the position of a wife under the applicable Jewish law, since even a slave would be released after seven years' bondage. Nevertheless, despite his justified indignation and powerful rhetoric, Justice Cheshin, like the other judges, did not find a way to intervene.

15. The court preferred to preserve the "real" purpose of maintenance payments rather than countenance, extending their function to discourage abuse of the power to withhold a divorce (*Mira Solomon v. Moshe Solomon* (1984), 38[4] P.D. 365).

16. *Plonit v. Ploni* (1997), 51(1) P.D. 198.

In the 1950s the Supreme Court rejected a widowed Muslim woman's petition for custody on the grounds that the Islamic sense of justice in regard to the good of the child must be taken into account (Raday 2000).[17] One of the judges rejected the petitioner's argument that the transfer of the child to the custody of her dead husband's sister was discriminatory, pointing out that the choice was between two women. However, in a more recent decision, the Supreme Court called upon the Sharia court to consider the professional opinions of social workers regarding what would be in the best interests of the child.[18]

Within the limits of the residual right to equality in family life, the Supreme Court has, in a number of cases, applied the principle of equality. In the early years of the state, immediately following the enactment of the Women's Equal Rights Law, the court canceled Jewish law rules when both parties had not expressly chosen to be governed by those rules, which created inequalities for women in the sphere of married women's property, domicile, and guardianship rights (Raday 1983).[19] In the 1994

17. *Braya v. Qadi of the Sharia Court* (1954), 9(2) P.D. 1193.

18. *Rayina Shaabani v. The Sharia Court* (1999), 99(1) Takdin 77.

19. However, the limited effectiveness of this guarantee is well illustrated by the case of *Halima Bria v. Qadi of the Sharia Moslem Court et al.* ([1955], 9 P.D. 1193). In that case, a widowed mother of three children who had remarried petitioned the High Court of Justice to desist from hearing an application to cancel her guardianship, on the basis of Muslim law. Under Muslim law a mother who remarries ceases to be the natural guardian of her children. The application to cancel Halima Bria's guardianship had been brought by the dead father's sister. The High Court of Justice refused to grant the petition. There was disagreement between the justices as to whether the provisions of the Muslim law discriminated against women. Whereas one of the three justices found discrimination, a second remained silent on the issue, and the third held there was no discrimination, "since the question was which of two women was to be given guardianship of the child." All three justices agreed not to invalidate the Muslim law as a relevant consideration. Only if it was proved that, in the final judgment, the Muslim courts had "intentionally ignored" the provisions of the Women's Equal Rights Law in judging the best interest of the child would the High Court interfere. The court dismissed the claim that a skillful *qadi* could find ways to disguise the fact that his decision was based on religious law and not on the principles of the Women's Equal Rights Law. In a more recent decision, the High Court of Justice required the *qadi* to take into account psychological opinion in determining the welfare of the child.

Bavli case, the High Court of Justice imposed on the rabbinical courts an obligation to abide by the principle of equality in the division of matrimonial property.[20] Justice Barak held that the Jewish law principle of separation of matrimonial property could not satisfy this requirement since it resulted in women's receiving a negligible share of the property upon divorce. The court's decision was in conformity with the Women's Equal Rights Law, which excluded only the matter of license or prohibition in marriage and divorce from the purview of the equality principle and not related matters, such as property, maintenance, and custody. The decision provoked violent opposition from religious groups and is not applied, in practice, by the rabbinical courts.

The Public Sphere: Political, Economic, and Military

The first gender-discrimination case to be brought before the courts after the State of Israel was established was the case of a man who was a member of the ultra-Orthodox Natorei Karta sect, who claimed that his prosecution for refusal to serve in the army constituted sexual discrimination, since a woman who held his religious convictions would have been entitled to an exemption from army service.[21] The Supreme Court rejected this claim, holding, among other things, that the Women's Equal Rights Law was intended to protect women, not men. It is not possible to draw policy conclusions regarding the stereotyping of women's roles from this case, as it was decided in the early 1950s prior to the development of feminist awareness in Israel and elsewhere.

The impact of religious values on public life was addressed in 1988 in the *Shakdiel* and *Poraz* cases.[22] The issue in *Shakdiel* was the decision of the minister for religious affairs and a ministerial committee set up under the Jewish Religious Services Law of 1971 to refuse to appoint Leah Shakdiel to serve as an elected member of a local religious services council, on the grounds that she was a woman. The issue in *Poraz* was the Tel

20. *Bavli v. Rabbinical Court of Appeals* (1994), 48(2) P.D. 221.

21. *Steinberg v. Attorney General* (1951), 5 P.D. 1061.

22. H.C. 153/87, *Shakdiel v. Minister for Religious Affairs et al.* (1988), 42(2) P.D. 221; Bagatz 953/87, *Poraz v. Lahat, Mayor of Tel Aviv et al.* (1988), 42(2) P.D. 309.

Aviv Municipal Council's decision not to appoint women to the electoral board for the Tel Aviv municipal rabbi. The opposition to these appointments was based on claims that, under Jewish law, women may not elect or be elected to public office. The women petitioned to enforce their right of participation, and their petitions were accepted by the court, which recognized women's right to equality as a "fundamental principle" of the Israeli legal system. Both appointments were to bodies established by legislation, which were hence, although dealing with religious affairs, clearly statutory civil institutions.

Undeniably, these cases established that women are entitled to equality of participation in state administrative bodies, even those bodies that deal with religious services. However, there are grounds for some hesitation regarding the impact of the two High Court of Justice decisions as regards the constitutional balance between equality and religion. Both decisions accorded the principle of equality to women, which they termed a fundamental principle, much less than hegemony in this balance. In *Shakdiel*, Justice Elon held that the principle of equality is to be "balanced against other legitimate interests of individuals or the public." Hence, he argued, "had there been a prohibition in the *halakha* against women serving on religious councils, . . . a compromise would have to be found between the two approaches. Although the municipal council is a civil statutory body and is hence subject to civil law, it deals with *halakhic* affairs . . . and thus it would be desirable to seek ways to bridge the opposing interests."[23] In *Poraz*, Justice Barak regarded it as the duty of the court to balance "the general principle of equality, on one hand, and particularistic interest in the appointment of an electoral board, which should be able to carry out its functions properly, on the other." He held that the balancing process was "horizontal, not vertical. . . . [W]e do not have a situation here of a clash, in which one of the principles predominates over the other. Equality is an important principle but it is a relative principle." Justice Barak went on to say that, even in this horizontal balancing process, the importance of equality is central and infringement will be permitted only if there is no other way to implement the particularistic purpose that underlies a

---

23. *Shakdiel*, at 242–43.

specific law. However, he made it clear that the principle of equality was determinative in this case only because there was, as a matter of fact, no real barrier to the proper functioning of a municipal rabbi if women sat on the electoral board.[24]

The court's readiness in the above decisions to ascertain whether the inclusion of women was prohibited by the *halakha,* as a relevant issue in determining the right of women to participate in these public bodies, indicated a preparedness to tolerate the encroachment of inegalitarian *halakhic* values in areas of public life: the bodies in question were, as the court itself stressed in both cases, public bodies set up under civil law. The Supreme Court could have furthered the cause of equality by deciding that, unless the legislature expressly provided otherwise, it was to be assumed that even if the inclusion of women was contrary to *halakha,* or even if no rabbi was willing to sit with a woman in a religious council or be elected by an electoral board that included women, the legislature did not intend to condone unequal treatment of women in this sphere.

In *Hoffman I,* in 1994, the High Court of Justice rejected the petition of the Women of the Wall (WOW) to pray at the Kotel (the Western Wall of the second Temple and a central national, cultural, and religious site for Jews) in a group, wearing prayer shawls and reading aloud from the Torah scroll, a manner of prayer customary for men but not for women and a subject of controversy among Orthodox Jewish authorities.[25] The women's prayer in this manner had been greeted with violent opposition from other Orthodox worshipers and prohibited by the secular authorities. Although rejecting the petition, the court recognized, in principle, WOW's right of access and freedom of worship, and Justice Shamgar recommended that the government make arrangements to enforce this right, with minimum injury to the sensitivities of other worshipers.[26] In

24. *Poraz,* at 336–37. Justice Barak relied on the prior decision of Justice Elon: "Justice Elon showed in the *Shakdiel* decision that there is no *halakhic* prohibition of participation by women in elections of functionaries to public office. It can be assumed that there are certain rabbis who think as he does and hence will be candidates for municipal rabbi."

25. *Anat Hoffman and Others v. Commissioner of the Western Wall* (1994), 48(2) P.D. 265 (in Hebrew).

26. Ibid., at 356.

1998, after a series of government committees had failed to find a solution, WOW petitioned the High Court of Justice again. The court, in *Hoffman II*, composed of Justice Beinish, Justice Strassburg-Cohen, and Justice Maza, directed the government to implement WOW's prayer rights at the Kotel within six months.[27] Orthodox Jewish political parties immediately presented a bill to convert the area in front of the Kotel into a religious shrine exclusively for Orthodox religious practice with a penalty of seven years' imprisonment for any person violating the current Orthodox custom of prayer. The attorney general requested a further hearing, and the president of the Supreme Court appointed an expanded panel of nine justices to reconsider the issue. The court held by a majority of seven to two that the members of WOW were entitled to pray at the Kotel.[23] The two minority justices who were opposed to recognition of WOW's right to pray at the Kotel were the religious justices on the court, Justice Tirkal and Justice Englard. The court also decided, by a vote of five to four, that, in order to prevent injury to the sensitivities of other worshipers, the government should make arrangements for a suitable prayer area for the members of WOW at an adjacent site, Robinson's Arch; if the government failed to do so within a year, the WOW members would have the right to pray at the Kotel. The four minority justices held that WOW's right should be implemented immediately in the Kotel Plaza.

The decision of the High Court of Justice in the WOW case has serious implications for the development of constitutional jurisprudence on public-sphere issues, which impinge on religious sensitivities. I was legal counsel for WOW in this case. My involvement was closely linked to my conviction that women are entitled to full personhood in all spheres of political and social life, including religious activities. It is, in my view, incumbent on the state and the courts to support women's right of

27. *Anat Hoffman and Others v. Director General of Prime Minister's Office and Others*, Tak-Al 2000(2), 846 (in Hebrew). I act as counsel for WOW. For a full discussion, see Raday 2003b.

28. Dangaz 4128/2000, *Prime Minister Office v. Anat Hoffman*, available at the Supreme Court Web site, http://62.90.71.124/files/00/280/041/g13/00041280.g13.HTM (*Re: Hoffman III*, 2003).

religious equality by refusing to subsidize or support religious activities that deprive women of this entitlement. The refusal of the court to accept the WOW petition represents a concession to the violent opposition by some religious fanatics to women's equal personhood in religion, at a site that is governed by state law and is of central symbolic importance on national, cultural, and historical as well as religious levels. It also indicates a weakening of the court's resolve in its application of the human right to equality in the public sphere, when this right impinges on religious sensitivities. Unlike the *Shakdiel* and *Poraz* decisions, although WOW's mode of prayer is not prohibited in the *halakha*, the court refused to justify women's right to equality. Furthermore, the leading judgment by Justice Cheshin and agreed to by Justice Or represents a departure from both their judgments in a previous case, where they had held in minority opinions that offense to religious sensitivities did not justify denial of the right of secular citizens to drive past a synagogue on the Sabbath, including at the time of services. It looks as though these justices' sensitivity to the right of the secular to equality in situations of religious coercion does not extend to religious women who want to exercise their right to equality within their religion.

Contrast with Gender Equality in Nonreligious Cases

There is a wide gap between the highly conservative judgments of the Supreme Court on the equality issues that impinge upon religious sensitivities and the more progressive decisions given by the court in those cases that do not. In 1990 the Supreme Court gave a decisive, unambiguous ruling on the supremacy of the principle of equality under the Women's Equal Rights Law: "Where there is no *expressly* contrary provision, the courts must prefer that statutory interpretation which is consistent with the principle of equality between the sexes."[29] Justice Bach, giving the lead opinion of the court, elevated the test for proof of discrimination to a level requiring strict scrutiny; he expressly pointed to the fact that there is insufficient awareness of discrimination when it acts against women and called on the courts to rectify this situation.

29. Bagatz 104/87, *Nevo v. the National Labour Court et al.* (1990), 44(4) P.D. 749.

This decision was a turning point,[30] and since *Nevo* the High Court of Justice has given a series of decisions that have transformed the principle of equality for women in Israel into something progressive and powerful.[31] The court went on, per Justice Cheshin, in a later case, to delineate the place of equality among legal principles: "The king of principles—the most elevated of principles above all others—is the principle of equality. . . . So it is in public law and so it is in each and every aspect of our lives in society. The principle of equality infiltrates every plant of the legal garden and constitutes an unseverable part of the genetic make-up of all the legal rules, each and every one. . . . The principle of equality is, in theory and practice, a father-principle or should we say a mother-principle."[32] In the last decade of the twentieth century, the court broke away from the limits of formal equality and incorporated concepts of affirmative action[33] and accommodation[34] into the principle of equality for women, and as integral parts rather than exceptions to it. The court has

30. The early legal actions brought by women for equality in public life were not successful. The failure in the early 1960s of the first claim brought by a woman to enforce her right to economic equality may have helped to discourage further litigation in this sphere: *Lubinsky v. Pakid HaShuma* (1962), 16 P.D. 304. This case, in which tax authorities assessed a married woman's income from an orchard that she owned together with her husband's income from salary for income tax purposes and refused her request for separate assessment, resulted in the Supreme Court's not only finding that the ruling could not be challenged because it was based on statute law but also holding that there was no sexual discrimination. It was not until 1977 that the next attempt at litigation was made. A petition was submitted to the Supreme Court by a legal apprentice. She claimed that refusal of the Law Society to reduce the length of legal apprenticeship in the case of absence for maternity leave, mandatory by statute law, in the same way it did for absence for military service discriminated against women. The High Court of Justice found it patently unproblematic to dismiss the petition, holding, in an uncharacteristically short decision (less than two pages), that there were no possible grounds for finding discrimination since women as well as men serve in the army.

31. For full discussion of the Supreme Court's equality jurisprudence, see Raday 2003c.

32. *IWN v. Minister of Labour* (1998), 52(3) P.D. 630, paras. 29–31 (Cheshin's judgment).

33. *IWN v. Minister of Transportation*, at 501; *IWN v. Minister of Labour*.

34. *Miller*, at 94.

secured equal retirement age for women,[35] adopted a concept of affirmative action, required admission of girl cadets to the pilot's course of the Israeli Air Force,[36] analyzed the need to prevent sexual violence against women in the context of women's right to human dignity and equality,[37] and imposed severe disciplinary penalties on public employees and army officers for sexual harassment.[38]

Against this backdrop of a strong equality concept, the Supreme Court's conservative reticence on all matters in which a decision in favor of women's right to equality will impinge upon religious sensitivities is evidence of the power that religious norms exercise. This power is felt not only in the Knesset, where it may be, as indicated above, a result of coalition politics, but also in the courts, where there is no direct power of the religious parties and, indeed, there is ostensibly a complete separation of powers.

Israel's Religious-Secular Dichotomy

There is a dichotomy in Israeli law between religious and secular values as regards gender equality. This dichotomy pervades the legal system at all levels. At the constitutional level, religious values have preempted the introduction of an explicit right to equality for women. The Knesset has put personal status law—license and prohibition in marriage and divorce—beyond the reach of the principle of equality, and the courts have not challenged it.

However, the High Court of Justice has established the right to equality as a fundamental right under the rubric of the constitutional right to human dignity. It has also required the religious courts to apply the principle of equality to issues of family law, other than license and prohibition in marriage and divorce, and did so with regard to the division

---

35. Bagatz 104/87, *Nevo*, 22.10.90.

36. *Miller.*

37. *The State of Israel v. Be'eri et al.* (1993), 48(1) P.D. 302. For discussion, see Hauftman 1995, 58–59, 233–34.

38. *The State of Israel v. Ben Asher* (1998), 52(1) P.D. 65; Bagatz 1284/99, *Plonit v. Chief of the General Staff* (1999), 53(2) P.D. 62.

of property upon divorce. As regards areas of public life connected with religious services, the High Court of Justice has imposed the principle of equality only insofar as it did not involve the infringement of a prohibition of Jewish law and did not inflame religious sensitivities to the point of violence.

In the regulation of reproductive rights and sexual violence, religious norms have also influenced the substance of legislation. As regards reproductive rights, the reliance on Jewish law principles has produced regimes regarding abortion and surrogacy that are permissive but within limits dictated by religious rather than social policy considerations. As regards preventing violence against women, the influence of Jewish law has been benign for women, and, indeed, in accordance with those principles, Israel was one of the first legal systems to prohibit marital rape.

In all other areas of law not directly related to religious values and norms, a strong concept of gender equality has been developed both in legislation and in the courts. Thus, in these areas, the legal system combines social accommodation for maternity and parenthood with equal-opportunity guarantees for women's participation in the labor force or the military, affirmative action in public-sphere economic activities, and protection against sexual violence as an inherent part of women's right to equality and human dignity.

The contrast between progressive and even radical legislative and judicial policy on matters of gender equality not related to religious norms and the traditionalist preservation of patriarchy in those matters that are related to religion bears witness to the rift between religion and human rights of women that dichotomizes Israel's democracy.

4. Legal Pluralism Versus a Uniform Civil Code

The Continuing Debates in India

MANISHA DESAI

Unlike most secular democracies, India does not have a Uniform Civil Code (UCC) to address matters of inheritance, marriage, divorce, maintenance, and adoption.[1] Instead, these issues are governed by religious personal laws. In India four religious communities—the majority Hindu, Muslim, Christian, and Parsi—have their own personal laws. Other religious communities such as Sikhs, Jains, Buddhists, tribal groups, and *dalit* or schedule castes are subsumed under Hindu law (Sunder Rajan 2003).[2]

The lack of a Uniform Civil Code for personal laws has come up for public scrutiny at various junctures following independence in 1947, including during the Constitutional Assembly when law minister Ambedkar resigned over it, in the 1950s when the Hindu Reform Bill was passed, again in 1986 during the infamous Shah Bano case—when the furor over it led to the passage of the 1986 Muslim Women's Protection Bill—and most recently in 2003 when the Bharatiya Janata Party (Indian

---

1. Thus, women of different religious communities have different rights around these issues. But all women are guaranteed the same economic and political rights as men in the constitution.

2. The schedule castes are the former untouchable castes, so named because the various castes so designated are enumerated on a schedule. *Dalit* (oppressed) is the word chosen by the schedule castes to refer to themselves. They were also called harijans (people of God) by Gandhi, but it was seen as a patronizing moniker and is rarely used today.

People's Party, or BJP) raised it. Its continued resurgence and abeyance reflect the contradictions of a secular, democratic, multireligious post-colonial state as well as the dynamics of reform and women's movements past and present.

The lack of a UCC in an otherwise gender-just constitution has been seen variously as the failure of the Constitutional Assembly;[3] a political, albeit appropriate, compromise of a multireligious nation-state (e.g., Sheth 1990); a failure of secularism (Bardhan 1997; Jayal 1999); and, more recently, as a case for legal pluralism (for example, see Agnes 1999; Chatterjee 1998; and Nandy 1998).

Legal pluralism is defined both in opposition as well as a complement to liberal legal theory, which as it developed in the West focused on a uniform and nation-state-based legal framework. This centrality of the state, legal scholars such as Santos (1995) argue, was a product of the denial of local and varied legalities based on customs and traditional practices.

But under contemporary globalization the increased flows of people, ideas, and practices across national spaces have brought these varied legalities into interaction and often conflict with each other in many countries. Today, "the national legal field is a quilt of legalities woven by national-local dialectics which interweave the hegemonic state legal thread with multiple local legal threads" (ibid., 250).

Such a legal pluralism is seen by many scholars as emancipatory because it challenges the Western hegemonic legality and recognizes the rich and varied legalities that have developed across the world. But I argue that the interaction and conflict between different legalities are neither new nor always emancipatory as far as women's rights are concerned. It depends on how, when, why, and by whom the varied legalities are framed.

My focus is primarily on personal laws and women's rights. I argue, first, that the lack of a UCC reflects modern and colonial and postcolonial practices of regulation rather than an emancipatory legal pluralism but, second, that such an emancipatory legal pluralism is not precluded, as

---

3. By "gender justice" or "gender-just laws," I mean laws that do not discriminate between men and women based on their sex.

evidenced by women's political mobilization, and can be furthered by a politics of cross-communal dialogue and solidarity.

Colonial Construction of Personal Laws

Bipan Chandra (1989) argues that in precolonial and colonial India religious communities did not have common interests or identities, as they were divided by caste, class, language, and ethnicity, among other differences. It is historians who misread these common identities into the past following colonial tendencies. The British colonial administration, faced with ruling and controlling a vast territory, with multiple customary laws, chose to develop a uniform set of administrative and criminal laws while leaving the "natives" to practice their diverse "personal laws." This separation between public common laws and private or personal multiple laws was devised by William Hastings in 1772 and reproduced the British cult of domesticity based on a similar public-private dichotomy (Mullally 2004).

Of course, colonial legality in India evolved over a century of complex negotiations among different actors in the process of change from the East India Company to the British Empire. The cartography of these changes would itself be an interesting analysis. But here, suffice it to say that over the years the colonial state formulated a strategy of "noninterference" in cultural matters. Such categorization belies the historical reality in which the colonial state actively constructed communities and a single set of personal laws for each of the four major communities.

As is widely documented (for example, see Agnes 1999; Bardhan 1997; Bose and Jalal 1997; B. Chandra 1989; Pannikar 1991; and Parasher 1992), colonial policies not only invented communal identities but entrenched them even further through codification of varied customary laws into one communal personal law per religion and later through political representation based on communal identities.[4]

Thus, in the colonial era we see a distortion of scale in which multiple local customary laws are scaled down, or up in colonial perspective, to a singular empirewide communal personal law in the context of an

4. In India religious identities are called communal identities.

imperial, transnational legality. This codification obliterated differences within religious communities, including some hard-fought rights against Brahmanic domination among an amorphous category called the Hindus, a group still hard to define. It also led to the privileging of certain scriptures over others as the basis of Hindu personal law. And British interpretation of scriptures became the valid interpretation, and a system that was flexible and diverse was made rigid and uniform. A similar homogenization also affected the Muslim community, whose customary practices had more in common with other non-Muslim communities in the same area than with Muslims in other regions.

Another distortion during the colonial era involved changing customs and practices that were orientational in nature, as guides for judgments, into laws that became the basis for judging diverse religious communities. In the precolonial period most regulation of personal matters was by nonstate local councils. As Agnes notes, "While precolonial society had anti-women stipulations, . . . the scriptures were not statutes and contained several contradictions and ambiguities both internally within each authority, as well as between authorities within a region. Further, the language and the context of these texts was open to several interpretations leading to diverse customs within a pluralistic society. Hence, it would be logical to infer that the customs and interpretations were not uniformly anti-woman and that there were spaces for negotiating women's rights" (1999, 64). But this situation changed with colonization. In the process of communal homogenization, the British were aided by historians and nationalists who projected eighteenth- and nineteenth-century realities onto earlier periods of history. The Catholic-Protestant struggles of Europe were mapped onto the Hindu-Muslim ones of India, and the British refused to recognize noncommunal views of Indian history. This communal history making in the eighteenth and early nineteenth centuries codified an open, mental map into a formal legal map that laid the groundwork for two-nation politics in the twentieth century.

Thus, the laws of British India entrenched identities, and the policies of the Raj politicized them. Lessons of history gave way to the politics of empire (Dhavan 1997, 45). The nationalist struggle took place in a terrain defined by imperial politics and thus reproduced the regulatory aspects of colonial law. With the emergence of the nationalist women's movement in the late nineteenth and early twentieth centuries, the nationalists were forced to consider the issue of women's rights. The women's movement first focused on suffrage for women and then on personal-law reforms. In 1934 the All India Women's Congress (AIWC) both demanded a reform of Hindu personal law and initiated discussion of a Uniform Civil Code.[5]

But the conservative and orthodox sections of the Congress Party vociferously opposed such demands based on patriarchal assumptions about women and their roles and relationships. The Congress supported only a very modified reform of Hindu and Muslim personal laws, which, as Kapur and Crossman (1996) note, did not lead to a discursive victory in terms of the understanding of and assumptions about women. Rather, these reforms further entrenched Hindu-Muslim differences. The reforms within both Hindu and Muslim personal laws made issues of women's rights secondary to male property rights. And the support of the conservative and orthodox forces was necessary for a strong nationalist movement. Hence, the concern over national independence outweighed women's rights.

Postcolonial Reproduction of Colonial Personal Laws

The colonial and nationalist legacy, together with the events of partition, meant that in independent India, the Constitutional Assembly had to deal with the legacy of politicized communities. As Dhavan (1997) notes, the choices before the assembly were limited. On one hand, the religious minorities, particularly the large Muslim minority, had to be compensated for their loyalties. On the other hand, members like Baba Saheb Ambedkar, a *dalit*, wanted a constitution that would be secular, not privileging any community but rather addressing all inequalities based on caste, gender, and communities. Members who were staunchly Hindu, such as K. M Munshi, were opposed to such caste and gender equalities.

5. The AIWC was one of the first organizational expressions of the nationalist women's movement in India.

So how did the Constitutional Assembly chart the course of personal laws? What was to be done with personal laws that were discriminatory to women and hence against the fundamental right of equality between men and women granted in the constitution? One solution was to codify all personal laws into a Uniform Civil Code, or a fundamental-rights solution, which would test the laws against the equality principle of the constitution, a courts-based strategy. But codification can be justificatory, not reformative. Any reformative Uniform Civil Code would require radical transformation and judgments among the different personal laws. And in a charged political climate, such a public debate could be used to chastise the Muslim community. This thought, of course, assumed that Muslim personal laws were more discriminatory toward women than other personal laws.

The second solution was statutory, reform of all personal laws by enacting legislation. The third solution was to leave each community to reform its own personal laws from its own inventive traditions as well as modernizing forces in each community. The third solution was adopted as an accommodating compromise, and the need for a UCC as a desirable goal was articulated in Article 44 of the constitution. Thus, a boundary-setting solution, more regulatory in nature, rather than a pathbreaking one, which could have been more emancipatory, was adopted. In protest, Ambedkar resigned as law minister.

At the end of the constitutional process many such questions were left unresolved. Among them were the issues of the Other Backward Castes,[6] which became politicized in the 1980s, and Kashmir, which is still unresolved. Nehru's own policies were contradictory, and while he wanted to celebrate diversity, his modernizing policies further antagonized communities. This communal resolution homogenized communities and all interests, and ties were seen through the lens of religion. Therefore, no interests that tied people across religions were seen or recognized. It also facilitated a modern communal ideology that dealt with

6. Other Backward Castes are groups just above the *dalits* but at the bottom of the caste hierarchy.

the issue of inequality at the level of the leaders and not the people, who are often its victims.

Women's Movements' Struggles for Personal-Law Reform

It is within this terrain of compromise, of a regulatory legal system with emancipatory aspirations, that women's movements mobilized to empower women. The first wave of the nationalist women's movement became institutionalized after independence, and many educated women were absorbed into the bureaucracy, professions, and even the parliament. Partly in response to the All India Women's Conference, Hindu personal law underwent some reform, and a reformed Hindu personal law came into effect in 1956 that protected the rights of private property more than women's interests. As Alam (2002) notes, this reform was not progressive or modernizing but continued the practice of homogenizing the varied communities. Moreover, the Hindu Reform Act's definition of a Hindu was anyone who was not a Muslim, Christian, Parsi, or Jew. The bill thus made a mockery of religious plurality and choice, as Sikhs, Jains, and *dalits* had no choice but to be Hindus. As Sunder Rajan (2003) notes, this reform was a victory of religious patriarchy.

Like the British in colonial India, the independent nation also homogenized different customary laws into a Hindu law meant more to unify the Hindu community like the Muslim communities. The UCC seemed to be forgotten in the task of nation building. The demand for a UCC was raised again in 1974 in the *Report on the Status of Women in India* as an important aspect of equality for women. The report was written as part of the UN's International Women's Year (1975) activities. The transnational space created by the UN, first through the International Women's Year and then through the International Women's Decade (1975–1985), facilitated a new global "gender-equality regime" that has not been explored fully by the women's groups in the case of personal-law reform.[7]

7. The "gender-equality regime" refers to the norms, conventions, declarations, and legal mechanisms for gender equality supported by the nearly two hundred member nations of the UN (Kardam 2004).

When the autonomous women's movement emerged in the late 1970s and early 1980s, the focus was on rape, dowry deaths, and wife battering (Desai 2001; Gandhi and Shah 1991; Omvedt 1994). Legal activism focused on laws related to violence against women that applied to all women. What brought the UCC back into focus was the now infamous Shah Bano case. At the heart of the case was the right of a Muslim woman to seek alimony outside the Muslim personal-law framework. Shah Bano, a sixty-three-year-old poor Muslim woman, was divorced by her husband of forty years. Under Muslim personal law she was eligible for alimony only for the period of *iddat,* that is, three months after the divorce. Hence, she sought alimony under Section 125 of the Indian Penal Code. The lower courts ruled against her, and her case made it to the Supreme Court. In 1985 the Supreme Court ruled that she was entitled to alimony under Section 125. But in its activist zeal the court noted that this maintenance would not violate the Koran and called for a Uniform Civil Code.

Similar rulings in previous cases had caused little furor. It was the climate of increasing Hindu chauvinism that led to the interpretation of the ruling as an interference in the religious affairs of the minority community. The uproar by the conservative factions of the Muslim community led the then Congress government, headed by Rajiv Gandhi, to enact the Muslim Women's Protection Act in 1986 that would ensure that personal issues would be decided only by religious personal law and not civil penal law. Rajiv Gandhi acted to ensure the Muslim vote and was not swayed by the strong mobilization of feminists, progressive Muslims, and other civil liberties activists opposed to the bill.

The women's movement saw this bill's passage as a loss for women's rights, particularly for Muslim women, and *Manushi,* a leading feminist journal in the country, initiated a debate on the Uniform Civil Code. It concluded that in the prevailing anti-Muslim climate, not just in the civil society but even in the Supreme Court, such a code would function only to rouse anti-Muslim sentiment. The debate went nowhere until a decade later when the right-wing Bharatiya Janata Party raised the issue as one of national integration, meant to chastise the Muslims for wanting to retain religious personal laws. The fact that Hindus, Christians, Parsis, and Jews also had religious personal laws was not noted by the BJP, nor was it connected to their patriotism.[8]

Now, however, there were multiple positions on the UCC. Sunder Rajan (2003) identifies the following main actors: constitutional secularists, who approve a UCC as a directive principle but not a fundamental right; the religious patriarchies of all communities, which are opposed to a UCC or reform in personal laws because it threatens the hierarchy of gender relations within families; minority communities, which oppose it on grounds of freedom of religion; Hindu political parties, which favor it to "remove" the privileges of minority, particularly Muslim, men (they envisage a UCC that would essentially replicate the Hindu personal law as the UCC); communitarians, who oppose the imposition of a UCC as a sign of coercive state secularism and favor instead a pluralist and decentralized polity; liberal secularists, who support a UCC on the grounds of egalitarianism, uniformity of law, and democratic politics; and women's groups, who oppose a UCC because of its political nature and are the only ones to highlight women's rights in the debate.

These various positions focus on two specific issues: the nature of secularism in India and women's rights in the context of personal laws. As a result of this two-pronged focus among the various factions, there are convergences between leftist-liberal secularists and the Hindu Right, who both support a UCC, and between secular communitarians, women's movements, and fundamentalist representatives of minority communities, who all oppose the UCC. Among the secularists there are two positions. One group (see, for example, Jayal 1999) has faith in the modernizing secularism of a separation between state and religion, while the other group (see Bhargava 1998; Chatterjee 1998; and Nandy 1998) favors the Indian version of secularism that is based on equality, tolerance, and respect for all religions, as outlined in the constitution and defined by Gandhi. Most of these groups do not address the issue of women's rights. It is primarily women's movements who focus on women's rights. It is to these debates that I now turn.

8. As the BJP dominated politics in the 1980s and 1990s, however, it did turn on the Christian community as well, and there were several anti-Christian mobilizations and even some gruesome deaths of nuns and an Australian pastor and his family.

As Sunder Rajan notes, the UCC debates in parliament and in public mostly focus on "uniformity versus minority rights, secularism versus religious laws, and modernization versus tradition" (2003, 156–57). Even though patriarchal norms and control of women's sexuality are central to many of the personal laws, women's rights were rarely raised even by women's groups like the All India Women's Conference after independence. It was only after the 1960s that the AIWC and leftist party women's groups began to call for equality for women in all realms, including personal laws.

After the Shah Bano case, this call became more complicated. Most women's groups agreed that all personal laws discriminated against women. Nivedita Menon (1998) outlines five positions among women's groups: a compulsory egalitarian code or a UCC for all citizens, reform from within communities with no state intervention, reform from within communities as well as legislation on areas outside personal laws, an optional egalitarian UCC, and reverse optionality, that is, all citizens to be mandatorily covered by an egalitarian code across personal and public domains but with an option to be governed by the personal laws of their religious community.

The first option has been given up by most feminists as too close to a Hindu Right position, and most favor either a wider civil code that will go beyond personal laws to address women's inequality in all laws and reform from within communities. Flavia Agnes (1999) has been the most vocal proponent of the "reform from within the communities" position. She argues that the UCC as currently conceived and articulated is specifically anti-Muslim and so does more to perpetuate communalism than women's rights.

By way of illustration she cites the consequences of the Muslim Women's Protection Act mentioned earlier. The constitutional validity of the law was recently put to rest by the Supreme Court's decision on September 28, 2001. Agnes argues that the very act that women's groups protested as disadvantaging Muslim women and excluding them from the protection of the constitution has so far worked in favor of Muslim women, as lower courts have interpreted the law to provide "fair and reasonable provision and maintenance." So Muslim women have been getting more support from the act, which was said to marginalize them, than the constitutional maintenance under Section 125 of the Indian Penal Code. Thus, multiple legalities can work in women's favor.

Although this outcome is an unanticipated positive consequence, it cannot be the only basis for emancipatory legality. Agnes sees it as a result of individual Muslim women's agency and notes that it is better to work for changes from within the community than to impose from above, especially in a context that is so highly communal and loaded against the Muslim population in general, and women in particular. Agnes also cites the efforts of the Christian community and the amendment of its personal laws in 2001 in support of her "reform from within" strategy.

There have been attempts by legal scholars, women's movement groups, and the government to initiate discussion about a UCC, and several model drafts have been formulated. As Agnes (1999) notes, most of the legal drafts are concerned with uniformity and regulation of sexuality than with women's and children's rights. The drafts of the women's movement, from the party-based movement and the autonomous movement, are based on substantive equality rather than formal legal equality and favor an optional code with reform from within communities. The party-based draft would also prefer legislation on specific issues covered by personal laws rather than a comprehensive code that would be less likely to deal with the issues of women's rights. Thus, feminists advocate shifting the terrain from personal laws to women's rights for which there is generally more support. Also as a signatory to the Convention to Eliminate All Forms of Discrimination Against Women (CEDAW), the Indian state is accountable for ensuring women's rights.

Agnes (1999) concludes that today most women's groups have moved away from a top-down UCC to a more cautious reform based on education and organizing. Sunder Rajan (2003) argues that this move away from a UCC and toward reform from within is not merely a strategic position. Rather, she argues, it reflects internal problems within the women's movement in India as well as theoretical commitments spelled out by communitarians.

Sunder Rajan draws on Flavia Agnes's (1997) and the Anveshi Law Committee's (1997) critique that the mainstream women's movement in

India is implicitly secular and fails to recognize internal differences and in so doing not only homogenizes the women's movement but also leads to the hegemony of the upper-caste majoritarian norms. Although women on the Left deny such accusations (for example, see Chhachi 1994), the issue as Sunder Rajan sees it is whether having separate religious laws is the best way to recognize differences among women. Another reason women have moved away from supporting the UCC draws on their conflicting position vis-à-vis the state. Here they borrow from communitarian arguments (primarily from Chatterjee 1998) to question the promises and premises of liberalism, nationalism, and citizenship as ways toward equality and justice.

Following such debates in the women's movements, many in the women's movement favor separating the issues of women's rights from the UCC, which has become a tool of alienating the minority communities, especially the Muslims. As examples, they cite legislation around specific issues such as termination of pregnancy, dowry prohibition, and so on that were won without communalizing them. But even within the movement, there has been no discourse over women's economic rights, and without it justice will not be meaningful for the majority of women who also happen to be poor.

Sunder Rajan (2003) posits an alternative that she argues will address issues of economic rights as well as get around pitting women between the state and religious communities: workplaces as spaces where women come together in public, in civil society, and build solidarities for other struggles. It is surprising that she goes back to this old leftist space and model of organizing as the solution when it has been critiqued by women's movements around the world.

Are there other avenues for women's rights aside from the state and religion? I explore some of the possibilities below.

Toward Emancipatory Legal Pluralism

The debates around the UCC and the new global gender-equality regime suggest several potential strategies for an emancipatory legal pluralism. As the UCC has failed primarily because of the hegemonic communalism at the national level, perhaps shifting scales to global legalities might prove useful. India is a signatory to CEDAW and other international women's rights conventions, albeit with reservations. These international treaty obligations can be used to ensure women's rights at the national level, as has been done by international networks such as Women Living under Muslim Laws in what Keck and Sikkink (1998) describe as a boomerang effect.

As Amien (2006) argues for the case of Muslim marriage legislation in South Africa, both the right to freedom of religion and women's rights or gender equality should be protected and held in equilibrium rather than in opposition, as has been done in the case of personal laws in India. In the South African situation, she argues, the right to gender equality is more entrenched in the constitution than the right to freedom of religion. And when there is a conflict between the two rights, rather than subordinating one right to the other, one can make judgments about whether all religious laws and practices are tantamount to religious freedom.

Another avenue for emancipatory legal pluralism is evident in the work of feminists and activists engaging in intercultural dialogues that challenge the distortions over time within all personal laws. Although this approach is clearly difficult to accomplish in an atmosphere of overt hostility against minority communities, which makes them defensive, it is necessary in a multiethnic country.

Mullally (2004), drawing upon Seyla Benhabib, makes a case based on a deliberative, democratic model. She argues that "women are often trafficked" between multiculturalism and gender equality. Rather than oppose feminism and multiculturalism, she proposes a two-track model of legislative reform and cross-cultural dialogue that recognizes the diversity of voices within any cultural or religious community and gives the right of expression to them all. Although these dialogues could be risky and have unintended consequences, as long as they meet the requirements of egalitarian reciprocity, voluntary affiliation, and the option of exiting any community, they can be productive.

Similarly, Santos argues that all cultures aspire to universal values and concerns and all are relative, so there is nothing to be gained by a philosophical posture of either universalism or cultural relativism. Rather, "against universalism we must propose cross-cultural dialogues on isomorphic concerns. Against relativism, we must develop cross-cultural procedural criteria to distinguish progressive from regressive politics, empowerment from disempowerment, emancipation from regulation" (1995, 339). Thus, for emancipatory legal pluralism we need a strategy that is neither universal nor culturally relativist but, as I have argued before (Desai 1997), moves back and forth between historically informed and contingent universalisms and particularisms, whose concern is against social oppression and human suffering. This approach requires a politics and process of knowledge creation that are collective, interactive, intersubjective, and networked. And many in India, both feminists and other progressives, have begun to engage communities in such dialogues. Perhaps potential solutions to the continuing UCC debates in India will emerge from them.

5. Institutions and Women's Rights

Religion, the State, and Family in Turkey

ZEHRA F. KABASAKAL ARAT

The United Nations defines globalization as shrinking space, shrinking time, and the disappearance of borders (*Human Development Report, 1999* 1999). We can clarify this description by noting that it involves increased human mobility and interaction, the creation of an integrated single market, and development of common norms and values. Defined as such, globalization appears to be a *process* that is *age-old* (dating from ancient times), *continuous,* and *irreversible.* Facilitated by technological developments in transportation and communication, as well as by some sociopolitical changes (for example, capitalism and colonization), this gradual process can peak at certain junctures (Z. Arat 2005).

Turkey has been an outward-looking country and active participant in the globalization process. The Ottoman Empire, ruling in three continents for six hundred years, not only integrated markets but also allowed for the coexistence of different religious and ethnic groups and their interaction. Various policies of modernization, which gained momentum in the mid-nineteenth century and were augmented by the nationalist leadership that established the Republic of Turkey in 1923, involved a deliberate effort to integrate Turkey into the Western world. Such efforts of integration and reform had important implications for women and intensified again in the period that followed the military coup of 1980.

In this chapter I focus on three institutions—religion, the state, and family—that have been crucial to defining and maintaining gender roles in all societies. I assess how patriarchal norms have been reproduced, transmitted, and enforced through these three institutions, especially by the state, in the Republic of Turkey. I contend that although the secularization goal of the Kemalist leadership made the state a counterforce of religion and allowed it to create some opportunities for women after the establishment of the republic, the policies followed gender norms that were not much different from the ones promulgated by conservative religious interpretations; in fact, the state and religion, together, supported a culture and family model that reinforced the power of men over women. After examining the impact of these norms on women's lives, I address some important developments that have taken place since the late 1980s and summarize the gender-related aspects of the recent legal reforms. I argue that the provisions favorable to women have been adopted by the parliament rather reluctantly, mainly to meet the conditions set by the European Union, which Turkey aspires to join, but also as a response to the pressure asserted by increasingly active women's groups.

Religion

As a legacy of the Ottoman Empire, the Republic of Turkey encompasses a diverse population. Nevertheless, as the religion of 98 percent of the citizens, Islam has been paramount in shaping the culture.

As a world religion, Islam cannot be defined in singular terms, and its gender ideology is open to interpretation as well. Moreover, the subordination and hardship of Muslim women are caused and reinforced by many factors and cannot be reduced to patriarchal religious norms. Nevertheless, the popular interpretations of the religion have placed women in a secondary position. Here, I will highlight only a few important references frequently *invoked* as proof of men's superiority over women, rather than providing a comprehensive analysis of the gender ideology of Islam.[1]

The Koran grants women property rights to be held under their own names, even after entering into a marital contract, but establishes an imbalance by assigning men inheritance rights that are twice the rights

1. For an assessment of women's rights in the Koran, see Z. Arat 2000.

of women (4:11). This element of inequality is often justified by Islamic jurists as enabling men to meet their Koranic responsibility of serving as the providers of their families (65:6–7). This sexual division of labor creates and maintains other gender roles that subordinate women, which are most profoundly expressed in verses that put men in charge of managing and disciplining women:

> Men are managers of the affairs of women
> for that God has preferred in bounty
> one of them over another, and for that
> they have expended of their property.
> Righteous women are therefore obedient,
> guarding the secret for God's guarding.
> And those you fear may be rebellious
> admonish; banish them to their couches,
> and beat them. If they then obey you,
> look not for any way against them. (4:34)[2]

The Koran does not require the concealing of women and the segregation of sexes, yet these practices have been considered religious requirements by Muslims in many countries, including Turkey. Such beliefs sometimes led to the seclusion of women and to the treatment of their presence in public places (without the company of a male member of the family) and interactions with other men as transgressions.

A Koranic verse that calls for two female witnesses in place of one man (2:288) has been frequently taken out of context, interpreted as implying men's intellectual superiority over women, used to exclude women from decision-making process, and employed as a justification of men's control over women's lives (Engineer 1992; Z. Arat 2000). The cumulative effect of these interpretations has been the designation of public affairs

---

2. The "authentic" intentions and meanings of the Arabic words translated here as "managers of the affairs" and "beat" have been subject to dispute among conservative and modernist exegetes. For various modernist and feminist exegeses, see Barazangi 1997; Engineer 1992; and Wadud 1999. For a brief review of the different interpretations of the verse, see Stowasser 1994, 1998.

and space as the domain of men and promulgation of the notion of an "ideal household" headed by a male provider and decision maker who keeps his wife and other female members of the family at home to raise children and fulfill other domestic responsibilities.

Although feminist and modernist exegeses would differ, local religious leaders perpetuate views that emphasize the subordination of women, as depicted in the following words of a mullah from an Iğdır village in northeastern Turkey: "A woman will never go to hell if she obeys the four principles of our holy Koran. First, a woman must not go out without her husband's permission. Second, she must not give things away without her husband's permission. Third, she must pray and fast in Ramadan. Finally, she must not listen to the voice of strangers except her immediate relatives. . . . When a husband is away, the devil is present in a woman, tempting her to overthrow her virtue" (Morvaridi 1992, 580).

The State

In the 1920s Mustafa Kemal and his followers launched a modernization project that involved the Westernization and secularization of society, thereby ending religion's function as a source of law. Kemalist policies encouraged women's participation in the public domain and improved women's education and employment opportunities, as well as their position in the family. The prowomen stance of the 1926 Civil Code, for example, ended some discriminatory practices such as polygyny, unequal inheritance rights, and men's ability to divorce by repudiation. Although these changes appeared to be deviations from the Ottoman state's and popular interpretation of Islamic law, the regime maintained the main tenets of the prevailing religious morality and perception of gender roles. Seeking economic development and Westernization, the republican leadership attempted to increase women's participation in the economy and public life and to curtail the power of religious rivals under the rubric of secularization, but the European legal codes and cultural norms that informed the Turkish modernization project were themselves patriarchal (Z. Arat 1994a). The limitations of this approach can be observed in laws and administrative policies pursued since the 1920s (ibid.), some of which are highlighted below.

The Civil Code of 1926

The Civil Code, adopted from Swiss law, embodied several articles and clauses that placed men as the first among equals. It identified the husband as the head of the union of marriage (Art. 152/I) and the representative of the union of marriage (Art. 154). He was assigned the right and responsibility of deciding the place of residence (Art. 152/II) and of providing for his wife and children (Art. 152/II). Although the father and mother shared the guardianship responsibilities, in case of disagreement guardianship was granted to the father (Art. 263). The wife's representative rights were limited to legal representation in matters that dealt with providing "the continuous needs of the house" (Art. 155). The wife could take a job or pursue a craft only upon the "explicit or implicit permission" of her husband (Art. 159/I), but the husband could require his wife to contribute to the family budget to "a reasonable extent" (Art. 190). Upon marriage the wife had to assume the husband's family name (Art. 153/I) and was held responsible for taking care of the house (Art. 153/II). The wife's secondary status was affirmed in Article 153/II: "To the extent that she can, the wife serves as the assistant and consultant of her husband to pursue the happiness of the family."

The Penal Code of 1926

Adopted from the Italian one, the Penal Code of 1926 included gender biases and restrictions imposed on women, most explicitly in areas of adultery and abortion. Adultery, which established grounds for divorce in the Civil Code, was also considered a threat to public morality and declared a criminal act (Art. 440–44). The separate definitions of and penalties for adultery for each sex revealed the gender bias: one incident of sexual intercourse was enough for a married woman to be charged with adultery (Art. 440), yet a continuous relationship with another woman that resembled the tie of a husband and wife was sought for men (Art. 441). Moreover, only if the accomplice was an unmarried woman could the husband be charged with the crime of adultery by his wife and punished by imprisonment for three to six months. If the accomplice was a married woman, however, his wife's complaint was not enough to bring up the charge; the adulterous wife's husband had to place a complaint as well. This law also denied reproductive rights for women by banning abortion and seeking prosecution of women who had abortions as well as those individuals who assisted them in the process (Art. 468–69).

Another discriminatory aspect of the Penal Code involved the way it classified crimes and felonies. For example, offenses that involved sexual violence against women were defined as "Felonies against public decency and family order," while other forms of assault against a person were placed under "Felonies against individuals." This "family-oriented" approach of the law also permitted pardoning a rapist if he agreed to marry his victim (Art. 423). Moreover, females' virginity and the honor of married women were upheld as public values and concerns in both the Penal Code and the Law on Police's Duty and Authority (No. 2559, enacted in 1934). The former devised the minimum and maximum sentences for sexual assaults according to the marital status and virginity of the victim, and the latter charged the police with the protection of *ırz* (chastity) and upholding the "public morality and rules of modesty" (Art. 2/I and additional Art. E). These duties, however, did not prevent the police from abusing their power and sexually assaulting women in custody or threatening them with rape to acquire a confession or information during an interrogation. Also, the obsession with honor and the classification of women according to their marital or virginity status have allowed the police to conduct "virginity tests" on women in custody (Amnesty International 2003b; Parla 2001).

The Labor Law of 1972 (No. 1475)

In Turkey employment has been regulated by a number of laws. The most comprehensive law that mainly applied to wage laborers was adopted in 1972. The law assumed a protective posture toward women workers and child laborers. Article 69, for example, imposed a ban on "night work" by women and children. Similarly, Article 68 prevented the employment of women of all ages and male children for work that took place underground or -water. It further barred women from jobs that involved physically demanding, dangerous, and poisonous activities, claiming that they would impair the reproductive function of women. Consequently, women have not been able to participate in better-paying jobs in mining, construction, and heavy-metal and manufacturing industries (Kazgan 1979).

The Labor Law also failed to assist women or accommodate their needs as mothers. Many important issues, including the following, were unaddressed: equal pay for comparable work, job security in case of pregnancy and childbirth, protection against sexual discrimination in hiring and firing and against sexual harassment, and provision of child-care assistance and facilities. The law attempted to protect maternity and motherhood by banning women from work six weeks before and six weeks after giving birth (Art. 70). However, it presented the maternal leave as a "ban" rather than a "right." It did not provide for a sufficient length of leave after birth in case of late delivery, and it allowed the employer to end the contract unilaterally at the end of the maternal leave (Art.13/a), thereby undermining the protective effect of the law. Labor laws addressed maternity leave differently for women in different occupations (for example, press employees, civil servants, and others) (*Women's Status* 1999, 93–94).

Emphasizing the socialization and transformative function of education, the regime supported women's education. However, the educational system also perpetuated the cultural norms and gender roles that considered child care and other household tasks as women's responsibilities (Z. Arat 1994b).

Despite their secular disposition, the discriminatory clauses of various laws and policies preserved the sexual division of labor and women's social and economic dependence on men. Even as it attempted to confine religion, the state subscribed to the same gender norms promoted and perpetuated by the restrictive interpretation of Islam. Thus, the state and religion, together, recognized men as providers and decision makers and defined women's *primary* and *proper* place as being in the home. This judgment reinforced the power of men within the family and allowed them to delineate what is proper for their wives and daughters.

Family and Family Honor

Perceiving women as an underutilized labor force, the Kemalist regime sought to increase women's contribution to the economy. Although the desegregation of sexes was the goal, the state continued to perceive the public domain as belonging to men. Since women's reproductive and domestic functions continued to be seen as their primary responsibilities, participating in the economy and making a living did not liberate even the "working" women.

A study by the Directorate General on the Status and Problems of Women indicates that in Turkey, a woman's employment is seen as acceptable and legitimate only after she fulfills her responsibilities as a wife and mother; urban women's participation in the workforce peaks for the twenty- to twenty-four-year-old age group and declines for the twenty-five- to twenty-nine-year-old age group as a result of getting married and having children (*Supporting Women's Enterprises in Turkey* 2000, 17). The average work life for a woman is eight years, after which she leaves the workforce for family-related reasons such as marriage, pregnancy, or to care for a sick family member (İlkkaracan 1998, 286, 291).

Women, too, tend to view employment outside the home as inappropriate and undesirable. The majority of working women indicate that they work because of family needs; otherwise, they would prefer staying home (Ecevit 1991; Tekeli 1982). Survey findings characterize Turkish women as "family and marriage oriented," meaning that their life plans are centered on getting married and having children (*New Production Processes* 1999, 176).

In addition, a woman's duties toward her family include the preservation of the "family honor." In Turkish culture the *namus* (honor) of a family is largely dependent upon the purity (especially sexual purity and virginity) of its women. This Mediterranean cultural norm is reinforced by the Islamic notion of *fitnah*, which beholds a disruptive potential in female sexuality and treats its containment as necessary to avoid sin and maintain order.

While family honor and social order are connected to the behavior of women, their protection is entrusted to men who are in charge of both the family and public affairs. The emphasis on honor not only restricts women's sexuality, behavior, and opportunities but also arms men with an extraordinary weapon. In addition to putting psychological pressure on women, men of the family—husbands, fathers, uncles, brothers, and so on—can invoke *namus* to justify violence against women and girls.

While the unequal treatment of the sexes in the Civil Code and the Labor Laws was often justified on the grounds of protecting women, no statutory arrangements were made to protect the wife or children against an abusive husband or father. A battered wife could claim continuous physical and psychological abuse to initiate divorce but could not raise criminal charges against her husband because no such crime was defined in the law. On the issue of abuse, the relationship between husband and wife was treated as a private affair, and the state did not assume a protective role.

The judicial system emphasized the importance of women's virginity. Noting that "the late discovery that the wife who was assumed to be virgin was not a virgin constitutes a 'substantial error in quality,' by the man, both subjectively and objectively," judges could treat the absence of virginity as legitimate grounds to annul a marriage (Feyzioğlu 1986, 123). Family honor was invoked frequently in cases of rape. If the woman was married, the courts tended to grant the husband's request for divorce, and if she was not, the family could agree to drop the charges if the rapist agreed to marry the victim (Feyzioğlu 1986). Forcing the victim to enter the union of marriage with her rapist has been pursued as a common strategy of restoring the family honor.

The Kemalist modernization project kept intact the culture that perceived women as symbols of honor. Women were expected to be Westernized in their looks and outlooks, but without neglecting tradition. As noted by Ayşe Durakbaşa, women were presented with conflicting roles and images: an educated professional woman at work, a socially active woman engaged in organizing clubs and associations, a properly trained mother and wife, and a feminine woman dressed in gowns and dancing at balls; they were encouraged to participate in the public sphere but remained restricted by some moral and behavioral codes that would ensure the preservation of "respectability" and "honor" of their families (Durakbaşa 1998).

I would further argue that the modernization project of Kemalism intensified the public preoccupation with *namus,* since it increased women's visibility in the public space and interaction between the sexes. In addition to family members, teachers, principals, and supervisors at work appointed themselves as the guardians of young women's behavior and sexuality, even specifying the quantity and color of lipstick a staff member could wear (Z. Arat 1998b). Until recently, some school officials would order the examination of girls whose virginity was in question. When the suicide cases of two high school girls brought the issue to public attention in 1992, to the amazement and protests of women's rights advocates, the female cabinet minister in charge of the advancement of women's rights defended the virginity tests as necessary and the protection of virginity as a responsibility of the state (Y. Arat 2000, 280).

Consequences of Religion, Law, and Family Culture on Women's Lives

The restrictive environment cultivated by religion, law, and family has resulted in a number of interrelated problems for women and prevented the achievement of gender equality.

Women's employment opportunities and participation in the labor force have been not only low but also declining: 72 percent of the female population aged fifteen and older was economically active in 1955, but the proportion fell to 39.6 percent in 2000 for females twelve and older (State Institute of Statistics 2004, table 5.2).[3] Nearly 57 percent of all economically active women work in the agricultural sector (*Statistical Indicators* 2003, tables 1.15–1.16), where they lack social security and unions and mostly (more than 88 percent) work as unpaid family laborers (*Women's Status* 1999, 35). Many wage earners do not have access to their own earnings, because the men in their families collect the payments (Berik 1984; *New Production Processes* 1999). Women's earnings tend to be lower in all economic sectors and occupations (State Institute of Statistics 2004, table 6.1), as do their promotion rates and representation in managerial positions (*Women in the Health Sector* 2000, 27; *Women's Status* 1999, 35–36; Kabasakal 1998; Acar 1998). A sex-based division of labor is common in factories, where women's work is separated from men's not only vertically but horizontally (Ecevit 1998, 277–78; 1991, 62). Consequently, the overall ratio of female to male earned income is 0.35 (*Human Development Report, 2007/2008* 2007, 331).

---

3. In 1975 the work age was reduced to twelve to accommodate apprentices. Hence, official statistics after 1975 include the twelve- to fifteen-year-old age group.

As a result of the economic liberalization policies led by the International Monetary Fund (IMF) (for example, privatization, freezing wages, and reducing government spending and employment), followed since January 1980, low-income families' dependency on female and child labor increased (Weisband and Öner 2007). The decline in government and private-sector jobs pushed women to seek employment in the informal sector, where jobs are insecure and marginal (*Urban Women* 1999, 29–37).

Education is an area in which women have made significant progress. Between 1935 and 2000 the illiterate female population (six years of age or older) fell from 90.2 percent to 19.4 percent. However, the progress has not been equal for both sexes. In 1935 females were 57.7 percent of the illiterate population; by 2000 this figure soared to 75.5 percent (State Institute of Statistics 2004, table 3.2). Similar gaps have been observed in educational attainment levels; schooling rates for girls decline as the educational level increases (Gök and Ilgaz 2007). Girls' access to vocational training tends to be lower, and the graduates of vocational schools designed for girls emphasize home economics and good housekeeping, which are not particularly marketable or demanded skills (Z. Arat 1994b).

Although women in Turkey acquired the right to vote and run for office in the 1930s, female representation in the parliament, cabinet, and other public offices has remained very low. Until the last elections parliamentary representation remained below 5 percent. A few political parties adopted quotas to guarantee women's representation in parliament but usually set them at a low 10 percent. Women's representation in local governments has been even lower, at less than 1 percent.

An amendment to the 1926 Civil Code set the minimum age of marriage at seventeen, yet parents can accept religious marriage contracts (*imam nikahı*) or go through the courts to change a girl's age to get around this law. Women are seldom able to choose their own partners. Especially in the eastern provinces, where kinship plays a stronger role in social relations, girls and young women are forced to marry according to certain patriarchal traditions such as *beşik kertmesi* (a girl is promised to a friend or the friend's son when she is an infant or toddler), *berdel* (the exchange of girls as brides between two families), "giving away" a girl as a bride to atone for a man killed in a feud, or marrying the younger sister of a deceased woman to her widowed husband upon her death. An abducted girl could be forced by her family to marry a man convicted of "taking [her] virginity." As mentioned earlier, the 1926 Penal Code allowed the charges to be dismissed if a rapist married his victim. The minister of the interior reported in 2002 that 546 men were allowed to benefit from this provision of the Penal Code (Amnesty International 2004, 10).

Family violence, both physical and sexual, has been rampant and largely accepted (ibid., 16). In a 1992 study that focused on the relationship among poverty, marital problems, and divorce, 53.42 percent of divorcées indicated beating as their reason for divorce, and 30.6 percent noted the husband's physical violence toward the children. Of the battered women, 84 percent were slapped, 70 percent were punched, 43 percent were severely beaten and hospitalized, and 55 percent were threatened with death (*Women's Status* 1999, 41–42). Battered women are usually left to their own means, and most of them lack even the support of their own families (Yüksel 1990).

Concern with protecting the family honor, which is connected to the behavior of the female members of the family, leads the male and older members of the family to control and restrict the attire, mobility, interactions, and conduct of girls and women. Violence is used both as a preventive measure and as a penalty. An extreme manifestation of this violence is "honor killings," which involve the murder of a girl or woman by a male kin in the belief that her improper conduct violated moral codes and shamed the family. The practice is most common in the southeastern region and among migrants from there. An estimated 200 women and girls are victims of honor killings in Turkey each year (World Organization Against Torture 2003).

The low value assigned to female life and several forms of discrimination against women (for example, lower nutritional intake, less or no access to health care, higher workload, and less leisure time) result in high infant mortality rates (36 per 1,000 live births) and high maternal mortality rates (130 per 100,000 live births). The lack of prenatal health care and medical personnel to attend births aggravates the situation. Only 64 percent of the married women ages fifteen to forty-nine use contraceptives, and while the average fertility rate is 2.2 (*Human Development*

Report, 2007/2008 2007, 244), it reaches 4.4 in the eastern provinces (*Women's Status* 1999, 39).

Post-1980 Developments

The coup d'état of 1980 led to a brutal three-year military regime that attempted to transform the economy and change the political culture completely. The policies of the regime have had lasting impacts and triggered other changes. Developments in five areas have been particularly important for women: Turkey's candidacy for EU membership, increased ratification of international human rights treaties, the growth of human rights activism and a women's movement, the rise of Islamist politics, and the revival of Kurdish nationalism.

The European Union

In addition to pursuing neoliberal economic policies, Turgut Özal, whose political party won elections and established the first civilian government after the coup, took bold political steps to facilitate the country's integration into the Western economies and the European Union. Turkey filed its formal application for EU membership in 1987 and entered into the jurisdiction of the European Court of Human Rights in December 1989. The number of cases taken to the court grew, and the court's decisions in favor of plaintiffs forced Turkey to recognize the normative framework followed by the court. The desire to join the EU also obliged the country to change its laws to protect human rights and harmonize them with other EU countries.

The impact of the EU candidacy on women has been mixed. While the EU's political criteria for membership (which include respect for human rights) helped improve the legal foundation for the protection of civil and political rights, its economic criteria (which emphasize privatization, competitiveness, and labor flexibility, thus in line with the IMF prescriptions) undermine job and social security (Z. Arat and Smith 2007). Although the antidiscrimination provisions in laws would benefit women, women carry the burden of economic "adjustments" at a disproportionate level, and as the last to be hired and first to be fired they find themselves pushed to the informal economy and marginal positions.

International Human Rights Law

Starting in the mid-1980s, Turkey increased its ratification of international human rights treaties. Turkey became a party to the UN Convention for the Elimination of All Forms of Discrimination Against Women (CEDAW) in 1986 and to its Optional Protocol in October 2002. In 1990 the Directorate General on the Status and Problems of Women was established as the national executive office to coordinate the state efforts and was eventually brought under the Office of the Prime Ministry. Various ministries and state agencies also formed offices focusing on women's issues (for example, the Ministry of Work and Social Security, State Planning Organization, and State Institute of Statistics) and on the implementation of other human rights treaties ratified by the state (for example, the parliamentary Commission on Human Rights, the state ministry responsible for human rights issues, and the Coordinating High Commission of Human Rights). These new offices and agencies have helped attract more attention to women's issues, but they lack the institutional power and funds necessary to accomplish significant changes.

Human Rights Activism and the Women's Movement

During the 1980s increased public awareness about human rights led to the formation of human rights organizations that focused on due-process rights, torture, and related issues. Also, a vibrant women's movement emerged, accompanied and enhanced by a proliferation of women's organizations (Sirman 1989; Ecevit 2007), some of which obtain grants from international foundations and the EU.[4]

A viable women's movement in the early days of the republic achieved women's suffrage in the 1930s, but the key women's organization was later co-opted by the Kemalist leadership. Women's groups were not visible again until the 1960s, and even then they usually operated as auxiliaries of left-wing organizations so that women's rights were not fully articulated or given priority.

---

4. A preliminary tallying of women's organizations around the country identified some 350 organizations in 2003 (see *Directory of Women's Organizations in Turkey, 2003*).

The new women's movement has emphasized consciousness-raising activities and independence. Although skeptical of the state agencies, women's groups embraced CEDAW and used it and other international human rights instruments to pressure the state to improve women's conditions, and at times they collaborated with state agencies (Ertürk and Kardam 1999; Ecevit 2007). They have established a coalition of women's organizations that regularly issue shadow reports submitted to the UN committee that monitors the implementation of CEDAW. Women's efforts, combined with the government's desire to improve Turkey's EU prospects, generated some legislation favorable to women, the most important one being a new Civil Code (discussed later in the chapter). Women also started to use the European Court of Human Rights to redress some violations; the court's decisions in favor of plaintiffs not only helped the victims but also informed the content of future legislation and amendments to the existing laws.

Islamist Groups and Politics

The 1980s also witnessed the rise of Kurdish nationalism and Islamist politics, which included organized militia groups as well as political organizations and parties. Islamist groups and parties challenged the secularist state's ban on wearing head scarves at universities and by public employees in government offices as a violation of religious freedom. These groups were forced to mobilize women wearing head scarves, since the head-scarf ban in universities was largely based on the rationale that the item symbolized religious repression. Islamist women, who wear large head scarves in a particular style that marks their political identity, framed the ban as a human rights violation. They claimed that it not only violated freedom of religion but also amounted to sexual discrimination by preventing women from enjoying their right to education and employment. In challenging the secularist state, demanding their right to enter public space to seek education and employment, Islamist women thereby also questioned the prevailing religious norms and interpretations that advocated a sexual division of labor, the segregation of the sexes, and women's domain as the home (İlyasoğlu 1998). Islamist women have also participated in the women's movement and collaborated with secular women's groups in pressuring the government on other issues such as the implementation of CEDAW and amending the constitution in favor of gender equality.The Adalet ve Kalkınma Partisi (Islamist Justice and Development Party) won landslide victories, both in November 2002 and in July 2007 parliamentary elections, and has been in power as a majority government since November 2002. Eager to achieve Turkey's accession to the EU, the AKP government continued with the legislative reform process established by its predecessors and accelerated privatization and other economic liberalization policies.

Kurdish Nationalism

The impact of the Kurdish nationalist movement has been more complex and discursive. The movement included a separatist armed guerrilla force, the PKK, which clashed with the military and turned the southeastern region into a war zone, as well as civic activism and lobbying activities in Europe. While women became subject to economic hardship, political repression, and violence, as all groups mobilized women, the traditional gender roles, which have been particularly intense in the southeastern region, started to change as well (Çağlayan 2007). The region witnessed the propagation of women's organizations and activism and produced a considerable number of women politicians and leaders.

Legal Reforms

As a consequence of changes initiated in the late 1980s the law has been reformed steadily in favor of gender equality. A milestone in the reform process was the Constitutional Court's decision of November 29, 1990, that itemized the articles of the Civil Code that violated the principle of equality of sexes protected in the constitution and as set forth in several international conventions to which Turkey had become a party (*Women's Status* 1999, 64). Two years later the court abolished Article 159 of the Civil Code, which made a woman's employment conditional on the husband's approval. It also annulled some provisions in other laws on similar grounds that they violated the principle of equality of the sexes. For example, provisions in the Penal Code that defined adultery differently for men and women were annulled in 1996.

The protection of women and children against domestic violence was incorporated into the Law on the Protection of Family (No. 4320), enacted on January 14, 1998. The law listed the forms of violence and unacceptable behavior (Art. 1), defined the state's obligations and the procedures it should follow, and set the penalty for the violators of the "protection decision" as imprisonment ranging from three to six months (Art. 2). Still, the law's title emphasizes the protection of the family rather than victimized individuals within a family, and its shortcomings became obvious in implementation. Enforcement officials overlook psychological violence, evidence is required to prove physical violence, preventive injunctions lack follow-up, and the law does not apply to acts of violence by ex-husbands (Diyarbakır Barosu 2006).

The new Civil Code (No. 4721), which entered into force on January 1, 2002, overhauled the 1926 Civil Code. It marked a drastic shift toward equality by employing the term "spouse" instead of gender-specific references—"husband" and "wife"—and by avoiding allusions to a sexual division of labor and responsibilities within marriage. The new law defines marriage as a union in which "spouses are obliged to maintain the happiness of the union together and attend to the care and education of the children jointly" (Art. 185). Together, they choose their domicile, manage the union, and contribute to the family expenses with their labor and wealth, according to their abilities (Art. 186). Both spouses represent the union throughout their life together (Art. 188). As for employment and work, "Neither of the spouses would need the permission of the other in choosing an occupation or work. However, the peace and interest of the union of marriage is considered in occupation and work choices and their performance" (Art. 1992). Article 202 also specifies a joint-property regime as the default for the wealth acquired by the spouses during the marriage—but not retroactively, as it applies only to the unions established after the law entered into force. The law maintains patrilineal norms by requiring a woman to take her husband's family name upon marriage, but it allows her to use her maiden name before the husband's last name if her written petition is approved by the Office of Population Registration (Art. 187).

The Regulation on Conditions of Work for Pregnant or Nursing Women, Nursing Rooms, and Daycare Nurseries, issued in 1987, entitles women to paid leave for medical checkups during the first trimester of pregnancy and one month after the delivery. Article 7 called for child-care accommodations:

> In workplaces that employ 100–150 female workers, regardless of their age and marital status, the employer is required to establish a nursing room, for infants to be dropped off and cared for and for lactating women to nurse children, in a place that is separate from the work area but no farther than 250 meters from the workplace.
>
> In workplaces that employ more than 150 female workers, regardless of their age and marital status, the employer is required to establish a nursery, for children aged 0–6 to be dropped off and cared for and for lactating women to nurse their children, in a place that is separate from the work area but close to the workplace. If the nursery is more than 250 meters away from the workplace, then the employer is obliged to provide transportation.

Despite the good intentions, the regulation and its 2004 replacement, which maintained the same provisions, have failed to create such facilities; in fact, they may have limited women's employment opportunities because employers tend to keep the number of female workers under 100 or 150 to avoid all child-care accommodation obligations (Acar, Ayata, and Varoğlu 1999, 9; Zeytinoğlu 1998, 192–93).

A new Labor Law (No. 4857), addressing maternity and pregnancy, was enacted on May 22, 2003, and entered into force on June 10 of the same year. Article 74 of the new law entitles women to paid leave for periodic medical checkups during pregnancy; increases the length of maternal leave to sixteen weeks (eight weeks each before and after pregnancy), extending to eighteen weeks in case of multiple births; in cases of late pregnancy allows women to take their unused time after the delivery; permits reduction in the workload during the pregnancy and extended leave as prescribed by a medical doctor; and entitles each woman with infant children to have up to one and a half hours of nursing breaks during each workday (the timing, frequency, and length of which are to be determined by the woman herself). None of these paid leaves can count toward the annual vacation of the employee (Art. 55), and the law imposes a fine on the employer or employer's representative who violates these provisions (Art. 104). However, the new Labor Law still prevents women from work that takes place underground or -water and assigns the authority of determining women's employment for "heavy and dangerous" or "night" work to a regulation that would be issued by the Ministry of Work and Social Security upon consulting with the Ministry of Health (Arts. 72 and 73, respectively).

The legislative reforms of the past decade also included amending the constitution. A law enacted on October 3, 2001, amended Article 41 of the Law on the Protection of Family, which states that "family is the foundation of Turkish society," by adding, "and it is based on equality of the spouses." The equality and nondiscrimination clause (Art. 10) was amended in May 2004 by adding a paragraph: "Women and men have equal rights. The state is obliged to realize this equality in life." Moreover, the amended Article 90 assigns priority to international human rights treaties over the laws of the country in cases of conflict (thus increasing the power of CEDAW).

Recent legal reforms include the replacement of the 1926 Penal Code, which was notorious for its tolerance of violence against women. The new Penal Code (No. 5230), enacted on September 26, 2004, recognizes and criminalizes several offenses against women. Article 102/2 recognizes marital rape, broadens the definition of rape beyond penetration of the vagina by the penis to include the use of objects, and no longer dismisses charges if a rapist agrees to marry his victim. The Penal Code also recognizes domestic violence *(eziyet)* as a crime punishable by three to eight years of imprisonment (Art. 96/2), penalizes the abuse *(kötü muamele)* of household members by other household members (Art. 232), and calls for imprisonment of the person who leaves and neglects a woman whom he impregnated (Art. 233/2). It also increases the penalties for some offenses, such as torture, if they include sexual acts and overtones (Art. 94/3), if the sexual abuser of a child is a person who is a guardian or in charge of protecting the child (Art. 103/3), or if the offense of "denying the freedom of movement of a person" is committed against a parent, offspring, or spouse (Art. 109/3/e). Article 105 defines sexual harassment, indicates a higher penalty if the harassment involves the abuse of a hierarchical or work relationship, and specifies a minimum penalty of one year of imprisonment if the victim was forced to leave work as a result of the harassment. In line with the article on equality before the law and justice (Art. 3), it eliminates discriminatory references and classification of offenses according to the sex of the victim. Although it does not recognize honor killings as a separate category of crimes, it includes "custom killings" *(töre cinayetleri)* (Art. 81/j), and the penalty for the murder of a parent, offspring, or spouse (Art. 81/d) is set at imprisonment for life with hard labor.

Although the overall tone of the new Penal Code still centers on the protection of state security more than individual freedoms and human security, it refrains from criminalizing acts for the sake of protecting public morality. Adultery is no longer a criminal offense, and the protection of chastity *(ırz)* is not addressed in the new law.

Successive governments have acknowledged but not seriously acted upon the need for shelters for battered women and children. Article 14 of a new Law on Municipalities (No. 5215, enacted on July 9, 2004) states, "All municipal governments of metropolises and municipalities with populations exceeding 50,000 shall open shelters for women and children." But the underfunded municipal governments, most of which are in serious debt, are unlikely to build shelters without strong financial support or a mandate from the state. Although 82 percent of the public favors state-run free shelters for battered women and children (E. Kalaycıoğlu and Toprak 2004, 59), municipal governments tend to be susceptible to the preferences of the local elite and are less likely to take radical actions that are protective of women. Despite the high level of domestic violence and relentless work of women's organizations against gender-based violence, as of September 2007 this country of more than seventy million people has established only a total of thirty some shelters for battered women (Y. Arat and Altinay 2007, 25).

Assessments and Prospects

The recent legal reforms were initiated mainly to meet the criteria set by the EU, but domestic pressure cannot be underestimated. The relentless efforts of women's organizations—engaged in lobbying, protest activities, consulting government agencies, and providing data—were consequential for the progressive content of the laws. The new laws are important for removing much of the legal support for discriminatory practices that had been in place since the 1920s. Nevertheless, they retain some discriminatory and restrictive clauses, and their effective implementation will require persistent pressure from national and international advocates of women's rights.

Perhaps owing to the pressure from women's groups, political parties introduced women's quotas, and practically all of them (including the AKP, which opposes quotas) increased the number of women candidates for the 2007 elections. Consequently, the percentage of seats occupied by women in the parliament increased to 8.7 percent (from 4.4 percent in 2002). Although it acquired only twenty-four seats, with nine of them held by women deputies, the political party that relied on a Kurdish constituency in the southeastern region has been the most impressive and the only one that approximated equal representation.

However, political parties' commitment to change and gender equality is not fully proven. Male leadership has been the norm, and female deputies tend to keep a low profile, especially within the governing party, the AKP, which often reverts to policy positions that reveal a traditional understanding of women's roles.

The predecessor of the AKP, the Welfare Party, headed by Necmettin Erbakan in the 1990s, attempted to close the limited number of shelters, defined women's primary roles as housewives and mothers, and supported segregation of the sexes and limiting women's economic participation to only four hours on two days a week (Güneş-Ayata 2001). The leaders of the AKP, some of whom were prominent figures in the WP but broke ties with the Erbakan group, claim to be reformed, that is, religious yet not Islamist. However, the parliamentary debates on women-related articles of the constitution and the Penal Code revealed the persistence of traditionalism among the AKP deputies, indicating that women may have more foes than allies within the ranks of the governing party. Their desire to keep adultery as an offense against public morality in the Penal Code, opposition to the failed constitutional amendment that would protect affirmative action toward gender equality, and insistence on keeping a provision of the new Civil Code that requires a wife to take the husband's last name are but a few instances that raise skepticism about the AKP's commitment to gender equality. Although women's rights supporters among AKP members and parliamentarians are not absent, their numerical and political strength has been neither clear nor reassuring. The resistance to change may be stronger at the local level. For example, a self-help booklet for newlyweds prepared and distributed by an AKP-run municipal government (in Altındağ, Ankara) demonstrated the persistence of patriarchal values. Promoting traditional gender roles, opposing women's education, and supporting men's control in the family, the booklet became a target of protests by women's groups in late 2005. Consequently, its distribution was stopped by an order of the national government.

The establishment of an ad hoc parliamentary committee to investigate gender-based and family violence was a progressive step, and the committee issued a comprehensive report with viable proposals. Most of the recommendations included in the report were incorporated into a circular, issued by the prime minister on July 5, 2006. The circular took a comprehensive approach to violence against women, including addressing inequalities in education and employment, and required all government agencies to take steps to combat it. However, the implementation of the circular's reforms was not followed up, and the questions raised in the parliament by opposition-party deputies fell on deaf ears and received no response from the government.

The judicial branch has not exhibited a consistent approach, either; in fact, some prosecutors and judges appear to be the old guard. Recent divorce cases show that the courts frequently ignore the new Civil Code or interpret it in a way that is unfavorable to women ("Whose Work Is Housework?" 2006).

Lacking rigorous support for their implementation among those persons in power, recent reforms require women's groups and women's rights advocates to be persistent and on guard. Improving women's conditions will also require cultural change because patriarchal norms are largely internalized by women.

Women's rights tend to decline as we move down from international law (for example, CEDAW) to national law and from national law to local laws and customs. Although improvements in national law would help, their effective implementation would require not only constant monitoring and pressure by women's organizations but also cultural transformation, which is more likely to be achieved by continuous work at the local grassroots level.

The emergence of women's organizations, such as KA-MER (http://www.kamer.org.tr), in the southeastern and eastern provinces, where honor killings have been most frequent, has been a critical step (KA-MER 2003 Report 2004; Pervizat 2003). KA-MER's activities range from creating employment opportunities to providing child-care facilities and helping women who are victims of violence. Most important, KA-MER organizes workshops where participants learn about their rights and the patriarchal foundations of their subjugation and daily problems. Participants also gain the self-confidence necessary to challenge these norms within their families and immediate surroundings. There are only a handful of KA-MER groups, located mainly in cities, but the demand for this kind of organization is increasing. Training only ten to twelve women every twelve or thirteen weeks may be a slow process, but it can have a snowball effect. With adequate financial and political support, KA-MER and similar organizations can effectively challenge patriarchal norms prevalent in the institutions of religion, the state, and family.

PART THREE

Family Law Codes Contested and (Re)constructed

6. Struggles over Personal Status and Family Law in Post-Baathist Iraq

JUAN COLE

The position of women and the shape of family law have been a key arena for cultural and imperial politics in post-Baathist Iraq, just as they were throughout the republican and Baathist period. Conflicts over the position of women had a global context in Iraq. On the one hand, the British colonialists had helped install a landed class that coded itself as traditionalist. This large conservative, pro-British landlord class and its clerical supporters were challenged in the 1950s and after by intellectuals, young officers, and workers adhering to the Communist and Baath parties, who deployed progressive, universalist, and international values. The Baath regime from 1968 created a significant population of highly educated Iraqi women. In this regard, it was one of a number of postcolonial Middle East states whose leaders often adopted "state feminist" policies that allowed them to undermine local elites and assert central state power through promotion of women's education and rights (Kandiyoti 1991a, 1992). This state project often contributed to provoking nativist countermovements stressing neo-patriarchy and local control by working-class or lower-middle-class men over their lives and families, as with the Muslim Brotherhood in Egypt or the Shiite movement of Ayatollah Ruhollah Khomeini (Goldberg 1992; Riesebrodt 1993). Where such nativist critics of state feminism later came to power, as in Iran, they often enshrined restrictions on women in the law.

The struggle over the place of women in the post-Baathist period from 2003 to a large extent also had a global context. The middle-class, educated

Iraqi women formed by state feminism saw the fall of the Baath government of Saddam Hussein as an opportunity to make further gains for women by shaping law and administration. The Bush administration also trumpeted the liberation of women as among its goals in Iraq, apparently unaware of the Baath Party's own relatively progressive stance on this issue. Bush's paternalistic rhetoric of imperial uplift for women had the advantage of appealing to American women and liberals, creating a potential constituency for his policies in Iraq among Iraqi women and progressive Arabs and Kurds, and appealing to evangelical tropes of anti-Muslim polemic.

Bush's marriage of convenience with the Shiite religious parties, the Islamic Da'wa Party, and the Supreme Council for Islamic Revolution in Iraq (SCIRI; the name was changed to the Supreme Iraqi Islamic Council in May 2007), however, set up a central contradiction, insofar as these partners had opposed Baathist state feminism and were dedicated to enshrining their conservative interpretation of Sharia or Islamic canon law in the Iraqi constitution and in the statute (Batatu 1986; Wiley 1992). American and Iraqi political actors broached these issues and fought over them most vigorously at two crucial junctures, the drafting of the Transitional Administrative Law (TAL) in January through March 2004 and the drafting of the permanent constitution in the summer of 2005. In the first of these turning points, secular women won significant gains despite strong opposition from leaders of the Shiite religious parties. In the second, these gains were significantly compromised. What political and social dynamics explain these different outcomes?

The fight in the Interim Governing Council over personal status law, which has implications for family law, broke out in January 2004. The grounds for the dispute were laid, however, when the IGC was appointed by U.S. Civil Administrator Paul Bremer the previous July. Bremer sought an alliance with the Supreme Council for Islamic Revolution in Iraq, in part because it had a trained militia of fifteen thousand men and could offset the power of the Baathists. So he gave seats on the IGC to SCIRI and its supporters, including the London and Basra branches of the Islamic Da'wa Party. The IGC had a Shiite majority, though a few members from a Shiite background were secularists. The religious parties' strong representation on the resulting body helped shape subsequent debates.

The IGC grossly underrepresented women, having only three among twenty-five members. In fact, the Iran-Iraq War, the Gulf War, and Saddam's repression of Kurdish and Shiite insurgencies had left Iraq with a female majority of some 60 percent. The strong patriarchal slant of the IGC was to create problems that winter. The United States tended to appoint men to high office, to exclude women, and to bow to vocal patriarchalists whenever challenged. Even where U.S. officials attempted to install women in significant offices, they were often blocked by the resurgent religious Right in Iraq. Coalition Provisional Authority (CPA) officials tried to install a female court judge in the Shiite holy city of Najaf in the summer of 2003, but her first attempt to preside over a case was disrupted by male lawyers, and her appointment never became a reality (Deeb 2004).

Among the women secularists on the IGC was Dr. Raja' al-Khuza'i, an obstetrician and the head of a maternity ward in Diwaniyah in the Shiite South, who had trained in London in the late 1960s and returned to Iraq in 1977. Al-Khuza'i, a fifty-seven-year-old mother of seven of Shiite heritage, was an early advocate of parliamentary democracy who rejected the idea of bringing back the monarchy and was supported by her colleague Songol Chapuk ("Women on Iraqi Council" 2003). Al-Khuza'i initially had a further ally in Aqilah al-Hashimi, a highly credentialed foreign policy expert, also a professional woman with a Shiite background. But al-Hashimi, who had served in the Baath Foreign Ministry, was assassinated in September 2003. She was ultimately replaced by Salamah Khafaji, a dentist from the traditional Shiite city of Karbala who was far more conservative than al-Khuza'i. At least the IGC had three women members. Bremer appointed none to the twenty-five-member constituent assembly initially charged with drafting the Iraqi constitution.

Al-Khuza'i's interest in women's rights and in the welfare of families put her in the mainstream of Iraqis, but her secularism did not. An Oxford Research Center poll that fall found that Iraqis said that what was most important in their lives was family (98 percent), religion (94 percent), and work (83 percent). Less than half felt that politics was important in the fall of 2003, though, interestingly, many more women (43 percent) felt it was crucial than did men (29 percent). This finding suggests that Iraqi women were more political at that point and perhaps felt they had more to lose by inactivity than did men. At the same time, Iraqis reported widespread respect for religious leaders (70 percent) (Cobban 2003).

Secular-minded Shiite women such as Aqilah al-Hashimi and Raja' al-Khuza'i had come to political consciousness in the nationalist and Baathist periods. The 1959 personal status code enacted by the new republic after a military coup toppled the British-installed monarchy had put all Muslims under a unified court system, though it appears to have allowed Christians to continue to follow their canon law. Prominent Iraqi women, who already had an organized women's movement with an upper-class character, played an important role in pushing for and shaping this law (Efrati 2005, 579).

> The law, enacted in 1959, included several progressive provisions loosely derived from various schools of Islamic jurisprudence. It set the marriage age at 18 and prohibited arbitrary divorce. It also restricted polygamy, making that practice almost impossible (the code required men seeking a second wife to get judicial permission, which would only be granted if the judge believed the man could treat both wives equally). And it required that men and women be treated equally for purposes of inheritance. When he was challenged by clerics over this provision, Abdul Karim Kassem, the Iraqi prime minister at the time, responded that the verse in the Koran calling for a daughter's inheritance to be half that of a son's was only a recommendation, not a commandment. (Coleman 2006)

The tendency in the Baathist period (1968–1990) was increasingly to put such matters under civil courts for all citizens (Human Rights Watch 2003; Joseph 1991, 178–79). The Iraqi Provisional Constitution, written by the Baath Party in 1970, made all citizens equal before the law without regard to religion, ethnicity, or gender. The Baath state also insisted on universal compulsory education for both boys and girls and instituted laws guaranteeing good treatment for women in the workplace. Women entered the workforce in great numbers during the 1970s and 1980s and were especially prominent in education, medicine, and medical research.

In 1978 the Baath government made some small alterations in the 1959 law on personal status, picking and choosing among Sunni legal rites and the Shiite Ja'fari legal code to find what its officials thought of as progressive provisions. Suad Joseph summarizes them: "For example, in cases of divorce, mothers were given custody of their children until the age of 10 (previously 7 for boys and 9 for girls) at which time, at the discretion of a state-employed judge, custody could be extended to 15. At that age the child could choose with which parent to stay. The code widened the conditions under which a woman could seek divorce" (1991, 184; see also Efrati 2005). An age of marriage for girls was also set, something lacking in the earlier law. The 1959 statute was not entirely secularized by the Baath government, despite its generally nonreligious commitments, so as not to alienate completely religious conservatives. Women in the Baath-sponsored General Federation of Iraqi Women admitted to Joseph in 1980 that the party put building the state and nation above women's liberation as goals. In addition to these small changes in personal status law, the Baathists did use legislation to promote a better position for women in society. Women had the same rights as men in the workplace with regard to "pay, pension, training, advancement. retirement, compensation and medical care" (Joseph 1991, 185). Women also gained the right to vote and stand for office in 1980, though, of course. Baathist elections were mainly for show, as with Soviet ones. Still, women did sit in parliament.

The late 1980s and the 1990s witnessed a general rollback in the rights gained by women in the 1970s. In 1988 Saddam enacted a law allowing honor killings of unfaithful wives. Charles Tripp argues that such decrees subordinated the universal rule of law to the private interests of the Saddami ruling clique. It was, after all, made up of men who liked their privileges. Women and their organizations were thus not subjects of rational-legal state legislation but recipients of Saddam's largesse, which he could arbitrarily withdraw (Tripp 2000, 227). In 1990 Saddam enacted a new penal code that made polygamy easier to practice and reduced women's rights with regard to inheritance and divorce. Article 427 allowed a rapist to escape punishment if he married his victim, and Article 409 was lenient toward husbands' crimes of passion, including murdering an unfaithful wife (Sandler 2003).

After the Gulf War, Saddam increasingly turned for support to tribal chieftains and Muslim religious leaders. Their growth in power led to new restrictions on women's freedom of movement. The crippling sanctions of the regime drove down family incomes and made it harder to send girl children to school. Women's literacy fell from 75 percent in 1987 to only 25 percent in 2000, according to UNESCO. Human Rights Watch argued that in the course of the 1990s, women and girls also suffered from increasing restrictions on their freedom of mobility and protections under the law (2003, n.p., n. 27). Both the declining economy and a weaker state more dependent on local patriarchal elites contributed to the marginalization of women in the public sphere. In collusion with conservative religious groups and tribal leaders, the government issued numerous decrees and introduced legislation that had a negative impact on women's legal status in the labor code, criminal justice system, and personal status laws. In 2001 the UN Special Rapporteur for Violence Against Women reported that after the passage of the reforms in 1991, an estimated four thousand women and girls had been victims of "honor killings." In recent years both the Kurdistan Democratic Party and the Patriotic Union of Kurdistan administrations in northern Iraq have issued decrees suspending laws allowing for mitigation of sentences in honor crimes, but the degree to which the suspension has been implemented is unknown.

Some secular-minded women saw the fall of the Saddam regime as an opportunity to gain significant advances in women's rights. In early December 2003, al-Khuza'i coauthored an opinion piece for the *New York Times* arguing for set-asides in the new Iraqi parliament for women representatives. Her commitment to this cause led her to favor caucus-based elections rather than one person, one vote, in the polls then scheduled for May 2004. Bremer and the IGC had agreed on this plan on November 15, 2003, as the country spiraled out of control and Washington recognized a need to install an Iraqi government. The caucuses would be drawn from members of provincial and some municipal councils that had been massaged into being through small unrepresentative elections held in provincial capitals among local elites willing to support the Americans and British. This plan was rejected by Grand Ayatollah Ali Sistani on the grounds that it was undemocratic and would not result in a government that reflected the will of the Iraqi people (J. Cole 2006). That is, Sistani saw the caucuses, which limited the electorate to handpicked members of provincial and municipal councils, as means by which the United States might shape the electorate and influence the constitution. In contrast, secular women like al-Khuzaʻi and the minority members of the IGC such as the Kurds saw them as guarantors that populist religious forces would not dominate the results.

Al-Khuzaʻi's progressive stances on women's rights were about to run into trouble. Already in December 2003 the women on the IGC had been forced to attend meetings wearing head scarves. It was clearly not the first instinct of either al-Khuzaʻi or Turkmen member Songol Chapuk. Throughout the country, religious paramilitaries had sprung up, both in Shiite and Sunni areas, which demanded that women veil in public. In the southern city of Basra, according to a series of articles by Ahmad al-Jawdah in the Pan-Arab London daily *Al-Sharq al-Awsat* in late December 2003, unveiled women were harassed, and liquor stores were closed. The poor security situation had an especially bad impact on women, imprisoning many in their homes and opening them to being kidnapped for ransom, as an estimated four hundred were in the fall of 2003. The behavior of U.S. soldiers, who often invaded homes and bedrooms, shaming Iraqi men by seeing their women in an intimate setting, also made many men more concerned with the veiling of women. It was reported that because U.S. soldiers so often kicked down bedroom doors, "One Iraqi says women in his village now sleep fully clothed, in case 'unbelievers' break into their houses at night. True or not, it is the kind of story that quickly spreads and poisons the image of liberation the allies want to cultivate" (Nelson 2003).

The Interim Governing Council had adopted the practice of having a rotating presidency, in which each of nine prominent members served for one month, going in Arabic alphabetical order by the first letter of the first name. In December the presidency was held by Abd al-Aziz al-Hakim. A younger son of the paramount grand ayatollah in Najaf in the 1960s, Muhsin al-Hakim, Abd al-Aziz had fled to Iran in the early 1980s. There he emerged after 1984 as the head of the Badr Brigade, later the Badr Corps. This organization was the paramilitary wing of the Supreme Council for Islamic Revolution in Iraq, an umbrella group that comprised a number of revolutionary Shiite movements expelled by Saddam Hussein from Iraq. The Badr Corps infiltrated Iraq to strike at Baathist targets all through the

1990s. The al-Hakims in Tehran were close to Iranian hard-liners such as Supreme Jurisprudent Ali Khamenei.

Abd al-Aziz al-Hakim came back to Iraq in April 2003. At that time he gave an interview to a satellite television station in which he spoke of the future he envisioned for Iraq. He said that at first there would probably be a period of pluralism and parliamentary rule. In the long run, he implied, Iraq's Shiite majority would establish an Islamic state. The al-Hakims grew close to Grand Ayatollah Ali Sistani in the summer of 2003. On August 29 Muhammad Baqir al-Hakim was assassinated by a car bomb in Najaf. He had been the leader of SCIRI since 1984. His younger brother, Abd al-Aziz, became the leader of the movement.

On December 29 al-Hakim called a meeting of the Interim Governing Council shortly before he was to cycle out of the presidency. At that point, as he no doubt knew, the three women members of the IGC were out of town. He introduced a resolution, Decree 137, that abrogated the 1959 law governing personal status, as well as subsequent amendments by the Baath regime such as the revision of 1978. Decree 137 put all Iraqis under the authority of their religious community's canon law with regard to marriage, divorce, inheritance, child custody, and other such personal status matters. That is, initially civil courts would judge Shiites under Shiite religious law, Sunnis by their code, and Chaldean Catholic Uniates by canon law. It was perhaps the intention that ultimately Sharia court benches would be established for this purpose. Similar systems are employed elsewhere in the Middle East, including in Lebanon and Israel, and had been characteristic of Iraq under the constitutional monarchy from 1921 to 1958.

Word of al-Hakim's legislation leaked out in early January 2004. An online summary of Iraq news revealed this headline in early January: "Civil Status Courts Must Apply Islamic Shariah, IGC Says" (*Iraq Press* 2004). The article said that under Saddam, personal status affairs needed to be registered at state-sponsored civil status courts and that many regulations were not in strict conformity with Islamic law. Indeed, all marriage, divorce, and birth certificates had to come from civil courts. One regulation required that couples desiring to marry had to appear before a civil court judge with two witnesses and had to comply with the court clerk's instructions in having a medical examination beforehand. In many Muslim countries clerics rather than civil court judges preside at marriage signing ceremonies *(nikah)*. In Iraq many Muslims, especially the ones opposed to the regime, went to clergymen for these purposes, refusing to deal with Saddam's courts. The resulting documents, however, had no official standing in the eyes of the state. The Sadr II Movement among the Shiites, founded by the martyred Ayatollah Muhammad Sadiq al-Sadr (d. 1999), was especially fervent in setting up informal Shiite courts (J. Cole 2003). Decree 137 abolished all the personal status laws and regulations instituted by Saddam Hussein and stepped back from any uniform legal code for such matters. The vice president of the Shiite Endowment Court, Jalal al-Saghir, argued, "The current law has nothing to do with Islam. It is the worst law ever since it gave women the right to willingly get a divorce. It also gave women equal rights with men in inheritance, contradicting Islamic law . . . [and] forced Iraqis to get married according to the Sunni Hanafi sect, including Christians" (Haris 2004).

The middle-class women of Iraq, many of them formed politically in the late 1960s through the 1980s when they enjoyed greater legal freedoms than most Arab women, refused to take the Shiite clergyman's démarche lying down. On Tuesday, January 13, 2004, the Iraqi newspaper *Al-Zaman* reported that they mounted widespread small demonstrations against the new law, saying that it "repeals women's rights" (see also Efrati 2005). About 100 women activists representing 80 women's organizations gathered at Firdaws Square in downtown Baghdad to protest the IGC decree. They were joined by Minister of Public Works Nasreen Barwari, the only woman member of the cabinet, who thereby joined a protest against the very government in which she served! Barwari complained bitterly about the "lack of transparency and democratic consultation" in the passing of Decree 137. The placards of the protesters were inscribed with phrases like "No to Discrimination, No to Differentiating Men and Women in Our New Iraq!" and "We Rejected Decree 137, Which Sanctifies Religious Communalism!" A Communist, Zakiyah Khalifah al-Zadi, complained that the law would weaken Iraqi families. The protesters objected that the IGC had ceded to the religious codes' jurisdiction over marriage, engagement, suitability to marry, the marriage contract, proof of marriage, dowry, financial support, divorce, the three-month "severance payments" owed to divorced wives in lieu of alimony, inheritance, and all other personal status matters.

On Thursday, January 15, protesters staged another round of street protests against Decree 137. The newspaper *Al-Zaman*, close to Sunni Arab nationalist circles, carried a number of essays by Iraqi intellectuals denouncing the decree as harmful to Iraq (Al-Jamil 2004). Some 150 prominent women also held a conference on the issue in which IGC members Adnan Pachachi, Dara Nureddin, and Nasir al-Din Chaderchi listened to what the Agence France Presse (AFP) called "the irate women" (2004a). Pachachi by that time had rotated into the presidency of the IGC. He and Chaderchi were old-time Sunni Arab nationalists of the 1960s variety (Chaderchi's father had had a small nationalist party in the 1960s), and Nureddin is a Kurdish court judge. Pachachi assured the women that the decree was not yet the law of the land and that there was still substantial dissension about it within the IGC. Conference organizer Nidal Abdul Amir said the conference was being called to "refresh" the legislators' memories, presumably about the importance of Iraqi women as a constituency. She complained, "I was hoping that all Governing Council members would participate, but they could not be bothered, while we had women come from all over Iraq." Al-Zadi, the Communist activist, warned that the decree was a Trojan horse for a clerical theocracy in Iraq. There were also small demonstrations in Baghdad in favor of the new law on personal status, with supporters saying that "Islamic law contains divine decrees and specifies clearly the rights of women" ("Debate Flares Up" 2004).

The middle-class Iraqi women activists, by their demonstrations and conference, had drawn attention to the issue in the United States. As had happened with regard to the Taliban regime in Afghanistan, congressional representatives became alarmed and decided to step in. Forty-four lawmakers, headed by Representatives Carolyn Maloney (D-NY), Eddie Bernice Johnson (D-TX), and Darlene Hooley (R-OR), complained about the IGC's implementation of Islamic law and urged the White House to step in to safeguard women's rights in Iraq (Lobe 2004). The Bush administration had made a paternalist theme of white men liberating Muslim women from the patriarchal domination of their own Muslim fathers, brothers, and husbands a keynote of its 'war on terror." In an election year the administration clearly hoped to use this issue as a way of blunting the advantage Democrats generally had with female voters. Decree 137 was threatening to blow up in Bush's face and to allow his political enemies in the United States to paint him as a purveyor of "medieval" Islamic legal restrictions on women in Iraq. Zakia Ismail Hakki, a retired judge, told the *Washington Post* that the resolution would "send Iraqi families back to the Middle Ages. It will allow men to have four or five or six wives," she said. "It will take away children from their mothers. It will allow anyone who calls himself a cleric to open an Islamic court in his house and decide who can marry and divorce and have rights' (Constable 2004). Maloney and the other women in Congress were particularly angered that Undersecretary of Defense Paul Wolfowitz (2004) had just published an opinion piece that neglected to mention Decree 137 and trumpeted the administration's liberation of Iraqi women.

The decree was also unwelcome in the Kurdish parliament, which met on February 6 and formally rejected the new law. Its statement stressed that it would abide by the civil uniform personal status law of 1959, as amended by the Kurdish administration since 1992. (Because of the American no-fly zone and Kurdish semi-independence from Saddam, the Kurds had been conducting their own administration for more than a decade.) A Kurdish representative on the IGC, Mahmoud Osman, himself rejected the IGC decree, saying, "The 1959 law guaranteed many just rights to women and affirmed their equality with men. The decision of the Governing Council turns over family law to religious laws for a decision, rather than to civil courts. . . . If we employed religious systems of law, matters such as inheritance and polygamy would not be just with regard to women" ("Parliament of the Iraqi Kurds" 2004). Osman's comments underlined the rift between the Kurdish North and the Shiite South. In the latter, Sharia law and obedience to the Shiite ayatollahs were popular values.

In contrast, Decree 137 picked up the support of the largely Sunni Iraqi Islamic Party (IIP), which had roots in the Egyptian Muslim Brotherhood. Muhsin Abd al-Hamid, its leader, became president of the IGC in February. He immediately weighed in on the need for a new constitution to be drafted that would reflect the Islamic character of Iraq (Krane 2004a). Alarmed, Bremer announced that Decree 137 could not become law until he signed it. Since he was a very lame duck, that statement might have only delayed matters until an Iraqi government took over sovereignty a few months later (Krane 2004b).

As February progressed, prominent women began speaking out against the lack of women's representation on the IGC and among the appointed ministers of the government. They also demanded that the new Iraqi parliament have seats set aside for women, as had been instituted in Pakistan in 2002. The proposals ranged from 25 percent to 40 percent of parliamentary seats. Worldwide, with the partial exception of Scandinavia, relatively few women serve in parliaments that do not have gender-based quotas, and Iraqi women notables were determined to have a voice. They were no doubt galvanized by Decree 137, which demonstrated to them where Iraq might go if parliament were virtually all male and dominated by religious parties. Safiya al-Suhail, the *shaykhah,* or clan leader, of the Banu Tamim, was especially vocal on the need for women's leadership. She had been elected by her brothers on the death of their father in the mid-1990s (Khalil 2004). Groups of women all around Iraq demonstrated on Wednesday, February 18, demanding that 40 percent of seats in parliament be reserved for women ("Iraqi Women Demand 40% Share" 2004). Around the same time, the Iraqi National Council of Women was established and met for the first time, with six hundred delegates at a convention center in Baghdad. It was addressed by al-Khuza'i, who argued again for having 40 percent of parliamentary seats go to women (Allam 2004).

The professional women continued to face significant opposition, as members of the Muslim parties and their supporters agitated for restrictions on women. On February 26 Jawad Kazim al-Anani, who had just been appointed to a high position in the Baghdad provincial government, issued a decree requiring enforced veiling of women municipal employees during business hours. One newspaper reported that he thereby deeply offended hundreds of female government employees. Some employees said that no formal action had been taken against them for not veiling, but they had received various forms of pressure to do so. Al-Anani was fairly quickly forced to resign, presumably by the CPA.

At the end of the month the Islamists suffered a defeat when the IGC abrogated Decree 137. An informed source reported that IGC member Raja' al-Khuza'i, who missed the first vote, had insisted that the directive be reconsidered in light of the angry public response to it. After a heated discussion the directive was voted down fifteen to five, with five absent. In the late-December meeting when al-Khuza'i and another woman member were absent, it had passed eleven to ten. The IGC members voting to retain Decree 137 were from al-Da'wa, SCIRI, and, presumably, the Iraqi Islamic Party. Supposed secularist Ahmad Chalabi instructed his nephew Salem Chalabi to join them on this issue (Fayyad 2004; AFP 2004b; Diamond 2005, 171–72).

The women's issue had been taken up as a stalking horse by both the Islamist and the more secular parties and male politicians, and the reactions to the news underlined the rift. In Kufa the young Shiite leader Muqtada al-Sadr renewed his threat to lead a rebellion if Bremer continued to reject the position that Islam be specified as the sole source of legislation in the new constitution, saying in his sermon, "America only came to harm Islam, but the occupiers will not be able to wipe out Islam. . . . I call on the believers to be fully prepared, when the orders come from the religious leadership, to challenge the occupation." He added, "I call upon the governing council to announce a rebellion against the decision, and I demand of Bremer personally to retreat from his statement against Islam" (Dergham 2004).

The struggle over Decree 137 and the reintroduction of religious personal status law in Iraq played out in a number of arenas simultaneously. It was only the first episode in a long-term struggle. It pitted leaders of Islamic parties such as Shiite cleric Abd al-Aziz al-Hakim against educated or notable women like Raja' al-Khuza'i, Nasreen Barwari, and Safiya al-Suhail (a Shiite physician, a Kurdish politician, and an Arab *shaykhah*, respectively). Al-Khuza'i crafted a parliamentary victory in the twenty-five-member IGC, but was helped in doing so by the other fissures that the decree had opened up. The Kurdish parties saw it as an attempt by Baghdad to dictate law to them, and that thought turned at least a majority of the Kurdish representatives against it. The Sunni Arab nationalists had a secular bent and feared the influence of the ayatollahs, so Adnan Pachachi and Nasir al-Din Chaderchi came out against it. With three women, the Communist delegate, the Kurds, and the Sunni nationalists on her side, al-Khuza'i was able to put together a fifteen-member majority and isolate the Islamists.

She gained this victory, however, with significant help from beyond the IGC. The Iraqi women's demonstrations and conferences had made the point to Pachachi and others that this issue was important to a significant constituency, and most of the IGC members had further political ambitions. The intervention of the U.S. congresswomen had signaled to the Bush administration that Decree 137 was a potential campaign issue in the looming election. It seems that U.S. Civil Administrator Paul Bremer and his staff weighed in behind the scenes with IGC members to convince them to repeal the decree. Bremer wrote in his memoir, "On February 27, the Islamists returned to the Council with the role of Islam still unsettled. In a surprise move, Pachachi opened the meeting by calling on one of the GC's female members, Dr. Raja' al-Khuza'i, a secular Shia doctor. She had brought a crowd of women and press into the council chamber, and proposed repealing Resolution 137. Caught off guard, the Council voted to repeal the resolution, which provoked loud ululations from the crowd and an angry walkout by the Islamist Shia members" (2006, 293). One author (Coleman 2006) wrote that Bremer quashed Decree 137 by fiat, but that description ignores the important role played by al-Khuza'i and Chapuk, the two secular women, in rallying their Sunni, secular, and leftist colleagues on the IGC. These negotiations were simultaneous with the crafting of the new interim constitution, or Transitional Administrative Law.

In the end, the religious parties and leaders accepted the outcome, in part because they recognized that they had been outvoted. In part, however, they also felt that further wrangling over the constitution and personal status law might delay the transfer of sovereignty scheduled for June 2004. Without at least a temporary settlement of these issues, no handover by the Americans was practical. They therefore acquiesced in the TAL and the abrogation of Decree 137, viewing it as a tactical defeat. A new parliament to be elected in January 2005 would craft a new constitution. The outcome of that election would be far more significant than the disputes within the IGC.

Al-Khuza'i lost the battle to reserve 40 percent of the seats in the new parliament for women. Although eighty countries set aside some seats for women, Bremer is said to have initially refused to consider the idea "out of a Republican ideology" (Braude 2005; Diamond 2005, 145). In the end, 25 percent of seats were reserved for women.

Despite opposing the only mechanism that would ensure women seats in the parliament, the Bush administration continued to underline women's rights as among the justifications for its presence in Iraq. On International Women's Day (March 12), Bush told an assemblage of 250 women from around the world (including Raja' al-Khuza'i), "The advance of women's rights and the advance of liberty are ultimately inseparable" (CPA 2004).

The United States cooperated with the United Nations and the IGC in appointing a transitional government under Prime Minister Iyad Allawi, an ex-Baathist and longtime CIA asset, which took office June 28, 2004. No women served in the highest executive offices of this government, and they received only six low-level cabinet posts (Hunt and Posa 2004). Since the Bush administration had adopted a rhetoric of women's progress, and since it appointed this government in cooperation with the UN, the outcome struck women's groups as incommensurate with Washington's rhetoric.

Women's rights and the personal status law emerged again as hotly debated issues during the drafting of the permanent constitution in the summer of 2005. In the January 30, 2005, election a parliamentary majority was gained by a coalition of Shiite religious parties, the United Iraqi Alliance (UIA). The Sunni Arabs largely boycotted the election. Grand Ayatollah Ali Sistani had insisted that the permanent constitution be drafted by elected delegates, and, although he was opposed by Bremer, he won on this issue. The outcome was that the religious Shiites and the Kurds dominated the constitution-making process. Sunnis had a largely consultative role and in the end were simply overruled on issues about which they cared, such as the question of a loose federalism versus a strong central government (the Sunni Arabs favored the latter). The committee was headed by a Shiite cleric from SCIRI, Humam al-Hamudi, a signal that the party was determined to shape the constitution in an

Islamic direction. Even though women were some 25 percent of deputies in parliament, only about nine of the seventy-one members of the drafting committee were women, and religious women dominated the delegation.

In August U.S. Ambassador Zalmay Khalilzad warned the Shiite religious parties not to put language in the constitution that was discriminatory toward women or minorities, presumably because of troubling reports that had reached him about the draft. According to a Kurdish member of the committee who leaked information to the Arabic press about the drafting process, the UIA, which wanted to do away with the 1959 personal status law, was engaged in a struggle with the Kurdistan Alliance, which wished to retain it. The Islamic Da'wa Party had opposed the 1959 law from the beginning, and the religious Shiites now had an opportunity finally to do away with it. The same source said that the Kurds viewed the law as not contravening the principles of Islam and as relatively progressive. He revealed that the Shiites also wanted stronger wording prohibiting parliament from passing laws that contradict the established principles of Islam, wording that the Kurds rejected (Fayyad 2005).

The Shiite religious parties proved too strong, however, for the United States and its Kurdish allies on issues of secularism. In a major dispute over whether Islamic law would be the fundamental source or only one of the sources of Iraqi law, the Shiite religious parties prevailed over the Kurds. The AFP attributed this victory to U.S. acquiescence, out of fear of being perceived by its Iraqi partners as hostile to Islam (2005). *Al-Hayat*, leaking details of the draft constitution, wrote:

> Also, an agreement was reached that Islam is the religion of state, and that no law shall be enacted that contradicts the agreed-upon essential verities of Islam. Likewise, the inviolability of the highest [Shiite] religious authorities in the land is safeguarded, without any allusion to a detailed description. The paragraph governing these matters will specify that Islam is "the fundamental basis" for legislation, though there will be an allusion to the protection of democratic values, human rights, and social and national values. A Higher Council will be formed to review

new legislation to ensure it does not contravene the essential verities of the Islamic religion. (see also Wong 2005)

Personal status law, concerning marriage, divorce, alimony, inheritance, and so forth, would according to this draft be adjudicated by religious courts in accordance with the religion or sect to which the individual belonged.

The recognition in the draft constitution of a special status for the grand ayatollahs in Najaf, the formation of a clerical council to vet laws for their conformity to Islamic codes, and the abolition of civil personal status law, forcing all Iraqis to live under the law of their religious communities (with all of the consequences for women that doing so might entail), provoked controversy in Iraq and in the United States. The plan struck many as far too close to the Iranian model, where the clerical Council of Guardians has review authority over legislation by parliament. Yet not everyone was appalled at this prospect. In Basra a thousand Shiite women demonstrated in favor of Islamic law, and others defended boys' receiving twice the inheritance that girls are awarded, as stipulated in Sharia, on the grounds that men have more financial responsibilities (R. Carroll 2005).

The text of the constitution that was finally approved specified in Article 1 that "Islam is the official religion of the state and is the fundamental source for legislation. It is not permitted to draft a civil statute that contradicts the established laws of Islam" (Arabic Wikipedia 2005). Most wireservice translations failed to convey the full force of this language, which made Sharia unchallengeable. The text goes on to say that no legislation may contradict the principles of democracy or "basic freedoms" spelled out in the constitution, either. These contradictions will likely result in enormous numbers of lawsuits if the security situation calms down and Iraq goes forward on the basis of this constitution. Given the influence of religious parties in Iraqi politics, the principle of the incontrovertibility of Islamic canon law could easily function as a Trojan horse, allowing the transformation of Iraq into an Islamic republic. Some observers have argued that Sharia is a flexible legal system and that all would not be lost for women if a progressive interpretation of it were implemented in

Iraq (Coleman 2006). Although it is true that Sharia can be flexible in the hands of reformers, the political momentum in Iraq has been enjoyed by hard-line fundamentalist parties such as the Sadr II Movement, SCIRI, the Islamic Da'wa Party, and the IIP. These parties, which so far have dominated the parliament, will appoint the court judges that interpret the law, and it is likely that their appointees will favor highly patriarchal rulings. Since the constitution recognizes the primacy of regional laws over federal ones, it is also possible that provincial confederacies will adopt an even more conservative interpretation of Sharia and impose it on women in those regional governments when they are formed (Al-Ali and Pratt 2006). MP al-Khuza'i, dismayed at the draft language, announced that she would emigrate: "This is the future of the new Iraqi government—it will be in the hands of the clerics. . . . I wanted Iraqi women to be free. . . . I am not going to stay here" (Filkin 2005).

As the constitutional drafting process continued long after the August 22 deadline, the Kurds, Sunnis, and Americans won a few concessions from the religious Shiite deputies on several other contentious points. The direct reference to the authority of the grand ayatollahs in Najaf was removed, as was provision for an Iranian-style clerical council with power of review over legislation to ensure its conformity with Sharia (Daragahi 2005). A compromise was reached on the issue of personal status and religious law, such that Article 39 read, in the end, "Iraqis are free to adhere to personal status [laws] in accordance with their religions or rites or beliefs, or their choice, and this matter will be organized by statute." Most observers took this language to mean that the individual could choose to be under the authority of Shiite law or Catholic law, or could choose instead to be under the 1959 civil code (without the Baath-era alterations?). Since the clarifying and enabling legislation has not so far been passed, however, its exact meaning remains undetermined. For instance, if parliament struck down the 1959 law and specified that all personal status matters had to be adjudicated under the law of some religious community in Iraq, that step would foreclose the option of choosing the more secular civil law. Indeed, Mariam Areyyes, a former member of parliament, complained in October 2006 that moves were afoot to amend the constitution in such a way as to put all Iraqis under religious law and abrogate the 1959 law (Fayyad 2006).

◆ ◆ ◆

The 2003 fall of the Baath government initiated a vigorous renegotiation of Iraqi national identity in which ambitious politicians sought to mobilize the populace on ethnic and sectarian grounds. In Arab Iraq, both Sunni and Shiite, fundamentalist religious parties grew enormously in importance. Movement away from the secular Arab nationalism of the Baath era toward Islamic politics inevitably raised the question of women's status. Although the Baath Party never secularized personal status or family law out of deference to conservative religious sentiment, it resorted to the stratagem of picking and choosing among Islamic legal rites in order to raise women's status within personal status law. It also passed laws giving women equality in other spheres of life. Baath officials had wielded a feminist state project as part of their challenge to local religious and tribal elites. Dissident parties such as Da'wa, SCIRI, the Sadr II Movement, and the Sunni IIP stressed renewed patriarchy as part of their opposition to the Baath legacy and their championing of local traditions. Religious fundamentalism as a modern phenomenon is highly correlated with a reassertion of patriarchy in the face of modernity. Female literacy and education and the entry of women into the urban workforce profoundly challenged men whose fathers had been the sole breadwinners and lords of their domestic domains. Conservative Islamic politics is a way for men to constrain women, promoting gender segregation (which effectively reduces their access to professional schools) and sometimes seclusion in the home, as well as promoting obedience to the husband within marriage. Many religious women find Islamic conservatism attractive, as well, insofar as it can protect them from predatory men in public and keep them from being reduced to sex objects or, worse, sex workers (the fate of many young Iraqi women widowed or orphaned by the violence of post-Baathist Iraq) (Phillips 2005).

SCIRI and the Islamic Da'wa Party made two major attempts to implement Sharia in the place of earlier codes concerning women and family. The first, the passage of Decree 137 by the IGC, met strong opposition from educated Iraqi women and the United States. It was defeated when Raja' al-Khuza'i proved able to make an alliance with the Kurds, the secular Arab nationalists, and the secular-leaning Shiites on the Interim Governing Council, isolating the Shiite fundamentalists. The behind-the-scenes role of the still-powerful Americans in this reversal helps account for al-Khuza'i's success.

Al-Khuza'i's 2004 strategy was no longer possible after the January 2005 election, in which the Shiite religious parties won a parliamentary majority. Although the Sunni Arab community boycotted the election, it was increasingly represented by the Iraqi Islamic Party and the Association of Muslim Scholars, according to opinion polls. The Bush administration continued to have an interest in promoting a mild state feminism in Iraq, both because it made for good U.S. domestic politics and because it might weaken the religious parties most closely tied to Iran. With the victory of the Shiite religious coalition in the 2005 elections, however, most of Washington's levers of power disappeared, and it was increasingly tempted to cooperate with the victorious fundamentalists.

The constitution drafting committee set up by parliament in June 2005 was dominated by the Supreme Council for Islamic Revolution in Iraq, which wanted Sharia to be the law of the land. Only a few of the committee members were women, and most of those women were elected from Shiite religious party lists. Raja' al-Khuza'i, a member of the committee, was isolated and rendered ineffective, lacking very many secular allies from either a Sunni Arab or a Shiite heritage. The Kurds proved willing to cede ground on the issue of Sharia to the Shiites, both because the latter were adamant and because they were more interested in gaining prerogatives for their Kurdistan provincial confederacy, which in any case would allow them to opt out of federal law on such issues. Only strong intervention by Ambassador Khalilzad produced a change in the wording of Article 39, allowing women to choose to be under the 1959 civil personal status law rather than the law of their religious communities. The ruling fundamentalist parties could, however, easily revoke that ability to choose if they repealed the 1959 statute. Even if it remains on the books, how cases will be adjudicated when the wife chooses one code and the husband chooses Sunni or Shiite Sharia is entirely unclear. So much of the constitution will depend on statutes to be enacted by parliament that the full meaning of Article 39 cannot yet be known. If religious parties continue to dominate parliament, as they have in the wake of both parliamentary elections, the MPs will likely adopt religious and patriarchal interpretations rather than secular feminist ones. Just as the Khomeini revolution undid the reform legislation of the shah's government concerning women and implemented Sharia, so the revolution in Iraqi affairs provoked by the American overthrow of the Baath era brought parties to power that championed nativist neopatriarchy and regional rights and traditions. They have thus overturned the policies both of Baath state feminism and of Bush's paternalistic uplift. Further, party loyalty has tended to trump gender considerations, so that the women in parliament have supported their Sharia-minded parties rather than agitating for women's rights. Iraq's security situation has deteriorated to the point that most women have more pressing anxieties than the ultimate implications of constitutional law, and many women from the working and lower middle classes increasingly view strict Islamic law as a potential guarantor of law and order.

7. Family, Gender, and Law in Jordan and Palestine

LYNN WELCHMAN

Recent years have seen considerable debates around developments in family law in Jordan and in the West Bank and Gaza.[1] The national liberation struggle in Palestine impacts distinctively on the discourse of gender and family law, while in Jordan the sovereign's historic investment in legitimacy within the country's tribal structures continues to challenge certain "globalizing" trajectories embarked upon by the authorities. This chapter focuses on the Muslim family laws that govern family relations for the majority population in both areas, in the context of vigorous ongoing national debates on law reform in the early years of the twenty-first century. The chapter examines interventions in support of and in objection to change in the law and the extent to which the existing law and arguments in the law reform debates variously invoke and contest the globalizing discourses around women's rights in the family as set out inter alia in the Convention on the Elimination of All Forms of Discrimination Against Women (CEDAW). To this end the chapter focuses on two particular areas: the age of capacity for marriage and a woman's right to divorce.

In their legal systems both areas maintain separate jurisdictions for personal status matters for recognized religious communities: it is official legal pluralism. Under this system the majority Muslim population is governed by a codification of provisions drawn mostly from the rules of the

1. My thanks to Nouf al-Rawwaf, Asma Khadr, Reem Abu Hassan, Maha Abu Dayyeh, Khadija Hussein, Ala al-Bakri, Shaykh Taysir al-Tamimi, and the Women's Studies Institute at Birzeit University.

four Sunni schools and legislated as state law for application by the Sharia courts. Recognized non-Muslim minority communities apply their own family laws in separate communal courts. In both areas the Sharia courts comprise first-instance and higher appeal courts.

In both Jordan and Palestine[2] scholars have used language that may also be associated with the family to describe the system of political rule. Thus, Hammami and Johnson note that in Palestine in the post-Oslo period "an ethic of familialism structures power" (1999, 324), while Amawi analyzes a 1997 speech by the late King Hussein of Jordan as illustrating the idea of "the nation as a collective family with the king as its head" linked to "the interrelatedness between the patriarchal family and the patriarchal state and the promotion of allegiance around these symbols of family and tribe solidarity in support of the state" (2000, 158). In their examinations the main focus is gender and citizenship in Palestine and Jordan, respectively; both treat family law as a key element in the construction of citizenship. Constructions of "the family" are also key in representations of national identity. With differences in structure and history as societies and political entities, Jordan and Palestine nevertheless share certain features of the regional pattern of "the privileged place of women and family in discourses about cultural authenticity" (Kandiyoti 1991a, 7) and populist ideologies that vigorously oppose changes to the position of women in the family when they are proposed through the medium of legislative amendments to existing codifications.

Thus, although there are differences in specific discourses arising from the different histories and constituencies of the areas, there are certain broad patterns. Objections to the proposed laws invoke biological determinism as well as monolithic and homogenous visions of Arab Muslim heritage and religious principle, populist representations of class difference, and the specter of family breakdown, growing numbers of unmarried individuals, and general moral dissolution stirred by Western agendas of antipathy and enmity to Islam and Arabs. References in this last regard to "international conferences on women" are not infrequent,

2. Used here to mean the West Bank and Gaza, rather than the historical area of Mandatory Palestine.

and accusations that such activities are supported by "foreign funding" invoke the same set of images. Proponents of change to the law similarly invoke religious principle and the need to protect the family, along with constitutional guarantees, the rights of women as equal citizens, socioeconomic change, and the realities of women's lives as necessitating changes in the law. Some invoke principles of human rights and specific international instruments to which the political authorities have adhered (or, in the case of Palestine, announced their intention to adhere when statehood is realized), while this discourse may be assimilated by opponents to the hostile Western agenda. There is considerable regional exchange among Arab legislatures on Muslim personal status law, and at the nongovernmental level there is also substantial regional exchange and cooperation, notably among the women's movements.

The Process in Jordan: Legislation and Debates

Jordan currently applies the 1976 Jordanian Law of Personal Status, which replaced an earlier 1951 law while maintaining broadly the same approach. The JLPS was first promulgated as a "temporary law" during the absence of a sitting parliament in a prolonged state of emergency after the 1967 war. The constitution permits the enactment of such temporary laws by royal decree based on cabinet decisions in "matters that require necessary measures that cannot be delayed"; temporary laws have to be presented to the first sitting of parliament when it reconvenes for confirmation, modification, or rejection (Art. 94 [1]). In June 2001 King Abdullah dissolved the elected lower house of parliament with a view to redrafting the Election Law and holding elections later that year. The elections did not in fact take place until 2003, and in the intervening period the government made substantial use of temporary legislation in a range of areas, including not only new penal legislation following the attacks in the United States on September 11, 2001, but also family law.

By the time a new House of Deputies was elected and parliament reconvened, more than a hundred temporary laws were in place awaiting discussion by the legislature. In the first stage of the process, in early August 2003, the House of Deputies turned eighty-six temporary laws over to its various committees; the exceptions were Temporary Law no. 82/2001 (*Official Gazette*, no. 4524, December 31, 2001, 5998) amending the Law of Personal Status and Temporary Law no. 86/2001 amending the Penal Code (*Al-Ra'y*, August 4, 2003).[3] The progovernment Jordanian press referred to an "undeclared alliance between deputies of the Islamist movement and the 'conservative' tribal deputies" (ibid.)—an alliance regarded by observers as more or less unprecedented—and some three hundred women were reported to have fasted outside the parliament building in protest (*Al-Dustur*, September 14, 2003).

The temporary law was subsequently referred to the House of Senators' legal affairs committee, where amendments were made (as discussed below); the upper house then approved the draft and sent it back to the House of Deputies. Progovernment newspapers cited observers as expecting Islamists to continue to reject the law but predicted that a "coalition with the conservatives who based their position on customs and traditions" would fail to materialize this time around (*Al-Ra'y*, September 2, 2003). In the event the lower house agreed to send the law to its legal committee for examination. The legal committee took almost ten months before sending the temporary law as amended by the Senate back to the House of Deputies with a recommendation to approve. However, the house rejected the law again, by a margin of just five votes, with those deputies voting against described in the English-language daily as "mostly Islamist, conservative and tribal deputies." The head of the Jordanian Women's Union observed that "such heated debates" take place only when the subject is women's issues: "We don't see the deputies take similar stands when it comes to laws that have a negative impact on citizens' lives such as raising taxes and prices or economic packages" (*Jordan Times*, June 29, 2004 [Rana Husseini]).[4] Although the substantive objections raised in the debate were similar to the ones presented for its rejection the summer before, there were institutional issues at stake for some deputies who objected to the opposition to the legislative decisions of the House of Deputies by the

3. The Penal Code amendments were also very significant for women's rights in the family.

4. The vote was forty-four of eighty-three deputies present.

appointed House of Senators (ibid. [Sahar Aloul]). Issues of procedure as well as substance thus affected the fate of the law.

Supporters of the aims of the law had generally articulated a preference for the presentation of such amendments through ordinary legislative procedures; some women's rights activists were nervous from the beginning at the prospect of the rejection of the amendments when parliament reconvened, a prospect possibly enhanced by the government's use of temporary legislation to push the amendments through. Nor had the implementation of the amendments become sufficiently "routine" and integrated to undermine the challenge mounted in the House of Deputies by those deputies who opposed the substance of the law (rather than the method of promulgation) when parliament reconvened. The fate of the amendments then rested on the convening of a joint parliamentary session of the two houses. Brown observes that the Jordanian system requires parliament to positively repeal temporary legislation issued in its absence if that legislation is not to remain valid; "parliamentary inaction constitutes acquiescence" (2002, 50).

The Process in Palestine: Legislation and Debates

In Palestine the post-Oslo (1994) political circumstances raised the possibility in the Sharia courts, as in other parts of the legal system, of the laws applied in the West Bank and Gaza being unified for the first time since 1948. Since the Israeli occupation of 1967 the West Bank courts had continued to apply Jordanian law to Muslim personal status matters (including the JLPS in 1976), while the Gazan Sharia courts applied a 1954 codification, the Law of Family Rights, issued when Gaza was under Egyptian administration. The Gaza code implemented some but by no means all of the family law reforms legislated in Egypt since the 1920s; no post-1967 Egyptian legislation was implemented in the Gaza Strip (Welchman 2000). The two laws of Muslim personal status in the West Bank and Gaza differ in some areas: age of capacity for marriage, ages of custody for children, some judicial divorce matters, certain succession provisions, and maintenance rights for a divorced woman.

The task of unifying both legal system and laws in the two areas of the West Bank and the Gaza Strip is an enormous challenge for the Palestinian

Authority and has preoccupied different sectors of civil society as well as the legislature. In the particular case of Muslim family law, the fact that there is no "Palestinian" law to "reform" distinguishes the situation somewhat from other contemporary efforts at reforming family law in the region, and was certainly a point raised by those individuals arguing from various perspectives for the need for a Palestinian law of personal status. On the other hand, there are many points of resonance with debates ongoing elsewhere: competing discourses of "authenticity" and "legitimacy"; the role of women in the national struggle and in processes of state building, linked with formulations of gender and citizenship; a perception of Islam as a shared national heritage; the (non)normative standing of international human rights principles and a "gender-equality" paradigm; understandings over the role of European colonialism and current globalizing trends; and the issue of "voice," that is, who is entitled to articulate (or, in some cases, even debate) the particular rules of family law to be applied. Although the debate was somewhat heated, the positions (and actions) of those persons involved practically in the law (as members of the judiciary, for example, or in legal advice centers) were clearly informed by the realities of life in transitional Palestine as well as by differently sourced frameworks of authority and principle.

Muslim family law became a focus of intense public debate in 1998 in light of the Palestinian Model Parliament: Women and Legislation, a project organized by a nongovernmental women's organization, the Women's Centre for Legal Aid and Counselling, with support and participation from a number of other civil society groups (Welchman 2003; Hammami and Johnson 1999; Sh'hada 1999). The Model Parliament provoked a reaction far beyond what was expected by those individuals involved in its activities, ranging from denunciations of particular proposals to criticisms of the debate's taking place at all. Some of the reactions from individuals and groups identified broadly as "Islamist" translated into personal attacks on women involved in the project—on their morals, their loyalty to the Palestinian national cause, and their religious beliefs. The exercise was portrayed by some as a "conspiracy" of hostile forces, linking the UN, the EU, and Israel, portrayed as actively denying Palestinian rights and seeking to weaken Palestinian resolve and unity through supporting and funding attacks on Palestinian Arab and Muslim values, family structures, and national unity; women leading the debates were portrayed as Westernized and removed from "authentic" Palestinian society and values (Welchman 2000, 368). The rights discourse was directly targeted (Hammami and Johnson 1999, 333). In their response to the Islamist attacks, nationalist politicians defended the exercise in statements where "typically, women's rights were linked to the modernist and nationalist project of state building" (ibid., 335).

After the second intifada, or uprising, began in September 2000, sustained interest in Muslim family law did not find similar public articulation, as groups previously involved had their energies and priorities drawn by the increasing hardship and brutality of daily life. Among other things, closures and severe restrictions on travel between different parts of the Palestinian territories all but put an end to the process of coordinated consultation and debate aimed at developing an agreed-upon framework for family law within major sectors of the women's movement, although a draft text was prepared by individuals (Johnson 2004, 157; Sh'hada 2005, 343–45).

By the summer of 2006 a draft text of personal status law, initiated by the Office of the Qadi al-Qudah (Chief Islamic Justice), was lodged at the Legislative Council after going through a series of consultations and reviews. Two other draft texts—one from Gaza and one from a coalition of civil society organizations—were apparently also subsequently submitted; in this chapter, it is the provisions of the draft text from the Qadi al-Qudah's Office that are considered by way of comparison to the Jordanian legislation, in an examination of the way the debates were proceeding in that period.

Marriage: The Age of Capacity

Limiting the practice of early marriage, particularly of girls, has long been a concern of social reformers, the feminist movement, and women's rights activists in the region, and is given weight in international instruments and the globalized discourse. Reformers focus on the physical and mental health risks to very young women and issues of their consent to the marriage and the loss or at least substantial limitation of their opportunities for education and work outside family labor.

The 1976 JLPS set the minimum ages of capacity for marriage at fifteen for females and sixteen for males in *hijri* (lunar) years. Relatively recent advocacy on raising the age of capacity above its current levels met with a certain amount of opposition voiced inter alia on grounds of religion and morality as well as on particular "social circumstances." Some of the interventions noted below express fears that raising the age of marriage further will in effect bar sexually mature young people from having lawful sexual relations (within the framework of marriage) and thus encourage immoral behavior. In some cases in the Jordanian debate, such warnings were accompanied by references to a Western agenda aimed at encouraging dissolute conduct among young persons and at limiting the birthrate in Arab Muslim societies.

For their part supporters of a change in the law held out the Civil Code's age of legal majority (at eighteen for both sexes by the solar calendar) as a target for advocacy and campaigning. Justifications for this objective were made both on the evidence of social science research into the effects of early marriage on young women and with reference to international instruments such as the Convention on the Rights of the Child. Others suggested that while the age of capacity should be raised to eighteen, the judge should retain the discretion to assess a female's circumstances in a particular case where her guardian requests permission for her to be married below that age. This type of formulation, which was in fact adopted in Temporary Law no. 82/2001, constitutes a partial return to the rules of the previous law, the Jordanian Law of Family Rights of 1951, when the approval of both the judge as well as the marriage guardian was required for a marriage below the age of full capacity (Welchman 2000, 108–21). In Temporary Law no. 82/2001 the age of capacity for marriage was increased to eighteen years by the solar calendar; the judge is empowered to permit the marriage of males and females below this age provided they are aged fifteen or older and if such a marriage realizes an "interest" or a "benefit" (*maslaha*) to be defined subsequently by the *qadi al-qudah* (Art. 2). A month later the chief Islamic justice issued the necessary directive setting out the bases on which a judge might permit such a marriage, which included attention to the consent and choice of the fiancée and the consent of the guardian, as well as the requirement that the marriage "prevents an existing cause of corruption" or "avoids the loss of an established benefit."

On the face of it this latter clause maintained a potentially very broad scope of judicial discretion in the matter of underage marriage. When the contents of Temporary Law no. 82/2001 were disseminated in Jordan prior to publication in the *Official Gazette* and implementation by the court, the print media gave substantial space to discussions on the rise in the age of capacity for marriage. In one article a sociologist and a professor (both men) supported the amendment on the grounds, among other reasons, of the negative impact of early marriage (particularly for females) on personal health and family relations, the opportunity for greater educational and productive capacities with a later age of marriage, and the idea that changing times and socioeconomic circumstances fully justified this change in the law (*Al-Dustur*, December 13, 2001). In the same piece two male lecturers in *fiqh* (Islamic jurisprudence) objected on the grounds, inter alia, that marriage is a right of females and males after puberty, that one of the aims of the amendment was to reduce the birthrate ("especially in Arab states"), and that the current problems concerned delays in marriage rather than early marriage, since there were some four hundred thousand single males and females in Jordan of all ages. One also warned against leaving such matters "in the hands of committees concerned only with human rights and child rights" to the exclusion of adequate *fiqh* expertise. Elsewhere, another Sharia academic insisted that the incidence of early marriage was actually very low, that there was no need "for this big media fuss," and that behind the pressures on "Islamic states" to raise the age of marriage lay "the tendencies of world conferences on women to facilitate the prohibited *(haram)* among adolescents; these are suspect calls for the corruption of Islamic society" (*Al-Dustur*, December 23, 2001). Sharia judges (who are responsible for applying the law) joined the public debate on both sides. One justified the amendment with *fiqh* arguments (including constraining something permitted in order to realize a benefit) and in light of social, cultural, and economic changes, including the longer period of compulsory education (*Al-Ra'y*, October 13, 2001). Another was more circumspect, warning that outside the cities marriage tends to take place below the age of eighteen, that the measure might be "shutting in front of them the door of the permitted *(halal)* and opening the door of the prohibited *(haram),*" and that he expected the exception (of permitting marriage below eighteen) to become the rule *(Al-Dustur,* November 7, 2001). Women's rights and social activists were more supportive, some stressing the risks of early marriage particularly to girls, others the need for *qadis* to be careful in their use of discretion to permit a marriage below eighteen *(Al-Ra'y,* December 20, 2001).

The caution expressed both by the last-mentioned judge and by women's rights activists turned out to be justified. By early 2006 the human rights group Mizan had launched "the country's first ever public campaign to raise awareness about the dangers of early marriage," having found that "the exception clause in the current law was widely abused."[5] Radio and television spots warned against the risks of early marriage and insisted on the substantive requirements of the law of the age of eighteen solar years.

In Palestine a broadly similar debate began a little earlier. The first *qadi al-qudah* and his successor showed little inclination to dispute the validity of moves to amend and update the applicable provisions on the age of capacity for marriage on the grounds of the public interest, taking into account problems familiar to those persons working in the Sharia court system. One of the first actions of Sheikh Muhammad Abu Sardane, in 1995, was to issue an administrative decree bringing the minimum age of capacity for marriage under Gaza's Law of Family Rights into line with the ages in the West Bank under the JLPS: fifteen *hijri* years for females and sixteen for males (Welchman 2000).[6] This order also required that the judge give permission for the marriage of females aged fifteen to seventeen and males aged sixteen to eighteen, a scrutiny no longer in force in the West Bank under the JLPS, as noted above.

5. Women's United Nations Report Network via the AGENDA Feminist Media Project, "Jordan: Rights Group Launches Drive to Curb Early Marriage," reproduced by Women Living under Muslim Laws, http://www.wluml.org/english/news.

6. Decision of the *qadi al-qudah,* no. 78/1995, December 25, 1995, valid as of January 10, 1996.

The current *qadi al-qudah*, Sheikh Taysir al-Tamimi, has shown similar interest in this issue. In an interview in 1998 he told a local newspaper that the Sharia courts frequently found fathers trying to marry their daughters off below the minimum age of marriage, using forged birth certificates; he also referred to the context of compulsory education, which "accords with the call of Islam to knowledge as an obligation on every male and female Muslim" (*Al-Quds*, March 8, 1998). Sheikh Tamimi's subsequent support for minimum ages of capacity matching the ages in the Jordanian amendments, accompanied by a provision for exceptions in particular cases, contrasts with the position taken by the then mufti of Jerusalem.

For its part, the Palestinian women's movement has raised concerns over the phenomenon of "early marriage," particularly of females. In 1996, just after the election of the Legislative Council, the Women's Affairs Technical Committee, an umbrella group representing a number of women's organizations, had identified as a lobbying priority the raising of the minimum age of capacity for marriage to eighteen, and in the summer of 1998 the committee launched a national campaign for that purpose (*Palestine Report*, March 8, 1996; *Sawt al-nisa'*, December 31, 1998). The resource documents prepared for the Model Parliament (Khadr 1998; Nashwan 1998) proposed a minimum age of capacity for marriage of eighteen by the solar calendar, on similar grounds of educational opportunities, the health risks to girls posed by early marriage, and for the sake of consistency with the age of legal majority and, in Khadr's case, conformity with the Convention on the Rights of the Child. Khadr held that there was a "quasi consensus" on the need to raise the age of marriage but also proposed that the judge be empowered, exceptionally, to permit the marriage of a person aged sixteen solar years or above "in circumstances where pressing necessity requires it." Nashwan's resource document proposed no such exceptions, but in the discussions at the final session of the Model Parliament in Gaza, a clause was proposed and voted on by participants providing that the types of cases in which exceptions would be made should be exhaustively specified in the law.

In the meantime, pending any changes to the substantive law, the *qadi al-qudah* acted within the sphere of his own influence in 2000 to tighten administrative control over the registration procedures for marriage in directives that appeared targeted at out-of-court marriages involving underage parties.[7] In the same year, however, in a fatwa entitled "Early Marriage," the Supreme Fatwa Council addressed the question of the validity of "early marriage, that is, the marriage of females of a young age," and whether an age of marriage for girls could be specified.[8] The Council examined the views of the traditional doctrines of the Sunni schools and held with the majority, determining that minors of both sexes could indeed be married, but consummation was not allowed if it would harm the female, even if she had reached puberty; here it cited the ages of twelve for the boy and nine for the girl as the ages before which the legal presumption holds that puberty has not occurred. It added that a minor girl should be married to an equal, a good man who would look after her affairs. The fatwa did not refer to the ages of capacity in the applicable statute law or the fact that it is a criminal offense to marry anyone off under those ages.

Two clearly distinct positions were thus articulated in regard to the age of capacity by the two most senior figures of the Palestinian Sharia establishment. In a seminar at the end of 2001 convened by the human rights organization Al-Haq, Sheikh al-Tamimi called on the Supreme Fatwa Council "to respect existing law, implying that some of its *fatawa* were in contradiction to the law" and that "the sharpest conflict was expressed in positions on the age of marriage" (Johnson 2004, 157). In 2005 the then mufti issued a further opinion on the subject, linking efforts to raise the age of marriage to Western cultural and legal concepts and opposing suggestions that the minimum age be raised to eighteen. In this fatwa he held that the minimum age should be linked to puberty, "which is very close to the ages of 15 for the female and 16 for the male," noting that individuals are free to defer marriage until after these ages. He noted that the existing law stipulates these ages as a minimum and that there were already problems with

7. Administrative directives no. 15/481, April 15, 2000, and no. 15/1358, November 11, 2000 (Welchman 2003).

8. Supreme Fatwa Council, no. 66/2000/5, May 4, 2000. See generally Labadi 2004.

families trying to avoid this limitation, in violation of the law, predicting an increase in such problems should the minimum age be set higher.[9]

Earlier drafts of a Palestinian personal status law produced under the supervision of the *qadi al-qudah* proposed the "classical" ages of *rushd*: seventeen for females and eighteen for males (lunar) as the ages of capacity, with exceptions allowed down to fifteen years. After further review and consultation, including by the Ministry of Justice's Bureau of Fatwa and Legislation, and further advocacy by women's rights campaigners, the 2006 draft set capacity for marriage at eighteen solar years for both males and females. Persons aged sixteen solar years could be married by the judge, provided the *qadi al-qudah* himself gave permission; marriage below sixteen was to be forbidden, and there was explicit reference to criminal sanction for those individuals carrying out a contract of marriage in violation of these requirements (Draft Arts. 8, 9, 10, 329). This proposition was bolder than the one in Jordan in regard to the minimum age of marriage and appears to reflect the effective impact of lobbying and professional consultations. There remained, nevertheless, the question of exceptions. Sheikh al-Tamimi has indicated that the requirement of permission from the *qadi al-qudah* rather than only from the court judge is needed to constrain the exceptional circumstances. The draft text did not suggest that the *qadi al-qudah* (as in Jordan) was to issue regulations governing the circumstances in which he would be entitled to exercise this discretion, although as noted some activists had called for him to do so. On the one hand, it is the case that the Jordanian approach appears to have been somewhat undermined by the wording of the ensuing regulations as relied upon by individual judges; on the other, the Palestinian *qadi al-qudah* appeared to rely on his own discretion, and the good faith of his successors, in deciding these matters.

Divorce: The *Khul'* Debate

Jordan's initial (1997) report to the CEDAW notes that "in the articles relating to marriage, repudiation, alimony and divorce, the Personal Status Act

---

9. In answer to the question "What is your opinion of early marriage and the debate around it?" in *Al-'Isra* (journal of the Dar al-Fatwa and Islamic Research over which the mufti presides), no. 60 (June–July 2005): 92–93.

gives men and women equal rights." In specific regard to divorce, it notes that "the wife has the right to handle her own divorce, provided that was specifically provided for in the marriage contract"—referring to the delegation of the husband's unilateral right of *talaq*—and goes on to detail the grounds on which a wife can seek a judicial divorce.[10] These provisions do not in fact establish women's "equal" access to divorce, but the fact that Jordan was already using this language may have presaged the 2001 law.

Temporary Law no. 82/2001 included a provision on judicial *khul'* closely modeled on the Egyptian provision of the previous year. *Khul'* is a form of divorce described as "divorce by mutual agreement" or "divorce for compensation." Essentially, it involves the wife's offering (or agreeing to pay) a consideration to her husband in exchange for his pronouncing a divorce *(talaq)*, which takes immediate effect as a final *talaq* and is therefore not subject to revocation by the husband during the *'idda* ("waiting period") of the wife following the divorce. The majority of traditional jurists concur on the principle of mutual agreement: it is the husband who issues the *talaq* in such a divorce, and his participation in the process means that his agreement is integral. A *khul'* is, in traditional Sunni law, a nonlitigious form of divorce; no grounds have to be established or recognized by the court; and the couple concerned agree and the divorce is effected, whether it occurs extrajudicially or the agreement is actually made or affirmed in court (possibly with the court's assistance in reaching an agreement). A variation of this nonlitigious *khul'* is in common use in both Jordan and Palestine in the form of *"talaq* in exchange for general absolution" where the wife waives her outstanding financial rights in exchange for the divorce.

In contrast to the preexisting law, Jordan's 2001 amendment enables the wife to obtain a *khul'* divorce from the court when her husband refuses to consent. To achieve this divorce she has to explicitly affirm that she "loathes life with her husband," that there is no way for their married life to continue, and that she is afraid that she "will not be able to live within the limits ordained by Allah because of this loathing"; she then has to "ransom" herself by waiving all her marital rights and "returning to her husband the dower she received from him." The court is to attempt

10. UN document, CEDAW/C/JOR/1, November 10, 1997, 24, 26.

reconciliation and, if unsuccessful, to appoint two arbitrators to pursue efforts at reconciling the spouses for a maximum period of thirty days, after which, if the spouses are not reconciled, the court is to rule in favor of the wife's divorce from the husband (Art. 126).

The Egyptian provision was a matter of substantial controversy, and the Jordanian parallel similarly attracted considerable attention. The debate reflects not only discomfort but vehement opposition among some to the idea of women being able to seek divorce without having to establish grounds to the court or to secure the husband's agreement to the divorce. One of the concepts evoked is *qiwama*, the idea of male authority or guardianship over women,[11] and specifically in this debate the authority of the husband over his wife. This idea is directly linked to assumptions and expectations of gender roles, with opponents warning of the dangers of women "ruling the family" and of widespread family breakdown.

In advance of the lower house's debate on the temporary law, a newspaper published a piece on the *"battle of al-khul',"* including a memorandum by a deputy from the Islamist opposition (*Al-Dustur,* August 31, 2003).[12] The memo focuses primarily on the need for the husband's consent and directly takes issue with the Jordanian debate about the question. It begins with arguments from the textual sources and judicial and legislative practice "until the start of the 21st century" when countries such as Egypt and Jordan allowed judges to grant *khul'* divorces without such consent. It notes that if the wife had received a large prompt dower, only rich women would benefit from the provision, while if it was a token dower (one gold dinar, for example) and the woman was required to return only that dower to her husband, it would be doing a great wrong to the husband (as "in reality nobody marries for a dinar"). The author asserts that "many believe" that the amendments came in response not to actual local needs but to "an agenda [set by] foreign Western thoughts, on recommendations from conferences or conspiracies aimed at destroying

---

11. The "meaning" of *qiwama* in the source texts is contested by modernist and feminist interpretations, but the idea of "authority" remains central to the meaning attributed by "traditionalists" in the Jordanian debate.

12. Memorandum by Deputy Nidal al-'Abadi, "Ma'rakat 'al-khul'."

the integrity of the family on the pretext of liberating women," with a specific reference to the Beijing conference. He criticizes the equality paradigm as going against the law of the family in Islam, insisting that *qiwama* and *talaq* are the rights of the husband, while maintenance is the right of the wife; giving the right of *khul'* to a wife whose husband is fulfilling all his duties toward her is "taking the wife's side over the husband's." He also underlines the need to narrow the doors of divorce rather than open new ones and observes that women are "mostly very emotional and quick-tempered," while men are ("mostly") more capable of being ruled by their heads and their reason, "which is why Islam gives men the right of *talaq* for the sake of family cohesion." A final point is that as currently applied, the *khul'* provision "usurps the right of the *qadi*" by obliging the latter to simply respond to the petition of the wife. The author's conclusion is to propose alternatives, including the simplification of establishing existing grounds for divorce on the petition of the wife.

The next day extracts were published from a roundtable on *al-khul'*, bringing together a female and a male deputy, a Sharia *qadi*, and a specialized Sharia lawyer (*Al-Dustur*, September 1, 2003).[13] All articulated support for the provision except for the male deputy, who was part of the coalition against the amendments in the house and who made remarks similar to the ones by the Islamist deputy the previous day, including a reference to "the Beijing and Cairo conferences where American interests prevailed." For his part the *qadi* argued for the validity of judicial *khul'* under the Sharia and blamed the "media frenzy" for contributing to a negative reaction in society, adding the role played by plays and films such as *How to Divorce Your Husband by "Khul'"* and *The "Khul'" Lawyer*. The Sharia lawyer argued that all forms of divorce go back to the idea of removing injury and said that in all of his experience he had never come across a woman who hated her husband for no reason: "If a wife doesn't have to give reasons [for seeking a divorce] this is a protection [of the intimate details] of married life." The female deputy argued that it was more

---

13. Roundtable convened by Nayef al-Mhaisen. The participants were, respectively, Deputy Nariman al-Rusan, Deputy Mahmud al-Kharabsheh, Judge Dr. Wasif al-Bakri, and Advocate Ratib al-Zhahir.

likely to be poorer women who benefited from the provision in situations where family breakdown had already occurred.

Elsewhere, the interventions of women's rights activists focused inter alia on the validity of the procedure under Sharia and the likelihood that it would be used as a very last resort and remedy by despairing wives needing a dignified and expeditious exit from their marriages. Some activists were concerned by delays in the proceedings in practice, which undermined the aim of a speedy remedy, difference in application of the provision by different judges, and difficulties faced by women who could not return their dowers; some held that the *khul'* law was an inadequate remedy in any case to the larger picture of family law in Jordan (*Al-Hadath*, February 15, 2003). In other press coverage opponents of the amendments criticized precisely the ease of the procedures, which according to one would result in "the corruption of many marital and family relationships and give rich women the right to rule in affairs of the home as the law has given them a sword hanging over the husband and his authority" (*Al-Dustur*, September 14, 2003).

Turning to Palestine, less than two months after the Egyptian provision on *khul'* was passed into law in the year 2000, the Women's Studies Institute at Birzeit University asked more than a thousand people whether they would like to see a law enacted in Palestine similar to the one in Egypt, enabling women to ask for a divorce if they waive their financial rights (Hammami 2004, 141). About a third of the respondents in the sample stated they would support it, with slightly (some 5 percent) more women than men in support. Significantly, however, many of those persons opposed (44 percent of women and 28 percent of men) expressed reservations not because of an opposition to women's right to divorce as such but rather because "women should not lose their property rights" in order to secure one.[14]

In the 2006 draft from the Qadi al-Qudah's Office, judicial *khul'* was provided for in terms rather different from the provisions in Jordan (Arts.

---

14. By comparison, 24 percent of females and 35 percent of males in the sample who opposed such a law did so on the grounds that "women should not divorce." Overall, Hammami found 71 percent of females and 61 percent of males supporting "women's right to divorce as such" (2004, 142).

184–85). The draft text proposed that if the husband refused to respond to his wife's request for a *khul'*, the judge could rule for a *khul'* "if he is convinced of the dispute *(khilaf)* between them or a reason that makes married life impossible." This caveat proposed to give the *qadi* considerable discretion at the beginning of the process; it would be he who determined that the marriage could not continue rather than accepting a unilateral statement to this effect from the wife. Nevertheless, he was empowered to make such a ruling only after he had appointed family arbitrators to attempt to effect reconciliation between the spouses in accordance with the rules applying to applications for divorce for "discord and strife," for a period of not more than four months. In effect, apart from the time limit, this text appeared to render the process of judicial *khul'* closely analogous to judicial divorce on the grounds of "discord and strife"; not only would the wife be required to submit to arbitration processes, but she was also not empowered to "insist" upon initiation of the process—at least, not textually. The textual allocation to the court of judicial discretion in the initiation of such claims contrasted to the position in Jordan (and in Egypt) and moved away from the more usual state-controlled efforts at "closure" and centralization of legal text.

◆ ◆ ◆

In both Jordan and Palestine, at the official level, there is a clear commitment to continuing to frame Muslim intrafamily gender relations in the authoritative discourse of "Sharia-based" law. The contested ground is the precise substance of this law and the precise nature of those relations. Hammami (2004, 134) finds the relationship between personal status law for Palestinian Muslims and Sharia to be a *doxa*, where "doxa stands for aspects of tradition and culture which are so internalized that they exist as unquestionable common sense beliefs and dispositions." Thus, the public opinion survey on which she bases this observation revealed a "profound commitment to *Sharia* as the basis for family law by both [men and women] but especially by women." At the same time, the data showed a growth in support for the principle of reform of Sharia-based personal status law, with more women than men wanting more rights to be given to women under Palestinian family law (ibid., 140). At issue is not so much the declared source of the law but its particular legislative expression, which brings in other underlying value systems as well as contending political constituencies. The *qadi al-qudah* has shown himself to be receptive to at least some of the advocacy goals of the women's movement, provided these objectives are shaped within the broad arguments of *fiqh*. The legislative debate lies ahead, in an uncertain time frame and political climate.

In Jordan the amendments to the JLPS passed as temporary legislation in December 2001 were distinguished by the involvement and consultation of the government-appointed Royal Commission on Human Rights in the drafting process, along with the Office of the Qadi al-Qudah. The procedural recognition of a human rights interest in personal status legislation is a very interesting development, notwithstanding criticisms that might be made of the mandate of the Royal Commission. The involvement of the commission can be seen as being in line with a tendency in Jordan (and elsewhere in the region) to move toward integrating (or accommodating or co-opting) human rights discourse and mechanisms within the government machinery.

In both Palestine and Jordan debates on family law have invoked issues of national identity and the expression in law of a set of gender relations—and in particular the "position of women"—describing a valorized notion of "family" considered integral to that identity. The substantial involvement of foreign and international donor agencies in funding a variety of activities in the women's sector is another factor in both contexts. This involvement may stimulate or facilitate emphasis on and advocacy for the international women's rights obligations of the political authority and at the same time be perceived or presented by opponents of such projects as evidence of "cultural inauthenticity" and an alliance with forces in the West hostile to and currently actively engaged in military aggression against Arab and Muslim peoples in the region. For some, the current context directly invokes colonial experiences in the Arab world. The particular contemporary (especially post–September 11) articulations and implications of the divisor of religion as constructed by powerful Western states challenge the structuring of successful international alliances in support of change as well as the domestic positioning of advocates.

8. Revisiting the Debate on Family Law in Morocco

Context, Actors, and Discourses

ZAKIA SALIME

In October 2003 King Muhammad VI of Morocco decided to reform the Sharia-based family law, *moudawana*.[1] The new Family Code transformed the Moroccan legislation of family law from one of the most conservative to one of the most progressive in the Arab world. Taking place only a few months after the Casablanca bombing attacks of May 2003, this reform was highly significant to the U.S.-led "war on terrorism" and came as a commitment of the Moroccan king to ally the country with the global fight against "terror" (see Salime 2007).

The new Code of the Family was presented by the king in a speech broadcast to the parliament in October 2003 and was introduced as a reform inspired by the Islamic Sharia, in a gesture to mollify the Islamists who had actively opposed the reform for two decades. While the media represented this reform as the goodwill of an enlightened and modernist king, in fact the reform was the outcome of two decades of struggle by the feminist movement. The purpose of this chapter is to revisit this debate.

1. The New Family Code makes several amendments to the *moudawana*, including the abolition of guardianship rights of men over women and the requirement of obedience for women, endows both husband and wife with joint responsibility in family issues, and raises the minimum age of marriage to eighteen for both sexes (it was previously fifteen for women and eighteen for men). Women can now initiate a divorce. Polygyny, though still authorized, is subjected to stricter conditions, and women's alimony rights are ensured until divorce is finalized, through a special state fund.

145

The feminist movement was instrumental in shaping the content and language of the new Code of the Family. This movement rose in the 1980s out of women's rights organizations mobilizing the UN conventions about women and a liberal rhetoric of gender equality and personal rights. Both the content and the language of the new Code of the Family was inspired by this rhetoric. The code recognizes the equal responsibilities and rights of husband and wife within a marriage. It abolishes repudiation and grants women the same right to file for divorce and to enter a marriage without a male guardian. Though polygamy is not outlawed, it is subject to strict limitations and is regulated by the court.

For such an achievement to be possible feminist groups had to negotiate the reform of family law by encountering competing discourses, agendas, and policies activated by three main players: the Moroccan state, which, far from being monolithic and bluntly patriarchal, was divided as to the importance of reforming women's status in family law; Islamist groups who had been activating a cultural relativist claim in order to question the feminists' claim to speak on behalf of *all* women and undermine the hegemony of the UN regimes of women's rights; and transnational organizations activating a modernist rhetoric on women in development.

It is the purpose of this chapter to relocate feminist activism within these competing agendas and discourses. I argue that family law has not only been the site for the repositioning of multiple actors on the global scene but also been the place of domestic contentions over definitions of democracy, modernity, and national identity. This debate is not new, however. It was launched in the context of the nationalist movement for independence and was, in postcolonial Morocco, carried on by women from both feminist and Islamist organizations in their negotiations of women's rights within their respective political parties and movements.

This chapter focuses on three historical moments of mobilization by feminist groups: the first is the nationalist movement under which women started for the first time questioning gender inequalities in Sharia law, the second is the 1992 One Million Signatures campaign led by feminist groups to reform the *moudawana*, and the third is the 1997 National Plan for Integrating Women in Development, a government project to reform the Code of the Family. I will conclude by discussing the meanings of the new reform in the context of the "war on terror."

Women's Status in the *Moudawana*

The *moudawana*, or Code of Personal Status, was promulgated in 1957, one year after independence. The code drew on a model of a male-headed family, with men having unilateral rights to repudiation and polygyny, and with women subject to their husbands or fathers. Hence, prior to the reforms of 1993 and 2003, many restrictions were imposed on women's rights within and outside of marriage. For example, to enter into marriage a woman required a guardian *(wali)*, either her father or a male relative, to consent to the marriage on her behalf (Moulay R'chid 1991, 56).

Further, the *moudawana* did not provide a woman with guardianship rights over her children or over rights to their father's legacy. Thus, a widow did not have the right to manage her minor children's inheritance; rather, it was managed by a judge until the children reached puberty. In divorce child custody was conditional on a woman's residing in the same city as the father and on her remaining unmarried (Bennani 1997, 161). Another inequity was that a husband's permission was required in order for a woman to enter into commercial activity. This requirement applied to all kinds of paid jobs. Though actually in conflict with the Sharia, which provides women with full rights to manage their own property, this discriminatory policy, implemented by the French in 1926, was incorporated into the *moudawana* in 1957 (Moulay R'chid 1991, 62). This situation contrasts, for example, with the one in postcolonial Tunisia, as described by Charrad (1996, 225).

Other limitations were imposed on women by the Ministry of the Interior from the end of the 1970s. For instance, prior to changes implemented as a result of the 1992 feminist campaign, a married woman was not allowed to request a passport without her husband's permission,[2] while a widowed, divorced, or single woman was required to provide a "certificate of good behavior" (Moulay R'chid 1991, 63; Bennani 1997, 165).

2. This ruling was effected by the Ministry of Interior in April 1990 and withdrawn in April 1994 (Bennani 1997, 165).

These measures, in absolute contradiction with the Moroccan constitution, are interpreted by Daoud (1993) as an official reaction to the recommendations of the Seventh Conference of Ulema, held in 1979 in the city of Oujda. The conference recommended the application of the Sharia, which government policy translated as exerting control over women's bodies and mobility. The *moudawana* encompassed still other discriminations: for example, in a mixed marriage a Moroccan woman could not pass on her nationality to her children.

Gender inequalities were also part of penal law, which contained two major discriminatory provisions. The first related to the benefit of mitigating circumstances offered to men who kill or injure their wives if the latter commit adultery. The second one related to adultery itself. Though adultery was condemned for both women and men, the law provided exclusively for husbands to take legal action against wives who commit adultery (Morocco 1995, 88). These examples show how significantly the legal status of women contrasted with their actual contribution to the economy and their presence in public life. They also testify to the urgency of changing the *moudawana*, which was the priority of women's rights groups since the end of the 1980s.

The battle over the legal status of women in Morocco was also shaped by the struggles of women across the North African region. Women faced similar exclusion from decision making in Algeria and Tunisia (Daoud 1993). The inequalities encoded in the *moudawana* are not specific to Morocco; the Algerian Family Law Code sustains similar inequalities, and the Algerian government's reforms have at times been even more regressive than the codes they were intended to address, as was the case with the new Code of Personal Status in 1984 (Paris 1989, 437; Charrad 2001). Nevertheless, despite many commonalities, each context presents unique circumstances relevant to the struggle for social justice and women's rights.

Some scholars link the revival of the independence-era Tunisian feminist movement to common trends that shaped feminist struggles in North Africa over the same period. These trends include liberalization in both the political and the economic realms and the resurgence of the Islamist project, which affected the three North African feminist movements in similar ways.[3] First, intellectuals played a key role in the women's movement in all three countries. For example, Fatima Mernissi (1989) of Morocco raised gender consciousness at both the academic and the political levels in all three countries through her publications, workshops, and research groups. Indeed, Mernissi has played a major role in the development of women's rights networks, linking activists and scholars from the Maghreb, which has helped bridge the gap between the production of knowledge and the concrete experiences of women in these three countries. She has also been instrumental in helping groups publish various documents (Paris 1989, 435–46). Second, the women's movement in the North African region shares a struggle for autonomy from political parties and governmental institutions. In Tunisia, Algeria, and Morocco in the mid-1980s, women began to wean their organizations from the political parties and student organizations that spawned them. Third, the women's movements in all three countries have appropriated the discourses of politics and religion—with Islamist women's organizations proliferating in the region from the mid-1980s until the early 1990s.

Women and the Nationalist Movement

The Moroccan women's movement emerged in the context of the nationalist struggle for independence, and then by the specific agendas of subsequent political parties after independence. The political climate during the 1950s was in fact more favorable to women's rights since it allowed women to question, in a very straightforward manner, the status given them in the Sharia as represented by Maliki jurisprudence. Al-Ahnaf (1994, 4) links women's demands concerning personal status laws in the late 1950s to the public reflection occurring within (the most progressive) women's wings of the nationalist movement.

The nationalist Party of Democracy and Independence (PDI, al-Shura wa al-Istiqlal) in 1944 created the first Moroccan women's association, the Sisters of Purity (Akhawat al-Safa). In their first congress in 1946, the Sisters of Purity addressed some of the prejudices faced by women before

---

3. See Paris 1989 for an examination of the influences on the women's movement in North Africa.

the court and asked for the prohibition of polygamy, the legislation of divorce, and the interdiction of early-age marriage (Daoud 1993, 248). In 1957 the PDI newspaper *Democracie* published a statement by a group of Moroccan women concerning gender inequalities maintained by the Sharia. The statement challenged the validity of Maliki jurisprudence and of the Sharia's interpretation of Islamic precepts and questioned the gap between the Sharia's affirmation of equality of men and women before God and the inequalities encoded by Maliki jurisprudence. Thus, for instance, the ulema were asked to explain the justification for a woman's testimony being equal to only half of a man's and for a woman's inheritance being half the amount of her male counterpart. The statement also renounced—not for the first time—polygyny, men's exclusive right to repudiation (unilateral divorce), the institution of marital guardianship, and women's absence from religious leadership (Al-Ahnaf 1994, 3). The same newspaper had earlier published a demand, signed by a woman called Souad, for full equality between men and women, for abolition of polygyny, and for equal inheritance rights for men and women (ibid., 3–4; Daoud 1993).

Though these demands came from the most progressive faction of nationalist women, this action was not mere elitist activism (Al-Ahnaf 1994). Indeed, women's liberation was part of the nationalist agenda framed by Allal Al-Fassi in his famous book *Al-Naqd al-Dhati* (Self-Criticism [1952]). As Al-Azmeh argues, it was evident in much of the Arab world's nationalist discourse that women's claim to full equality and citizenship corresponded with the nationalist movement's agenda, which incorporated gender equity as part of the modernization project. The political and social vocabulary of the peak period of nationalism and socialism was modernist and reformist and did not include religious or pious terms. The fight against what is now called the West was then a struggle against capitalism and imperialism, not a fight against "cultural imperialism" as it is understood now (Al-Azmeh 1996, 42). The inclusion of women's issues on the nationalist agenda was supported by both Moroccan nationalist leaders and the ulema. The alliance between the ulema and nationalist leaders was in fact the outcome of the latter's adherence to both the religious teachings of Qaraouine University and to the broader political Salafi school of thought.[4] The Salafi school first emerged in the Middle East at the end of the nineteenth century as a call to reform Arab society. Thinkers and scholars such as Jamal al-Din al-Afghani and his student Muhammad Abduh led a movement of thought and interpretation of the ulema to modernize Arab society and enhance the status of women.

Salafi thought shaped the movement of independence in North Africa, and more particularly the Moroccan nationalist movement. Moroccan nationalist leaders such as Al-Fassi called for reactivating *ijtihad,* that is, "the reinterpretation of scriptural and other foundational texts" (ibid., 12). As an Islamic concept *ijtihad* was co-opted by nationalist women and was instrumental in their call for reforming women's status in the Sharia. This opening of the Sharia to public scrutiny during the nationalist struggle allowed women's issues to be part of the discourse on the liberation process and linked religious teachings to the fight for independence and modernization—supported by even the mainstream ulema. For example, in 1956 Abderrahman al-Touzani, one of the ulema from Qaraouine, addressed the king in an open letter, urging him to reverse the "archaic laws including the ones based on the Maliki dogma" (Al-Ahnaf 1994, 4).

Women's demands were not only brought into play by the nationalist discourse but also the spontaneous expression of women's effective participation in the nationalist struggle for independence (Baker 1998). However, it is notable that after Moroccan independence, neither the recognition of women's role in the nationalist movement nor the nationalist consensus on women's rights was maintained. The Personal Status Code, prepared by the Ministry of Justice in 1957 and reviewed by a council of experts headed by Allal Al-Fassi, did not incorporate the ideal of an egalitarian society championed earlier by the nationalist leaders. Despite women's roles in the struggle against French and Spanish colonization, and even though three main figures of the nationalist movement were part of the council reviewing and revising the code, the final version remained faithful to Maliki

---

4. Qaraouine University was founded in Fez in the ninth century and became one of the most prestigious centers of knowledge in the region for sciences, literature, and religious studies. By the time of the French occupation, the teaching had been reduced to the repetition of an admittedly traditional interpretation of the Sharia.

jurisprudence. Thus, as Mernissi notes, "At the dawn of Moroccan independence, the nationalist leaders, who had undergone torture in prison so that equality and democracy could reign, designed the future Moroccan family without consulting the central element of that family—women" (1989, 2).

Indeed, the revised document was even more regressive than the one proposed by the Ministry of Justice (Al-Ahnaf 1994; Daoud 1993). Daoud explains this disregard by nationalist leaders of their commitment to women as part of a strategy to reunify Morocco and construct a nation-state subject to one juridical frame. The return to Maliki *fiqh* (Islamic jurisprudence) was meant to repair the division between the Berber and Arab populations introduced by the French under the so-called Berber Dahir (decree) of 1930 (1993, 255; Al-Ahnaf 1994, 5). The revised document introduced some small reforms, including a fixed minimum marriage age of fifteen for women, the elimination of forced marriage, and women's right to *mut'a* (alimony) in case of abusive repudiation (Moulay R'chid 1991, 53; Al-Ahnaf 1994, 6). However, the *moudawana* also maintained polygyny and marital guardianship. The core of the struggle later led by women's groups centered not on the insignificance of these reforms but on the religious establishment's claim as to the divine origins of the *moudawana*. The argument that the *moudawana* is a direct expression of the Sharia cast all attempts to change it as efforts to undermine its sacred character.

Two Decades of Struggle Against the *Moudawana*

Starting in the 1970s, the women's wings of various political parties proposed reforms to women's status and contested the discrepancies in men's and women's access to education, to equal wages, and to political participation. These actions failed to attract even the support of the affiliated political parties and have generally remained unheard by the government and the parliament. The Union de l'Action Feminine launched the first public campaign against the *moudawana* in 1992, following an initial unsuccessful attempt to put an end to the practice of repudiation in 1987 (Brand 1998, 69–70). Leading UAF members such as Latifa Jbabdi were already well known through their publications in the Arabic magazine *8 Mars*, created in 1983 by the same group of women who established the UAF. This publication was the first Arabic-language feminist magazine in independent

Morocco and was supported by the Organisation d'Action Démocratique Populaire (OADP), the party of affiliation of most UAF members. From its first issue in 1984 the paper underscored the diversity of roles Moroccan women undertake and addressed the conditions women face in the workplace and within the family. Articles have considered taboo subjects such as the political detention of women, violence against women, and rape and sexual harassment. The magazine has also provided information on global women's events and on the government's position vis-à-vis various conventions relevant to women's rights.

The UAF's 1992 One Million Signatures campaign occurred within the context of an electoral campaign and a climate of constitutional reform. The official discourse of democratization during this period kept women as political actors at the margins of the discussions. However, the UAF used the political atmosphere to propose a reading of both the constitution and the *moudawana* as they pertained to women. So, for example, the UAF contested the *moudawana* in terms of both the Moroccan constitution, which enshrines full equality for all citizens, and in terms of the Sharia, which prescribes full rights for both men and women. This campaign continues to this day to provoke virulent debates between women's groups and their opponents.

The UAF began its One Million Signatures campaign with a mailing to the political parties and the president of the parliament, urging representatives to take into account women's issues in their discussions concerning constitutional reform. In the document the UAF reminded the representatives of the state's obligations to the international community as stated in the Copenhagen Convention[5] and its commitment to implement the Nairobi resolutions.[6]

---

5. The 1980 UN Copenhagen conference on women convened to examine the progress made by member nations in terms of women's advancement and rights midway through the UN Decade for Women, which targeted "equality, peace, and development." In 1987 Moroccan women's organizations affiliated with opposition political parties held meetings and organized workshops to pressure the government to ratify the Copenhagen Convention. Many women's organizations used the Copenhagen Convention to legitimate their action (Daoud 1993; Moulay R'chid 1991).

6. The 1985 UN Nairobi conference was held to review and appraise the achievements of the UN Decade for Women. The conference also laid down the strategies to be

The UAF mailing argued that the *moudawana* was obsolete because of the concrete evolution of Moroccan society and changes affecting family structure and called for the adaptation of the *moudawana* to these changes. The UAF also challenged the exclusive reliance on Maliki jurisprudence and called for a reactivation of *ijtihad* as a source of legislation. The UAF document called for the Moroccan Constitution to establish women's rights and requested a quota of 20 percent women in all elected institutions (Al-Ahnaf 1994). In a press conference given by UAF members on March 7, 1992, the newspaper *8 Mars* announced the campaign to collect one million signatures protesting the *moudawana*.

Like the UAF, the Association Démocratique des Femmes du Maroc (ADFM), created in 1985, was secular and leftist but supported by a different faction of the political Left. Moreover, it was the first women's organization established independent of a political party. Though ADFM committee members were affiliated with the Party of Progress and Socialism, the initiative to create the ADFM came from the collective action of individual women, not from the party. The ADFM declared total independence from any official party's political agenda or perspective. Its first campaign against the *moudawana* in 1992 occurred in the context of the creation of the Union du Maghreb Arabe.[7] Through the UMA the ADFM helped launch a "Maghrebian" women's network, the Collectif 95 Maghreb Égalité, along with nongovernmental organizations (NGOs) from Algeria, Tunisia, and Morocco, in order to provide women of the Maghreb with a regional voice. Collectif 95 called for a truly democratic Maghreb that recognized women's rights and their claim to full citizenship.

---

implemented up to the year 2000 for the promotion of women, with a particular focus on women's economic security and welfare in the developing world (United Nations General Assembly 1994). Following Nairobi, the Ministry of Social Affairs organized workshops to develop strategies for improving women's condition in Morocco. The strategies developed by a group of experts were submitted to a national committee for approval in 1987 (Daoud 1993).

7. The UMA was created in Marrakech in February 1989. Morocco played a leading role in the formation of this union, which was intended to be a geopolitical and geoeconomic region made up of Algeria, Tunisia, Libya, Mauritania, and Morocco (Lacoste-Dujardin and Lacoste 1991).

As women's rights advocates, members of Collectif 95 aimed at lobbying their respective governments to support the ratification of the Copenhagen Convention without reservations. By acting within a framework of international resolutions, the group intended to disarm opposition framed by demands for cultural authenticity and particularism; it called for the establishment of a "unified platform for a non-discriminatory codification of women's rights in the Maghreb" and published a book titled *One Hundred Measures and Provisions for a Maghrebian Egalitarian Codification of the Personal Statute and Family Law* (1995). Besides producing this proposed universal codification of personal status laws in the Maghreb, the group published many reports and studies on the state of women's rights in the three countries. The ADFM helped in providing regional coordination and held workshops and conferences to address women's absence from decision making and to devise strategies to support women's political participation, all the while networking with women's NGOs to support the petition campaign against the *moudawana* (Daoud 1993, 335).

The Achievement and Limitations of Women's Mobilization

The UAF's One Million Signatures campaign called for the following changes: the suppression of the marital guardianship and acknowledgment of legal competency for women at the age of twenty-one, granting men and women mutual responsibility and equal rights and obligations within the family, equal guardianship rights for men and women over children, the right of women to keep the conjugal home in case of divorce, the abolition of polygamy, the abolition of repudiation and regulation of divorce through the courts, equal rights of women to obtain a divorce from the courts, and the indisputable right to an education and to work (Daoud 1993, 333; Brand 1998, 70; Al-Ahnaf 1994, 10). To achieve its goals the UAF used various strategies, including media blitzes and the creation of local neighborhood-based committees in different cities and towns to sensitize the population through direct contact (Daoud 1993, 337). The group also organized countless meetings, conferences, and workshops outlining the campaign to the public and created a network linking many Moroccan women's groups and women's wings of the various political parties in support of the petition. This mobilization was highly effective;

according to UAF members, more than one million signatures were collected in a few months.

But although the UAF campaign appeared highly successful, a parallel mobilization was also occurring—Islamist activists in the educational institutions collected three million signatures against the campaign (ibid., 338). However, the major attack against the campaign came from the Islamist newspapers. *Al-Raya* was the first to publish a reaction to the One Million Signatures campaign. As the mouthpiece of the Reform and Renewal Movement (Harakat al-Islah wa al-Tajdid) headed by Member of Parliament Abdelilah Benkirane, *al-Raya* condemned the petition against the *moudawana* as a "conspiracy against Islam" and called for political leaders and the ulema to take a public position against it. The tension between leaders of the UAF campaign and the Islamist activists reached its peak when a group of ulema writing in *al-Raya* called for the death penalty to be applied to the leaders of the campaign for apostasy (Al-Ahnaf 1994, 14).

Most of the political parties, nationalist as well as socialist, remained silent as the battle lines for and against the *moudawana* were drawn, though some, including the Istiqlal Party, had already enjoined their female members to withdraw from the UAF network. The political parties feared that support for the campaign would give credit to the OADP, the main political party supporting the UAF campaign (Daoud 1993).

The reaction of the Islamists brought into question another fundamental dimension of the state. The Moroccan Kingdom is based on the definition of the religious sphere as one of the responsibilities of the king. The king is defined as "commander of the faithful" *(amir al-mu'minin)* and represents the highest spiritual as well as temporal authority. The Islamists' activities and statements encroached on the king's religious responsibility and sphere of authority. A reaction to the Islamists' claims by the king was therefore vital for the monarchy to restate its jurisdiction and legitimacy over both the political and the religious arenas. In his speech to the nation on August 20, 1992, King Hassan asked women to end their campaign and to address their demands to him by writing to his cabinet. He reiterated his exclusive rights regarding issues relating to the *moudawana* and its application and announced the creation of a committee of forty-four women, which he invited to present its demands at the palace in September 1992. However, the forty-four women included only one representative from the UAF; the majority were from various state departments or from the king's cabinet and the political parties and had played no role during the One Million Signatures campaign (Al-Ahnaf 1994, 18). The committee members representing women's organizations were primarily from the Union of Moroccan Women, headed by Princess Fatema Zohra since its creation by the palace in 1969. In his public speech to these delegates, the king acknowledged that the *moudawana* was in need of reform and that the ulema would be in charge of studying the project and examining women's demands.

In general, observers were not very optimistic about the king's intervention, which many saw as constraining women's mobilization and their ability to influence the political arena. The king's speech was interpreted as an order to stop a successful campaign that was polarizing Moroccan society during a period when the government was searching for a national consensus on constitutional reform (Daoud 1993; Al-Ahnaf 1994; Denoeux and Gateau 1995). Closing down the campaign in this manner, and effectively precluding gender issues from the constitutional debates, clearly indicated that the operative definition of democracy in Morocco did not include the constituency of women. King Hassan's intent was to distance the debate on the *moudawana* from the political level of parliament and government and render it a matter for the individual attention of the monarch (Al-Ahnaf 1994, 17). The king's intervention also clearly showed the divergent sources of authority over women and the complex articulation between those sources. As Bennani notes:

> The legislation regulating the different aspects of social life of Moroccan Muslim women is characterized on the one hand by the diversity of the sources of legislation and on the other hand, by the incoherence and contradiction between these different sources. Besides the constitution, which is the highest source of legislation, many other particular codes from various sources regulate each aspect of women's lives. Some of those sources stem from the French colonization; others are inspired by the Islamic Sharia; others are marked by the international legislation concerning women's rights. (1997, 146)

The king's intervention brought into play his role as supreme authority in the arena of family law, wherein women's personal status is considered the responsibility and domain of the monarch. Indeed, when the king
appointed his council to study women's demands, women were entirely
removed from the discussions of the council, which was composed primarily of conservative ulema who ultimately made what most activists
consider insignificant changes to the *moudawana* (Al-Ahnaf 1994, 23).

The changes addressed four areas. First, the new code limited the
power of the male guardian *(wali)* by requiring a woman's signature on
her marriage contract, and it eliminated guardianship of mature "orphan"
women. Second, guardianship of children upon the death of their father
went to their mother and not to a judge, as was formerly the case. Third,
divorce, while still the exclusive right of the husband, now required the
presence of both parties to register the divorce. The permission of a judge
was stipulated in cases of repudiation, and a *mut'a*, a compensatory sum,
was due to a repudiated woman in case of unjustified divorce. Fourth,
while polygamy was maintained, it required permission from a judge,
and the first wife (or wives) had to be informed (Al-Ahnaf 1994; Morocco
1995; Bennani 1997; Brand 1998). These changes did not come close to the
demands of women's groups, having been shaped by a traditional conception of the family that did not reflect any of the changes that have significantly impacted Moroccan society (Miadi 1997, 210). Many observers
believed that women's groups had failed in their struggle to implement
women's rights and were deceived by the political parties and co-opted by
the palace (Denoeux and Gateau 1995).

However, the positive impact of the campaign cannot be denied. It is
my contention that it succeeded in changing the public status of women
and redefining their relationship to both the religious and the political arenas. First, the king's invitation to women constitutes official recognition of
a new status of women not simply as housewives but as citizens and opinion leaders. The public invitation for women to address their demands
to the monarch without mediation was the first step toward establishing
women's identity as full political agents. Second, the feminist campaign
was successful in challenging the status of the *moudawana* as a sacred and
therefore inviolable text. The king's promise to examine women's demands

vis-à-vis the *moudawana* redefined the document as open to revision and reform. Third, the feminist campaign allowed a renegotiation of power relations among the state, the political parties, and women's groups. The latter emerged as political agents through their struggle to get parliament and the government involved in the debate over the *moudawana*. Finally, women publicly claimed their right to read and interpret Islamic texts, which has resulted in various women-centered interpretations of them. This last point has important implications for Islamist women as well as for secular feminists by delegitimizing the exclusive mediation and interpretation of Islam by men for women. This change in itself constitutes a revolution with long-term consequences.

The New Code of the Family: The International Conjuncture

Currently, Moroccan gender debates are shaped by different political and cultural challenges. The main challenge is the resistance of Islamist groups to the perceived hegemony of universalist women's rights and global feminism. The United Nations' agenda on women is challenged by the Islamists' claim of "cultural authenticity" and the framing of gender debates by Islamist activists and scholars in terms of an opposition between Muslim "self" and non-Muslim "other." However, as Narayan shows, cultural polarizations are also not new—they are grounded in divisions created by colonial forces to justify their domination and ongoing in postcolonial political, economic, and social struggles (1997, 14). But even though such oppositions are not new, the forms of contemporary contestation are certainly shaped by the postcolonial world's resistance to new currents within the global agenda on women's rights—including the recent coalition of the feminist movement in Morocco and transnational women's rights movements—and the adoption of a transnational discourse and priorities by the Moroccan movement. The inscription of the feminist movement within this universal frame is challenged by the Islamist call to fight imperial domination, which they see working through transnational agencies (Chukri 2000; Mufid 2000).

Divisions within the Moroccan state have also impacted state gender policy; this ambivalence has found expression in the state's reluctance to ratify certain international conventions on women's rights. For example, though Morocco ratified the Convention on the Elimination of All Forms of Discrimination Against Women in 1993 (preceded by Tunisia in 1985 and followed by Algeria in 1996), the three countries have expressed reservations that CEDAW conflicts with the Sharia and fails to take into account religious and customary laws. And though other spheres are no longer legislated by the Sharia, women's status remains within its dictates.

These contradictions and divisions spurred the battle over the implementation of the National Plan for Integrating Women in Development, elaborated by the government in 1999. The plan targets "removing the conditions of inequality between men and women" by changing the *moudawana* (Morocco 1999). The plan aims to introduce major changes in family law by limiting polygamy and abolishing repudiation, providing men and women with the same guardianship rights over children, ensuring economic security for divorced women and their right to keep the conjugal home, and abolishing marital guardianship. In support of these changes the plan referred to the Beijing Platform for Action and the CEDAW convention. However, since its presentation to the media in 1999 by the prime minister, the national plan has polarized Moroccan society and underscored primary cleavages within both the government and civil society. Within the government, the state secretary in charge of the family, childhood, and social protection is championing it, while the Ministry of Religious Affairs and the mainstream ulema have declared it to be contrary to the teachings of the Sharia. Within civil society, the fight over the plan has Islamist women's groups acting as a major force for mass mobilization.

The demonstrations of March 2000 highlighted this polarization not only within the women's movement between Islamist and feminist agendas but also within the government. More than one million people took to the streets in the cities of Casablanca (in opposition to the plan) and Rabat (in support of the plan). Seven out of forty-three ministries took part in the march to support changing women's status in the *moudawana*. The roots of these polarizations go back at least to the eighties and debates over the legitimacy of universalistic conceptions of women's rights versus cultural particularism and the negotiation of women's status within the framework of the Sharia (Kandiyoti 1997; Afkhami and Friedl 1997).

♦ ♦ ♦

The forgoing discussion has emphasized the complexity of Moroccan women's struggles to change their status in the family law over the last decades. These struggles were not new; they were shaped by earlier nationalist discourse of modernization and women's emancipation.

The context of the current women's rights struggles in Morocco is shaped by competing frameworks of globalization of women's rights and global Islam. The complex relationship of women's groups to the state is evidenced by divisions within the state concerning women's rights but also by the new prerogatives of the "war on terror."

Studies have shown that certain political processes increase the political space available to women's organizations even when the state actively represses other sectors of civil society (Alvarez 1990, 262).[8] A case in point is the Casablanca bombing of May 2003 by a group of Islamist radicals and the way increased world attention on Morocco shifted the balance in favor of reforming women's status in family law. Gender was central to the repositioning of the Moroccan state at this juncture. It was in fact through the reform of family law that the Moroccan monarchy truly recovered its image as a modern and "moderate" regime, the Casablanca attack notwithstanding (see Salime 2007). Yet, although this code constitutes the most significant gain women have made since independence, it also reconfirms the place that gender holds as a marker of political and cultural identification of the state in the current conjuncture of the U.S. global war on terrorism, which itself is delivered with a discourse of modernization, democracy, and reforms in the Middle East. This discourse in itself remains an obstacle to women's acting as full citizens in their own right.

Feminist theory has shown that gender, race, and sexuality inform definitions of citizenship and national identity, especially when state power is challenged or negotiated (Enloe 1989, 2004; Joseph 2000a; Moghadam 2000; Charrad 2001; Hoodfar 2004). In Morocco, the women's rights legislation—its promulgation in 1957, its initial reform in 1993, and its "radical"

8. Indeed, it is important to recognize that the reform of the *moudawana* came at the expense of setbacks to other rights and freedoms, including the right to information.

reform in 2003—has been the primary site on which the postcolonial state has negotiated national identity within the dual framework of modernity-tradition and authenticity-moderation. The revised Code of the Family bears witness to how political tensions are played out and may unfold in the gender field (Salime forthcoming). In Morocco these representations were articulated by the *moudawana* and the way it had grounded national identity in the gendered values of extended kinship and patriarchal family (Charrad 2002). Before as well as after its reform, the *moudawana* has been the primary vehicle through which the Islamic identity of the state is defined. Thus, any fundamental change in the code implies a fundamental redefinition of state or political ideologies.

9. Straddling CEDAW and the MMA

Conflicting Visions of Women's Rights
in Contemporary Pakistan

ANITA M. WEISS

Pakistan became a state party to the United Nations Convention on the Elimination of All Forms of Discrimination Against Women (CEDAW) in 1996,[1] and, as such, it pledged to review its existing laws and social institutions to eliminate discrimination against women.[2] Three years later, a relatively progressive government came to power in the wake of a coup d'état led by Gen. Pervez Musharraf, who resigned as the country's president in August 2008. Shortly before his government was ready to file Pakistan's first CEDAW report, the tragedy of September 11, 2001, struck, and the ensuing war in Afghanistan began.

Pakistan had been embroiled for four decades in social conflict, much of it focused on the rights of women, and in the post–September 2001 situation the turmoil did not abate (Weiss 1999, 2003). The clash of conflicting

1. The UN adopted CEDAW in December 1979, and it entered into force in 1981 (see United Nations Division for the Advancement of Women 1979).

2. I am deeply indebted to the many people who kindly met with me and shared their views in Pakistan during October–November 2003 and August–October 2004, and in particular to Zulfiqar Gilani, Akbar Zeb, and Sikander Sherpao for their guidance, enthusiasm, and support, and to Nilufer Javaid and Ayesha Attique for their assistance with translations. I appreciate the support of the Center for Asia and Pacific Studies and the Center for the Study of Women in Society at the University of Oregon that helped make this fieldwork possible.

visions of women's rights held by different groups escalated with the victory of an Islamist coalition, the Muttahida Majlis-e-Amal (MMA), in the October 2002 elections in the North West Frontier Province (NWFP).[3] It was the first time in Pakistan's fifty-five-year history that an Islamist political party had won a significant election.[4] The social and political implications of this event are staggering, for Pakistan is but one of many Muslim states that are grappling with balancing the demands of modernity and globalization with the often contradictory demands of their local populace. A number of new and proposed laws and policies in the NWFP directly challenged federal legislation, the most powerful and transformative of which concern the rights of women.

This chapter assesses the progress that has been made by the federal government of Pakistan to implement CEDAW and compares these efforts with laws and policies proposed or promulgated by the provincial NWFP government of the Islamist MMA, which was voted out of power in the February 2008 elections. These contrasting actions taken by the federal and provincial governments have enormous implications for women's rights, for while the MMA coalition is no longer in power today, it created important precedents of priorities that such Islamist provincial governments in Pakistan might undertake in the future.

Identity politics is the driving force behind the debate over women's rights in Pakistan. The rise in support for populist Islamist political parties is representative of the trend in Muslim sentiments throughout the Middle East and Asia. Many now conclude that the secular governments of the past century not only did a disservice to Muslims—by denying them the opportunity to live under Sharia (Islamic law)—but also sold them short by not prioritizing Muslim values as alternatives to global capitalism.

---

3. The MMA held 70 of 124 seats in the NWFP Provincial Assembly. There were 23 female members of the assembly, one of whom, Ghazala Habib (PML–Sherpao Party), won a general seat. The others were appointed to seats reserved for women, based on proportional representation of total seats won by distinct parties. Thus, the MMA had 13 female members, and the combined opposition had 10.

4. I use the term "Islamist" to refer to political groups and parties that aim to implement norms and laws consistent with their interpretation of Islam in the event they come to power.

Popular sentiment widely holds that the resultant social, political, and economic crises that their communities now face cannot be resolved by following Western styles of governance but only through recapturing the faith and incorporating it into a political agenda. When Islamist governments are elected—as in the NWFP elections of 2002—such scenarios often juxtapose these emergent local Islamist agendas with laws existing at the federal level and find the latter lacking. This dilemma is the most compelling when we consider laws relating to the rights of women.

Background to the Phenomenon of the MMA in Pakistan

When Pakistan became an independent state as a result of partition of the former British India in 1947, its greatest advocates were those individuals supporting a homeland for the Muslims of South Asia so they would not be at risk of living under the threat of Hindu hegemony. The most religiously oriented groups, particularly the Deobandis (the precursor of the Jama'at-i Islam), did not initially support the creation of Pakistan on the basis that Islam could not be constrained within the borders of a modern nation-state. The country was not even initially declared to be an Islamic republic; that designation came only with the second constitution in 1965. The third constitution, promulgated in 1973 after the divisive 1971 civil war, finally included other references to Islam and the supremacy of Islamic laws. The third constitution also mandated the establishment of the Council of Islamic Ideology to ensure that no laws in Pakistan contradict the Sharia.

No substantive program of Islamic reforms existed in Pakistan prior to President Zia ul-Haq's implementation of his Islamization program in February 1979. Those reforms included the establishment of a *zakat*-based welfare and taxation system, a profit-and-loss banking option in accordance with Islam's prohibitions against usury, a new educational policy, and an Islamic penal code—including the controversial Offense of *Zina* Act in the Hudood Laws—that had far more implications for women than men.[5]

5. For further discussion of Zia's Islamization program, see Weiss 1986, 11–16; for an updated discussion, refer to Weiss 2003, 586–90.

However, the Islamization program under Zia ul-Haq was pursued within a rather complicated ideological framework. His stance contradicted the popular culture in which most people were "personally" very religious but not "publicly" religious. An untoward outcome was that the state fomented factionalism with its Islamic policy by legislating what was Islamic and what was not. Islam itself could no longer provide unity, as it was now being defined to exclude previously included groups. Shi'a and Sunni disputes, ethnic disturbances in Karachi, increased animosity toward Ahmediyas, and the revival of sectarian and intraprovincial tensions can be traced to Pakistan's having lost the ability to use Islam as a common moral vocabulary (Weiss and Gilani 2001, 11). Importantly, too, the state attempted to dictate a specific ideal image of women in Islamic society, one that was largely antithetical to the one existing in popular sentiments and in everyday life.

The debate has escalated in the past two decades over the role that Islamic law should play in the country's affairs and governance and over government intervention in the personal practice of Islam. Implementation of Sharia remains a high, identifiable political priority, especially in the NWFP. When members of the MMA parties vowed to fellow Pashtuns in 2002 that if elected they would implement Islam, they found a sociopolitical climate very willing to listen. In addition to having witnessed—and largely opposed—military attacks on neighboring Afghanistan a year earlier that were supported by the federal government in Pakistan, Pashtuns in the NWFP have been frustrated by the escalation of local onslaughts against purported al-Qaeda operatives but whom many perceive as being indigenous freedom fighters lacking ties to global terrorism.[6] The NWFP has remained mired in poverty, while the Pashtun majority has witnessed its cultural hegemony waning. Many people pointed out to me the creeping "Punjabization" of social hierarchies that has been increasingly

---

6. Amnesty International reported the arbitrary detention of hundreds of people suspected of having links with "terrorist" organizations and their transfer to U.S. custody in the context of the Pakistani government's support of the U.S.-led "war on terror" (Amnesty International 2003a). Nowhere are people more acutely aware of this fact than in the NWFP, where the majority of raids have occurred.

manifest in the NWFP in the past twenty years. The Pashtun concept of a leader's being "first among equals" has been eclipsed by Punjabi practices of elites considering their constituents as inferiors who should serve *them,* which has elicited noticeable resentment against many incumbent politicians. Hence, the political landscape was ripe for change, and unprecedented numbers of voters were receptive to the message of the MMA in the fall of 2002.

CEDAW, Legal Changes, and the Rights of Women

Prior to its ratification of CEDAW, Pakistan had become a state party to a number of other gender-focused UN human rights instruments, beginning with the 1953 Convention on the Political Rights of Women (United Nations High Commissioner of Human Rights [UNHCHR] 1952). It went further than some of the requirements of the convention on the consent to marriage, minimum age for marriage, and registration of marriage (which it did not ratify) by instead promulgating the 1961 Muslim Family Laws Ordinance to regulate marriages and restrain polygamy. The MFLO required the registration of all marriages and written permission from a man's wife (or wives) before an arbitration council would decide if he could marry an additional wife. It abolished divorce by repudiation *(talaq)* and provided other safeguards for women in the event of a divorce. The constitutionally mandated Council of Islamic Ideology had undertaken review of the ordinance but would not publicly release its assessment— written in the 1980s—until recently, as more conservative groups would have lambasted the fairly liberal opinions expressed in the report and further polarized the country around the issues of women's rights.

Pakistan later became a state party to the UN Convention on the Rights of the Child of 1989, the 1993 Vienna Declaration that "recognized women's rights as human rights," the 1994 Cairo Population and Development conference's Programme of Action, and the 1995 Platform for Action in Beijing (UNHCHR 1989, 1993; United Nations International Conference on Population and Development 1994; United Nations Division for the Advancement of Women 1995).

The women's movement in Pakistan played a key role in the government of Benazir Bhutto's ratification of CEDAW in 1996. Critical elements within the convention attest to this ratification as a watershed point for the Pakistan women's movement, such as Article 1 that requires states to create policies to eliminate discrimination against women, including "any distinction, exclusion or restriction made on the basis of sex which has the purpose of impairing or nullifying the recognition, enjoyment or exercise by women . . . on a basis of equality of men or women, of human rights and fundamental freedoms"; Article 2, requiring states to establish "legal protection of the rights of women on an equal basis with men"; and Article 7, which ensures that women have input into "the formulation of government policy and the implementation thereof." Article 5 merits special attention here, as it urges state parties to the convention to take "all appropriate measures to modify the social and cultural patterns of conduct of men and women, with a view to achieving the elimination of prejudices and customary and all other practices which are based on the idea of the inferiority or the superiority of either of the sexes or on stereotyped roles for men and women." Additional articles in CEDAW assert that women are to enjoy the same conditions and access to education as men (Article 10), that women are to be accorded "a legal capacity identical to that of men" in civil matters (Article 15), and that there be no discrimination "against women in all matters relating to marriage and family relations" (Article 16).

In its ratification of CEDAW the government of Pakistan declared that its constitution would be supreme and supersede any contradictions with the convention. Yet its constitutional framework is inconsistent on women's rights (Weiss 2003, 586). The 1973 constitution affirms that the state is committed to eliminating exploitation and guarantees that "all citizens are equal under the law," prohibits "discrimination on the basis of sex alone," and promises that "steps shall be taken to ensure full participation of women in all spheres of national life." Yet laws passed during Zia's Islamization program (1979–1985) are also a part of Pakistan's constitutional makeup. The Islamic penal code, selectively gleaned from Islamic jurisprudence, focused on enforcing punishments for three kinds of crimes explicitly outlined in the Sharia: theft of private property, consumption of intoxicants, and adultery and fornication *(zina)*. The most controversy swirled around the latter, *zina,* both because the ordinance governing it made no legal distinction between adultery and rape and because its enforcement was highly discriminatory against women. The Law of Evidence, promulgated in 1983 and subsequently upheld only in cases concerning economic transactions, would have restricted women from providing evidentiary testimony in certain kinds of cases and require corroboration by another woman in other kinds of cases. Regardless, the law clearly gives men and women different legal rights and, at the least, underscores the state's view that women and men are not equal as economic actors.

Islamic laws are based mainly on the Hanafi school of jurisprudence, though on occasion the state has turned to decisions based on other schools as well. However, two kinds of laws that deny women the same rights as men are derived from Sharia and, as such, are considered immutable: inheritance and evidence or legal witness.

The former is based on verse 11 of the Qur'an (in the chapter "Women"), which is commonly interpreted as stating that a male shall inherit twice as much as a female. As Pakistan's constitution requires that no laws can contradict the injunctions of Islam, the prevailing sense is that Pakistani law cannot grant complete equality in inheritance to men and women. Pakistan has no accepted secular systems of wills; inheritance is determined based on the school of jurisprudence to which a deceased subscribed.

The issue of evidence or legal witness is more problematic. The controversial Law of Evidence was promulgated by Zia's government based on verse 282 in the Qur'an (in the chapter "The Cow").[7] However, in practice this verse has been interpreted in a number of ways, and current case law in Pakistan does not restrict women's testimony except in certain kinds of financial cases.

One point that many people believe is an issue of legal discrimination in Pakistan, but actually is not, concerns consent and guardianship at the time of marriage. Pakistani case law had previously been ambiguous on

---

7. A common translation of the Qur'anic verse on which the Law of Evidence is based is: "Call in two male witnesses from among you, but if two men cannot be found, then one man and two women whom you judge fit to act as witnesses; so that if either of them commit an error, the other will remember."

this point, sometimes ruling in favor of a father who opposed a daughter's marriage on the basis that he is her guardian *(wali)*, other times ruling in favor of the new bride and her husband. But a number of different rulings in the late 1990s established a clear legal precedent: in Pakistan, based on Hanafi interpretations of Islamic law, once a child is legally considered an adult, the only consent necessary for a marriage to occur is the agreement of the man and woman entering into the marriage. Consequently, a parent's objection to the marriage of an adult child is not relevant to the law. As an extension of this interpretation of a woman's rights as a legal adult, the nationality law has been revised so that a Pakistani woman's children can "inherit" her nationality irrespective of her husband's nationality (although her husband still cannot).

In the years following Zia's demise in August 1988 that saw Benazir Bhutto and Nawaz Sharif jockeying for power, no pivotal legislation was passed that further affected the rights of women one way or the other. The 1991 Shariah Bill, greatly watered down from what both Zia and Nawaz had initially proposed, was promulgated, declaring Islam as the supreme law in the land but without any further stipulations. The mandate to reserve seats for women in parliamentary elections expired, and neither Benazir nor Nawaz resurrected it, a big disappointment for women's rights activists.[8] They clamored for the Hudood Ordinances—and particularly the *zina* clause—to be repealed, but it didn't happen, either.

It was the Musharraf government, which came to power in a coup in October 1999, that revived the issue of women's empowerment as a key component of its policies to promote Pakistan's progress. It established distinct quotas to promote women's greater participation in public arenas of society: 5 percent for women in government service, 17 percent for women in the national and provincial parliaments, and 33 percent for women in most tiers of local government. It formalized the National Commission on the Status of Women, sought national consensus on the National Policy on Women, and overall set in motion a series of reforms to promote women's rights consistent with globalized norms articulated in CEDAW.

8. The Pervez Musharraf government reinstated the policy of reserving seats for women in elections held in 2001.

In response to growing demands to reform the Hudood Laws, the federal government promulgated the Protection of Women (Criminal Laws Amendment) Act 2006 in November 2006. A key priority was the removal of *zina bil jabr* (adultery without consent) entirely, and the provision regarding *zina* was moved to the Pakistan Penal Code. Provisions would be included to prevent malicious, baseless charges of *zina*, and when a charge filed was found groundless (or if the woman was not found guilty), the charge of *qazf* (false accusation of *zina*) would then apply to the person making the charges. Section 8 (6) definitively states that "no complaint under this section shall be entertained . . . against any person who is a complainant or a victim in a case of rape, under any circumstances whatsoever." We can see how the federal government is cognizant of its standing in the global community in its reform of the Hudood Laws. For example, in explaining the reasoning behind deleting the punishment of whipping for certain offenses, the act goes beyond merely stating that as the Qur'an and Sunnah do not provide for any explicit punishment, therefore "the State is authorized to make this change in conformity with the Islamic concept of justice." It positions itself within the global arena when it continues that this change is also being made in accordance with "the evolving standards of decency which mark the progress of a maturing society."

Another bill on women's rights—to ban antiwomen practices such as forced marriages, marriage in exchange for vengeance, and deprivation of women's inheritance—was submitted to the National Assembly on February 13, 2007. This bill, the Prevention of Anti-Women Practices (Criminal Law Amendment) Bill 2006, seeks to end the "social, political and religious excesses against women." Although it was not expected that the acrimony that shrouded the bill in the fall of 2006 would surface over this one (many Islamist groups have publicly supported banning many of the actions this bill sets out to ban), the National Assembly has yet to move on transforming the bill into becoming a promulgated act.

The state had apparently been reluctant to file its mandatory report to the CEDAW committee on its efforts to eliminate discrimination against women likely because it knew that without moderating some of the laws passed during Zia's regime—such as criminalizing the act of being raped or giving women second-class status in financial transactions—its report would be harshly condemned.[9] Pakistan finally submitted a combined initial, second, and third report to the CEDAW committee on August 3, 2005, which was taken up for review in the thirty-eighth session of the CEDAW committee in the spring of 2007.[10] In its CEDAW report, the Pakistan government identifies a number of obstacles, quite forthrightly, that it faces in eliminating discrimination against women and in implementing the convention, notably prevailing sociocultural norms, the existing patriarchal system, legal guarantees that are often not translated into concrete actions, and the society's feudal values.[11] It argues that most of the substantive challenges lie in implementation, especially at the grassroots level, due to locally perceived cultural restrictions and political necessities to appease certain groups. Not surprisingly, throughout its queries in response to Pakistan's report, the Expert Committee on CEDAW consistently requested clarification of what reforms the state was contemplating to attempt to rectify these injustices.

Laws in Pakistan do not condone discrimination against women. In effect, the view from the vantage point of the federal government is that it has done a fairly good job in reforming laws so as to provide equal

---

9. I had seen different versions of Pakistan's draft CEDAW report by that time. On September 7, 2001, the then secretary of the Ministry for Women's Development told me that the CEDAW report was in the midst of being proofread and she expected it to be submitted shortly.

10. Full details of the review can be found at http://www.un.org/womenwatch/daw/cedaw/38sess.htm.

11. These concerns are stated as follows: "i. A number of sociocultural norms influence women's status and perception of self in the community and are a hindrance in the implementation of laws safeguarding women's status and enjoyment of basic human rights; ii. [The] prevailing patriarchal system, cultural norms and feudal values in the society continue to influence the role of women in the community; iii. The legal guarantees often do not get translated into concrete actions due to prevalent social and cultural norms/practices in the society; and iv. Domestic affairs are considered a private matter and incidents of family/domestic problems are usually hushed up; Community conciliatory committees have been set up; Trained case workers have been posted in different localities to provide initial marriage and family counseling services" (United Nations Division for the Advancement of Women 2007).

legal rights for women, but it is limited in what it can do in the arena of inheritance (broadly defined) and challenged in its efforts to eliminate or even dilute culturally constructed discriminatory attitudes and practices. Regardless, it has repeatedly stated that its vision is "the achievement of gender equity and equality; social, political and economic empowerment of all Pakistani women at all levels; a just, humane and democratic society; and economic prosperity through sustainable development." I want to note that it "hedges its bets" by also including as its goal "[the] empowerment of Pakistani women, irrespective of caste, creed, religion, or other consideration for the realization of their full potential in all spheres of life, especially social, economic, personal and political and in keeping with our Islamic way of life" without identifying any of the particulars of the latter highly contested point (Pakistan 2002, 2).

The MMA Coalition

The Muttahida Majlis-e-Amal that came to power in the provincial government of the NWFP in November 2002 was a coalition of six Islamist parties: Jama'at-i Islam, Jamiat ulema-e-Islam (Fazlur Rehman group), Jamiat ulema-e-Islam (Sami ul-Haq group), Jamiat ulema-e-Pakistan, Markazi Jamiat Ahle Hadith, and Tehrik Nifaz Fiqah Jaferiya (a Shi'a party).[12] These parties had joined together in early 2000 as the Pakistan-Afghanistan Defense Council, in response to the West's criticism of the Taliban, transforming themselves into the MMA after the United States attacked Afghanistan in October 2001. The constituent parties decided to make an alliance "to implement an Islamic system and to protect Islamic values" with the objective of ensuring the "supremacy of Islamic Law and enactment of legislation according to the recommendations of the Islamic

---

12. In mid-November 2003 one of the MMA's constituent members, Tehrik Nifaz Fiqah Jaferiya, was banned as a terrorist organization. The Jamiat ulema-e-Islam (Sami ul-Haq group) dissociated itself a few times from the MMA coalition on the grounds that it was not being treated equally with the other senior partners, the Jama'at-i Islam and the Jamiat ulema-e-Islam (Fazlur Rehman group). However, it stressed that no ideological differences separated it from the coalition; it merely wanted to play a greater decision-making role and hold more cabinet positions in the provincial government.

Ideological Council" (MMA 2002). Only the Jama'at-i Islam had much experience previously in contesting elections, and with limited success (Nasr 1994, 2001, 2002).

The MMA identified four priorities in its campaign agenda to contest the October 2002 elections: promote the Islamization process, greater provincial autonomy, rename the province "Pukhtunkhwa," and social issues (for example, lower unemployment and inflation rates). Its "Election Manifesto" pledged to support reforms that would provide "real constitutional autonomy" to the provinces by removing "all powers resting jointly with the Federal and Provincial Governments" in Pakistan's constitution (MMA 2002). This pledge was of particular importance to the overall agenda of the MMA, for to implement a number of its goals it needed to ensure it had the power to pass legislation in those domains. In particular, it was seeking to cross lines where it could pass legislation to structure an individual's degree of religious piety, though indeed it would have been the MMA's interpretation of piety. Significantly, much of that legislation bears directly on women's rights.

The MMA identified explicit goals of an Islamic polity, including provision of rights to women "according to the Qur'an and Sunnah and to enable them to play their role in society," to arrange for "healthy entertainment and mental, psychological and moral mentoring of the youth," and to end "unwanted restrictions on independent journalism and freedom of speech, and that journalism be made according to religious and national values." A key campaign promise was to institute an *effective* process of implementing Sharia laws in the province (ibid.).

Six months after taking office the MMA government passed the provincial Shariat Law (June 2, 2003), which, though similar, has two key differences from the federal Enforcement of Shariat Act of 1991: whereas the federal law states that no law should be in contradiction to or against Islam, the provincial law states that all issues should be decided according to Sharia and that Sharia extends to all arenas of law. It emphasizes "advocating virtue and forbidding evil" *(amar bil maroof and nahi anil muunkar)* and states that legal and constitutional protection is necessary to ensure these objectives. Additionally, "all local courts would interpret and execute all laws falling within the jurisdiction of the Provincial Government strictly according to Sharia," and in the event laws can be interpreted and implemented in more than one way, then "the courts would adopt that interpretation which is closer to Sharia" (MMA 2003). That *local* courts were now to be given jurisdiction to interpret laws according to Islam was revolutionary, as these tasks thus far had been shared between the constitutionally mandated Council of Islamic Ideology and the Federal Shariat Court. No distinct school of jurisprudence *(fiqh)* is mentioned in the provincial Shariat Law; mention of *fiqh* and Sharia appears to presume a shared understanding of what would constitute them, though albeit in practice it may not be so.

The provincial Shariat Law also proposes various fairly detailed measures for the enforcement of Islam in education, culture, the economy, the system of justice, and governance. It states that mass media should be used to promote Islamic values and teachings and calls for the creation of commissions to examine educational, judicial, and economic institutions in the province to ensure conformity with the requirements of Islam.

The MMA government laid out hundreds of other explicit, detailed goals to promote Islamization in the NWFP. There was a distinct emphasis—critics claim an undue emphasis—on gender segregation under the MMA leadership: girls were to study in separate schools from boys, only female physicians were to treat female patients, and all new mosques were to have separate areas for women. MMA representatives claimed that creating an Islamic context would itself solve many prevailing social problems. However, these ideals were being conveyed in a resource-poor social context, where schools often don't have furniture, teachers, or books and female literacy rates are appallingly low; there are not enough doctors to begin with (let alone female doctors), and families are often reluctant to seek out medical care, especially for girls; and women in this area do not usually go to mosques to offer their prayers.

The justification generally offered for such gender segregation was that it would enable women to live better lives, in accordance with Islam. A female MMA member said, "There is a growing need for female doctors to treat female problems. In this way demands of modesty and *purdah* during treatment can also be fulfilled. Also they should observe *purdah* so that Allah is happy with their services."[13]

The MMA has said male doctors ideally should not perform electrocardiogram tests on female patients, as the test requires a doctor to touch the chest of the patient. MMA detractors have argued, however, that this recommendation is being taken to the extreme and that some male doctors are refusing to treat female patients altogether. MMA representatives, in countering this charge, contended to me that this situation would be an ideal scenario but that, in order to implement this recommendation, there must first be many more female physicians and hence the need to establish a female medical college in the province, which they had initiated.

The MMA government also explicitly addressed women's rights within the family. To their credit, they condemned the Pashtun customary practice of *swara*, whereby disputes, especially when murder is involved, are resolved by the family of the murderer giving a female in marriage to someone from the family of the victim,[14] deeming it against Islam. They also condemned honor killings and the trafficking of women (ibid.). Yet some of their stances contradicted federal law, such as the statement in the draft Islamization agenda that declares that "divorce, which is also an unwanted act in Sharia and destroys many families, should be declared as a punishable act." Consistent with the position held by the Jama'at-i Islam, the MMA leadership criticized the 1961 Muslim Family Laws Ordinance, claiming that it includes two un-Islamic clauses: the requirement to *register* divorces (on the basis that it is not required in Islam) and the requirement for a man to acquire permission from his first wife before he can marry a second wife (ibid.). One MMA leader told me that "as women cannot control their husbands' sexuality, it's better that he has a legally binding

13. Speech by Rehana Ismail, MMA MPA, at a reception at the Lucky Marwat School, NWFP (n.d.).

14. The assumption is that the former belligerent will not harm the victim's family if one of his family's own women is in that household and that long-term peace is ensured once there are children from that marriage. However, in practice, the life of a girl given in *swara* becomes a living hell, for the strong, lingering animosity toward the murderer is taken out on the girl. Even very young girls have been given in *swara*.

second marriage than run around with ten other women."[15] Needless to say, this point is a highly controversial stance within Pakistan today and inconsistent with federal law.

The MMA also voiced concerns about cultural issues and social change, which have largely fallen into two categories: disdain of Westernization and the elimination of obscenities (which it deems a product of the West) and implementation of a reward system for honest behavior. In the former category they banned music in government buildings (which, as they are often locales for wedding celebrations, also precludes music from being played at such ceremonies as well) on the basis of its being un-Islamic. They had limited success in eliminating vulgar film posters and vulgarity in local Pashto films.

Many of these stances and recommendations can be critiqued as mere "window dressing," light efforts by an Islamist-oriented government to try to garner popular support for its ideology. However, the seriousness of these efforts emerges when we analyze a pivotal piece of legislation the MMA introduced to ensure implementation of both the Shariat Law and various other goals to promote Islamization: the Hisba Act. An analysis of the Hisba Bill reveals just how different the MMA's stance on women was from the position of the federal government of Pakistan as well as from globalized views on women's rights.

The MMA introduced the Hisba Bill shortly after implementing its provincial Shariat Law. This controversial bill would have created a new ombudsman's office to "advocate virtue" and, with the assistance of a Hisba Force, ensure that "social evils, injustices and the misuse of powers could be checked properly." The MMA maintained that the Hisba Bill would eliminate non-Islamic practices from the province and bring "justice to people's doorsteps," while critics feared that it could result in an overwhelming vice squad that would compromise human rights in the process of requiring a rigid conformity to regressive practices considered to be "Islamic" by its advocates.

Then provincial information minister Asif Iqbal Daudzai told me that the MMA's Hisba Bill would help bring about a just Islamic society and be

15. Personal interview in Islamabad, November 4, 2003.

beneficial for women: "We are trying to eliminate social diseases. We have banned *swara*. We have banned *talaq*.[16] Hisba will enforce this. The Shariat Bill will be completed by Hisba."[17]

The Hisba Act, through the Hisba Force that it was initially to have created, was to have ensured "compliance of Islamic moral values at public places, discouragement of lavish spending on wedding parties and other social occasions, suspension of business activities and games at prayer times, and a strict enforcement of Islam in all walks of life of the people, government institutions and private businesses and societal activities" (Pakistan Institute of Legislative Development and Transparency 2003, 16). The Hisba Force was proposed to be a sort of vice and virtue patrol, similar to that which the Taliban had established. Nothing like it has ever existed in Pakistan, and it is difficult to imagine its potential for effectiveness and the possibilities for overreaching its mandate.

An MMA provincial minister told me that the MMA government, with its Hisba Act, was trying to Islamize those subjects that did not come under the Federal List,[18] and was seeking to implement laws in those areas where the provincial government had authority to act.[19] However, the federal Council on Islamic Ideology and federal Supreme Court judgments have explicitly stated that the Hisba Bill overstepped those boundaries.

Surprisingly, the Council of Islamic Ideology, the constitutionally mandated institution charged with determining whether existing and

---

16. *Talaq* (repudiation), the act of divorce by a husband stating three times that he has divorced his wife, was already banned by the 1961 federal Muslim Family Laws Ordinance. However, the Jama'at-i Islam has long advocated the repeal of the MFLO on the grounds that it has many aspects that have nothing to do with Islam. The MMA has stated that a month must pass between each time *talaq* is pronounced, and only then is a divorce finalized. There is no requirement in the provincial law that such divorces be registered.

17. Personal interview in Peshawar, November 2003.

18. Specific governance concerns are listed under the Federal List. All others revert to the domain of provinces.

19. Personal interview in Peshawar, October 29, 2003. The ongoing issue concerns federal and provincial authority surrounding the Concurrent List and Federal List and when distinct items should be removed from the Concurrent legislative list and authority for them be allowed to devolve to the provinces.

proposed laws are in accordance with Islam, made a judgment on the proposed Hisba Bill in September 2004. It deemed that under Paragraph 23 of Article 12 of the Pakistan Constitution, the bill was unconstitutionally vague. What is surprising about the judgment is that it was made at all: the Council of Islamic Ideology had been notorious for not making judgments on controversial laws. As noted earlier, it took decades before publishing a judgment on the 1961 Muslim Family Laws Ordinance. To do so would be to take a firm position on interpreting Islam one way or another, something that the council had previously been reluctant to do.

The judgment made on the Hisba Bill, however, did not rule on the act's Islamic credentials per se.[20] Instead, the judgment was concerned specifically with the possibility of the Hisba Force opening the door to havoc *(mufasid)* because it raised the possibility of posing contradictions between the Qur'an and the Sunnah. This force may have created a dangerous condition of indeterminacy in the law (Pakistan 2004; "NWFP Government" 2005). The judgment's greatest concern seems to have been with the arbitrariness that may have resulted.

Its greatest unease was with the goal of establishing a Hisba Administration at all. It stated that there was a danger of the Hisba Administration being misused, especially as there was no consensus or agreement on the moral and ethical issues it was supposedly implementing. It could not do so on an ad hoc basis, and arbitrariness would bring disgrace to the institution. Importantly, the judgment recognized that existing Civil Courts and Shariat Courts have checks and balances against arbitrariness built into them, which the Hisba Bill lacked.

Subsequently, the MMA revised its Hisba Bill, ostensibly on the basis of the Council of Islamic Ideology's guidelines, and then adopted the new version on July 14, 2005. Under the revised Hisba Act, the *mohtasib* (ombudsman) had the authority "to protect Islamic values and etiquettes; to ensure that government publications are useful for the purposes of upholding Islamic values, and forbid government servants from acting against Sharia." The vagueness initially cited by the Council on Islamic

20. I am very grateful to Juan Cole for helping me translate the judgment on the Hisba Act.

Ideology remained, as the law did not specify what these things were: whose vision of etiquette, what school of *fiqh* defined Sharia, and who finally decided if something was Islamic or not.

There was indeed little difference between the two versions. Iqbal Haider, secretary-general of the Human Rights Commission of Pakistan and a former federal minister for law, argued that the provisions in the revised bill, with the exception of Section 23, were "already covered by the existing laws on the list of both federal and provincial statues on the same subject and having the same objects and purposes" (2005, n.p.).

Merely three weeks later, on August 4, 2005, the Supreme Court of Pakistan opined that the new Hisba Bill was unconstitutional on the grounds that it was "vague, overbroad, unreasonably based on excessive delegation of jurisdiction, denying the right of access to justice to the citizens and attempting to set up a parallel judicial system," and it directed the governor of the NWFP (who is appointed by the federal government) not to sign the bill in its present form. The court took umbrage that the Hisba Bill went too far and that "private life, personal thoughts and the individual beliefs of citizens cannot be allowed to be interfered with."

The MMA tabled a discussion of the new Hisba Act on October 10, 2006. This date, however, was two days after the devastating earthquake that claimed more than eighty thousand lives in Pakistan, most of whom were in either the NWFP or Azad Kashmir. The MMA was widely criticized for pushing this controversial bill through at a time when the country's focus was on responding to the devastation. In the year that followed, the MMA government repeatedly stated that its focus was on earthquake relief and not on advancing the Hisba Act. But if indeed that were the case, then why was the act tabled in the provincial parliament on October 10?

Conflicting Visions of Women's Rights?

In the Pakistani context, both the federal government's and the MMA provincial government's actions hold the potential to have enormous implications for women's rights. When the federal government sought to revise the Hudood Laws in September 2006, they were thwarted by the MMA, which called the reforms un-Islamic (and threatened to resign from the National Assembly and boycott the government). A revised Hisba Act was introduced in the NWFP legislature in November 2006, just days apart from the federal government's promulgation of the Women's Protection Act that finally reformed the Hudood Laws. The Supreme Court, on February 21, 2007, determined that it now had objections to only two clauses, so the Hisba Act could now be promulgated.

We should bear in mind that there are tangible interests at stake in how the provincial MMA defines women's rights in ways that differ from what the national MMA espouses. The provincial MMA's Pashtun base does not see itself in a globalized context: its optic is far more immediate and concerned with Pashtun cultural preservation and values. But in the national context, where the majority of the population—though fairly conservative—steers away from the extreme rhetoric of the provincial MMA, the MMA has moderated its actions and its rhetoric. There is no mention of gender segregation, no call for a national Hisba Act.

A number of the policies proposed by the provincial MMA government *would* intrude into the domain of international treaties that the federal government has joined, and particularly into the requirements of CEDAW noted earlier. The provision of separate facilities in a resource-poor environment—capital as well as personnel—that prioritizes men *is* discriminatory. It is one thing for the MMA provincial government to have decided it would negate federal policies, but it is another thing when doing so overflows into the arena of international agreements. The MMA provincial government could no more decide that the torture of prisoners would be acceptable, or that child marriage should be encouraged (which would negate Pakistan's position as a signatory to the UN Convention on the Rights of the Child), as to promote discrimination against women, which would be in contradiction to the federal government's pledge when it acceded to CEDAW. When some NWFP Union Councils decided that women would not be allowed to vote in the August 2005 local elections and MMA provincial leaders did not step in to ensure women's electoral rights, the provincial government became party to an unabashedly discriminatory practice. This practice, indeed, is a direct contradiction to the requirements of the international treaty CEDAW to which Pakistan is a state party.

Culture wars have been ripping Pakistan's social fabric asunder for some time. The federal government has articulated its development priorities for Pakistan within a global framework: skills training, poverty-alleviation strategies, improvement of the educational infrastructure, and promoting the empowerment of women. But it cannot leave behind the patois of Islam, as doing so would provide the MMA or other Islamist parties with the opportunity to claim they are the only viable Islamist alternatives on the political landscape. During its tenure in office (2002–2007) the provincial MMA leadership actively tried to quell people's fears that it was moving in extremist directions. However, although their gender politics may have met with less opposition in the NWFP than elsewhere in Pakistan, in part it may be because women in this cultural context are powerless within the family as well as the larger society. The provincial MMA was myopic, as it based the very core of its identity politics on the continuing submissiveness of women rather than seeking to make women partners in Pakistan's public future. When they pushed for reforms that would particularly affect women, such as allowing girls to use fingerprints instead of a picture on the secondary-school enrollment form, we must question if it is empowering—enabling a girl to go to school—or ultimately detrimental, as it perpetuates the stereotype of women as property.

The current scenario in Pakistan is sobering, for here the state and its opposition appear unable to agree on a major reform to "protect women," while most of the rest of the world is grappling with how to implement legal reforms and policy changes to eliminate discrimination against women. We must continue to question whose identity is being affirmed by the MMA's stance on gender politics. Are gendered power relations between men and women so rigid that there is indeed populist support for their views? Why do they insist on interpretations that promote exclusion of women and limitations on their rights, as well as reiterate fears of uncontrolled promiscuity in the event the *zina* laws are amended?

Disputes over legal reforms to promote the empowerment of women in Pakistan are certain to continue until there is a national consensus—which

I do not see coming—on what the concept "women's rights" actually means. The ideological and substantive differences we have seen manifest in the exchanges between the provincial Islamist government of the MMA and the federal government of Pakistan are contestations over power but fought to the detriment of women's lives.

.

PART FOUR

Women's Roles and Family Relationships Renegotiated and Redefined

10. Gender and Law(s)

Moral Regulation in Contemporary Bangladesh

SHELLEY FELDMAN

Feminist analyses of women's behavior and increasing attention to technologies of self have enhanced appreciation for how women negotiate their social worlds. Such appreciation recognizes women as social agents rather than victims and implicitly acknowledges the constraints on women's behavior set by extant social mores. Although it is crucial to understand how women, as active and engaged social agents, negotiate among the different social mores that shape their lives and opportunities, it is also critical to understand the conditions that constitute their choices and to think broadly about rule making and the expectations that constitute behavior. This understanding is especially important if we are to recognize the normative assessments, regulatory practices, and institutional apparatuses that historicize and contextualize women's everyday lives.

This normative context includes what Corrigan and Sayer acknowledge as "the cultural content of state institutions and activities . . . [and] the state regulation of cultural forms" (1985, 2). In their formulation, the state is not examined solely as a territorial domain or set of institutions but, rather, following Abrams (1988), as the accomplishment of rule. As they put it, state formation incorporates the "meanings of state activities, forms, routines, and rituals—for the formation and regulation of social identities [and,] ultimately, our subjectivities" (1985, 2).

Arenas where state practices are enacted include civil, religious, and customary law. These distinct, if overlapping, codified systems of rule offer sites for interrogating the institutionalization of behavioral ideals and the legitimacy of accompanying sanctions for noncompliance. Understanding these normative spaces appreciates how systems of regulation and rule hold people to certain "obligatory" behaviors, provide space for opposition to such behaviors, and, importantly, legitimate sanctions against those individuals who transgress normative expectations.[1] In Bangladesh customary practices may parallel, challenge, or engage religious and civil law in ways that (re)produce social mores and gender inequalities, as well as overdetermine some forms of behavior while also providing spaces for their transgression. Together, customary, civil, and religious law reveals both the discrete and the overlapping character of disciplinary practices and moral regulation.

Embodied in relations of inequality—of gender, class, ethnicity, and sexuality—normative practices do not prefigure social practices but realize them. Thus, I mean that social mores are realized in their accomplishment and when viewed as social practices can help reveal both regulatory and disciplinary forms of rule as well as the difficulty of drawing a deep divide between these practices. Dorothy Smith (1987) refers to such normative practices as relations of rule where gender relations are characterized by regimes of control. In this frame, sanctions secure particular relations of rule and refer less to how systems of rule are constituted and more to how they are implemented. Implementation in this context is instantiated in law and provides the institutional face of social regulation. Examining institutional practices, particularly the contradictions that emerge at the intersection of civil, religious, and customary law, can expose institutional opportunities and constraints on women's autonomy and behavior and add an important complement to what we can learn directly from women.

As we learn from analyses of purdah, or women's seclusion, purdah is often understood as an effect or outcome of religious or customary practice rather than as an expression of normative expectations, disciplinary

---

1. This position differs from one that claims that women's subordination is situated in patriarchal norms rather than in the institutional sites of their instantiation, including Muslim Family Law (Mansoor 1999).

rule, or moral regulation. Purdah is thus assumed to explain or justify intrahousehold or labor-market inequality rather than to mark a gender relation where women negotiate normativity and bargain with social expectations through adaptation and resistance (Feldman and McCarthy 1983; Kandiyoti 1988). Examining civil, customary, and religious practice as aspects of a normative environment can help to reveal the meanings and values that women hold and how their assumptions are embedded in tensions over rights, gender, equality, and morality.

To be sure, the intersection of civil, religious, and customary law is refracted through a changing political and cultural economy with contradictory effects for women. In 1980s Bangladesh, for instance, as women realized greater autonomy through recruitment strategies by a growing movement of nongovernmental organizations (NGOs) and an emergent entrepreneurial class, and as they negotiated greater civil freedoms, they were often confronted by violent reactions from their family or kin, on the streets, in the workplace, or as members of civil society organizations. These challenges to their autonomy were justified by religious or customary practices that were presumed to prohibit women's mobility. In some instances, the decentralization of bureaucratic authority that characterized the period increased the authority of the *shalish* (village council) in its control of women's lives. By the 1990s, political changes included the increasing representation of religious parties in the cultural politics of daily life, especially in the media, public schools, and madrassas, where their authority is framed in a discourse of morality.

I will argue that encoding institutional regulation in a discourse of morality, particularly one that is legitimated in a religious idiom, offers a window on regulatory relations that shape how women negotiate their mobility. I assume that contemporary regulatory relations incorporate the complex and contradictory practices of civil, religious, and customary law, a premise that supports the hypothesis that although constitutional reform is needed to institutionalize gender equity, reform in the legal arena alone may continue to elide how customary and religious laws contribute to the regulation of women. Constitutional reforms are thus not likely to provide a sufficient restraint on those men who perpetuate violence against women, even were they to be implemented fully, since this strategy would leave unattended religious and customary practices in constructing relations of rule.

Following a brief elaboration of the insights of Abrams (1988) and the collective contributions of Corrigan and Sayer on the cultural and moral economy, I highlight the changing institutional character of civil, religious, and customary practices in contemporary Bangladesh. I then share examples from Bangladesh to reveal how these practices shape women's lives.

Moral Regulation

Corrigan (1981, 316) argues that human sociation is a product of social relations that normalize difference. He bases this claim on three foundational points. First, tradition is not fixed but refers instead to a changing set of practices and valuations (Hobsbawm and Ranger 1983). Second, these practices and valuations change in specific rather than determinant ways in the context of intra- as well as international inequality. Third, such practices and valuations are never totalizing, even as they are instantiated as hegemonic. Framed thusly, moral codes of behavior ought to be understood as social constructions rather than ruling principles that are embedded in natural law.

Importantly, these moral codes foreground how economic practices are influenced by social norms and how these norms in turn are compromised by economic forces. This link between the moral and political economy situates how changes in economic relations portend ongoing transformations of valuing women's lives. For example, in Bangladesh, as elsewhere, neoliberalism often requires every person to secure his or her own subsistence. Thus, when individual autonomy displaces the family wage and the household economy, women and young unmarried girls must often secure work to contribute either to family subsistence or to their individual reproduction, demands that can compromise meeting normative expectations and customary practices premised on subsistence production, the male family wage, or both.

This view is neither determinist nor functionalist but instead historicizes moral regulation as a denaturalization of power relations to signal the disciplinary quality of social control. As Corrigan recognizes, "It is *not* necessary for a dominant group to accomplish total belief and commitment amongst the dominated, but that the world of 'public' evaluations and judgments should be such that rituals . . . confirm the correctness, truth and validity of the Obvious" (1981, 327). And, as he rightly emphasizes, moral regulation is "exercised through preferred forms and modes of social relations and practices" where state agencies establish the range of what are proper ways of public performance (ibid., 326). The law, whether customary, religious, or civil, embodies and legitimates these proper public performances, even as each recognizes structures of inequality that are premised on patriarchal, class, or ethnic difference.

The power of these different legal formations and their moral suasion depends on *self-restraint* and *self-discipline* to reproduce normative behavior. This statement is made not to suggest that legal institutions do not "act" to control their publics but instead to emphasize their dual and often less recognized contribution—to establish the context to secure particular "ways of being" and appropriate forms of engagement. In Bangladesh, women navigate the different meanings attendant to their appropriate role by drawing on customary practices and religious codes while operating in circumstances that make it increasingly difficult to maintain particular expressions of modesty. Conversations with young, often rural, working women, for example, reveal that they continue to observe purdah by observing it "inside" in ways that allow them to "carry *purdah* with them" while not wearing a burka (Feldman and McCarthy 1983). Women explain their behavior in these ways to show how they operate within the same normative regime as those women who wear burkas.

Presenting oneself as a *purdahnashin* (an observer of appropriate female behavior) is also an effort to avoid class harassment, especially among young garment workers who represent a significant section of young urban workers. Identifying with the values of propriety and respect that accrue to middle- and upper-class, often nonworking, women, and moving about appropriately "covered," enables working-class girls to challenge their collective reputations as loose, immoral prostitutes in ways that draw on class-based regulatory regimes that have long been understood as part of patriarchal ideology. In these ways, women who cannot afford to stay at home, or don't want to, or who cannot afford the accoutrements of purdah, can nonetheless live according to its rules by shaping and adapting its expressions according to their needs, interests, and desires. Here a system of moral regulation helps to unravel how normative assessments carry situated meanings rather than fixed or natural expressions of gender difference.

In the following section we will see that for women, expressions of female modesty are increasingly necessary since even democratic and secular parties have incorporated and promoted Islamic idioms in representations of everyday practice. The democratically elected government of Khaleda Zia, for example, in coalition with the Jamaat-e-Islami, contributed to greater adherence to expectations about appropriate Islamic comportment through sustained media representations. Arguably, this shift can be viewed as a partial response to changes in Bangladeshi geopolitics represented first in relation to Pakistan under military rule during the Zia and Ershad period (1977–1990), then in alignment with the larger Islamic community, and today, following the Gulf War, the invasion of Afghanistan, and the Iraq war, increasingly among countries who oppose U.S. intervention. Nonetheless, however interpreted, it suggests a constitutive relation between the cultural and political economy.

The Legal Context

With the partition of India in 1947, Pakistan (including Bangladesh, the former East Pakistan) was established as a new state for Muslims. Yet from the beginning Pakistan was defined as secular with respect to recognizing all religious practices. In broad outline, the inheritance of English common law provided the pragmatic rationale for claiming a secular state. But in the immediate post-1947 period secularism was compromised since Islam provided the substantive rationale for Jinnah's two-nation theory connecting West Pakistan and East Pakistan and the partition of the subcontinent.

Moreover, given linguistic and ethnic differences between East Pakistan and West Pakistan, Islam was assumed to be one of the only grounds upon which a national project could be imagined. Not surprisingly, with limited autonomy for East Pakistan between 1947 and 1971, its civil and religious law mirrored West Pakistan's, and even today personal status laws continue to be based on legislation enacted in Pakistan despite what is arguably a changing institutional environment in Bangladesh.

Following a brutal, and some would say a genocidal, struggle for independence, Bangladesh adopted its own constitution on November 4, 1972, and established fundamental rights and nondiscrimination in all aspects of state and public life. Article 10, on the participation of women in national life, states it as follows: "Steps shall be taken to ensure participation of women in all spheres of national life." Article 11, on democracy and human rights, frames the issue this way: "The Republic shall be a democracy in which fundamental human rights and freedoms and respect for the dignity and worth of the human person shall be guaranteed [and in which effective participation by the people through their elected representatives in administration at all levels shall be ensured]."[2] Article 19, too, directly addresses the question of equality of opportunity: "The State shall endeavour to ensure equality of opportunity to all citizens, and . . . shall adopt effective measures to remove social and economic inequality between man and man and to ensure the equitable distribution of wealth among citizens, and of opportunities in order to attain a uniform level of economic development throughout the Republic." But, perhaps unsurprisingly, Article 29, Clause 3, reveals the administration's unwillingness to challenge paternalism as a structural feature of social practice since even as it recognizes equality between the sexes, it also clearly delimits its meaning by reserving for members of one sex any class of employment or office that it considers "by its nature to be unsuited to members of the opposite sex."[3]

The framing of the first Bangladesh Constitution was guided by the principles of secularism, democracy, and socialism even as the new government and bureaucracy recognized religious and customary law from the prepartition period. Thus, from its beginning, Bangladesh sought to craft a set of legal practices—legal pluralism—that could accommodate

2. Changes in this constitutional provision, indicated by the brackets, were introduced in 1975 and removed in 1996.

3. This and other provisions indicate that equality is a relation that is culturally rather than universally interpreted.

state or civil, religious, and customary law.[4] It meant recognizing the 1949 Objectives Resolution, which was passed to enable all Muslims "to order their lives in the individual and collective spheres in accord with the teachings and requirements of Islam as set out in the Holy Quran and the Sunna," while continuing to uphold its constitution (Choudhury 1969, 35, cited in Menski 2003, 3). Islamic and other religious family laws continue to be implemented through the statutory courts and remain the first recourse for personal status cases for all religious communities, even as personal status laws govern different religious communities (Menski and Rahman 1988).

In 1977, under Ziaur Rahman, the Constitution was amended to remove the principle of secularism that had been preserved in "Part II: Fundamental State Policy"[5] and replace it with "absolute trust and faith in Almighty Allah" (Bangladesh Legal Profile n.d.). Zia also inserted "Bismillahir-Rahman-ir-Rahim" (in the name of Allah, the Beneficent, the Merciful) at the beginning of the constitution and inserted the statement, "The state endeavors to consolidate, preserve, and strengthen fraternal relations among Muslim countries based on Islamic solidarity." Despite his reinsertion of religion as the identifying feature of the Bangladesh Constitution, Zia supported international pressure to recognize that women's participation was central to accomplishing what was, at the time, understood as economic development. As he would say, "One cannot think of any development strategy for a society that does not explicitly take into account the roles and status of half of its human resources" (in Kabeer 1991, 46). It is arguable whether Zia's commitment to "women's development" was actually a concern with the social and economic security of Bangladeshi women or a recognition of the benefits to be garnered from millions of dollars in donor assistance available for women's programs and projects. Moreover, with the UN Decade for Women framing much of the international development discourse, there was significant

4. Today customary law still guides relations between the Bangladesh state and the Chittagong Hill Tracts.

5. Article 41, on fundamental rights, addresses freedom of religion and the freedom of each religious community to establish, manage, and maintain its religious institutions.

pressure from Western aid agencies to comply with the goals of improving maternal and child health, reducing population, and enhancing women's education. Although investments were often spent on what were traditionally defined as women's activities, particularly on efforts to reduce population, they also opened new opportunities for women and met some of the economic needs of the rural and urban poor (Feldman and McCarthy 1984). It is during this period of women's increased access to NGO resources and employment that women spoke of "internal purdah" or their "carrying purdah with them" as they navigated the streets of a town or city unaccompanied by a male companion or young boy. Such expressions expose both a transgression of normativity and a reframing of its disciplinary authority.

President Ershad, too, would continue to give rhetorical space to the role of women in development. In a speech in 1987 he would frame it this way: "Bangladesh has made a special attempt to educate the female half of the population, to make them self-reliant and give them a chance to participate in the building of society" (Kabeer 1991, 46). He would also amend the Constitution in 1988 to insert Article 2(a), declaring Islam the official state religion: "The principles of absolute trust and faith in the Almighty Allah, nationalism, democracy and socialism meaning economic and social justice, together with the principles derived from them as set out in this Part, shall constitute the fundamental principles of state policy." As stated in the Eighth Amendment of 1988, "The state religion of the Republic is Islam, but other religions may be practiced in peace and harmony in the republic." This change was controversial[6] and a dramatic blow to the liberal and feminist interests that, by the 1980s, had become a significant voice in public debate. Yet, the political conflagrations over the failure of democracy and the institutionalization of military rule— from Zia Rahman (1977–1981) to General Ershad (1982–1990)—did not sustain debate against the amendment, even as it contributed to weakening Ershad's legitimacy.

---

6. Although there is no necessary contradiction between Islamic belief and gender equality, in this case the politicization of Islam led to fundamentalist readings of the Koran and increased hostility to women who sought any form of public participation.

Among secularists the most popular interpretation of the Eighth Amendment was as a compromise to enable the military to co-opt its strongest and most organized opposition, the religious Right in the form of Jamaat-e-Islam. While the Jamaat was the largest Islamic movement opposing the secular, pluralist impulse of the Constitution, it was not the only one. Interviews with the secular opposition revealed the following: "Bengalis are not a fundamentalist people, look at our struggle with Pakistan, we are not like them"[7] and "Religion will not dominate us" (Feldman 1988, 1990). When queried about the consequences for women, the reaction was similar: "It will not make us over as in Pakistan under Zia-ul-Haq; we are more syncretic." Although some feminist groups, notably Naripokho and Oikyobaddho Nari Samaj, protested against the amendment, others jeered and harassed them at the rallies they organized.

While current evidence does not enable me to conclude that the Eighth Amendment was a turning point in the cultural climate of the country, it is clear that by the early 1990s many people from the university and the NGO community, representing institutionalized efforts to realize gender equity, recognized the increasing religious character of everyday practices, whether it was the required reciting of prayers before public meetings or on government television. As Sultana Kamal notes, "Military regimes in Bangladesh have patronized extreme religious based political parties and encouraged a political culture charged with strong communal, anti-secular sentiment" (2004, 72). This statement is supported by conversations with rural professional women who offer a similar account of the changing cultural climate and who now choose to don the burka "to avoid the hassle of moving about freely."[8]

Discussions with secular academics and members of the NGO community were framed in a slightly different voice: rather than a concern with the constitutional shift toward Islam, people expressed anxiety and resignation about "the chemistry" of their social world. This stance was

7. This statement was framed in the wake of the Zia ul-Haq regime (1977–1981) and the introduction of the Zina and Hadood ordinances.

8. Field notes from discussions with women working with the Integrated Rural Development Programme and the Health Ministry (1978–1984, 1988–1990).

especially evident in discussions of the behavior of young daughters. As one colleague recounted, "I feel like I must demand that my daughter 'behave and dress more traditionally' if only to avoid being identified as 'different.'" Other seemingly small changes contributed to reorienting daily life in the idiom of Islam. For example, Ershad introduced the Zakat Fund to raise the poor tax in accordance with the teachings of Islam, the workweek was altered from Monday through Friday to Sunday through Thursday in recognition of Jumma prayer, and religious programming was extended on government television, a practice that has continued under the democratic administrations of Khaleda Zia and Sheikh Hasina.

Interestingly, Ershad ratified the Convention for the Elimination of All Forms of Discrimination Against Women (CEDAW) in November 1984, although with reservations on several of its Articles (2, 13.1[a], and 16.1[c] and [f]) on the basis of their conflict with Sharia.[9] Each of these reservations has to do with articles referring to equality between women and men, particularly with regard to women's rights in marriage, divorce, and maintenance, as well as in the guardianship of children and inheritance.[10] Ershad also supported the 1985 Family Court Ordinance that established a system of family courts at the local *zila* (district) and *thana* (subdistrict) levels. This change gives greater authority to local communities with exclusive jurisdiction over matters relating to the dissolution of marriage, the restitution of conjugal rights, dower (a sum of money or property given to the bride by the groom in consideration of Muslim marriage), maintenance, guardianship, and child custody (Asian Development Bank 2004).

9. See, for example, Article 2 that condemns and seeks policies to eliminate discrimination against women. Article 13.1 concerns equality of men and women in relation to benefits, whereas Article 16.1 suggests eliminating discrimination against women in all matters relating to marriage and family relations, including guardianship, wardship, trusteeship, and adoption.

10. The government's failure to support the substantive claims of Articles 2, 13.1(a), and 16.1(c) and (f) suggests that interpretations of marriage, divorce, and maintenance that challenge local gendered norms and conventions regarding what is deemed appropriate Islamic behavior can blur the boundaries and effects of Sharia, customary, and civil law for women. In these contexts, one system can either reinforce or contradict another, but together they serve to frame disciplinary and sovereign power.

However, the move toward decentralization can also consolidate the rule and control of the center, as its legitimacy is often at the behest of central administration, especially when the system is coordinated through clientalist relations.[11] Moreover, the Family Court Ordinance decentralizes authority and, in its implementation, can overlap with the regulatory practices and relations of customary law in ways that legitimate what are arguably narrow interpretations of personal and marital behavior. It is to this point that I return below. Here, emphasis is on the institutional formations and regulatory regimes that characterize legal recourse and what the conflation of legal and customary expectations and practices means for women. One might hypothesize that for women, and for rural women in particular, the decentralization of authority constrains their access to an impartial hearing, especially in communities with large hierarchically arranged conservative religious constituencies who judge women by "fundamentalist" interpretations of their rights.

Despite the inauguration of democratic elections in 1991, and the coming to power of Khaleda Zia and the Bangladesh Nationalist Party, Islamic parties retained a strong base of support, most notably through their alliance with the BNP. In the 1991 parliamentary election, for example, despite winning only eighteen of three hundred seats, the Jamaat-e-Islami in an alliance with the BNP enabled the sharing of the thirty reserved seats for women that were to be nominated by parliament. In July 1992, a private member's bill was introduced in parliament to criminalize acts that "defile" the Koran or the name of the Prophet. Although the bill was rejected following criticism both in and outside of parliament, it nonetheless sustained the place of political Islam in the cultural and body politic of the BNP. Even after withdrawing support from the party, Jamaat continued to issue fatwas against progressive and secular voices and, by so doing, supporting a regulatory regime that framed the contours of

11. Such administrative reforms reflect efforts to recast rural power under a national administration where the devolution of authority enables individual regimes to form alliances with rural or religious communities and the private sector. These relations help to configure a support base and state legitimacy while ensuring central control of governance practices (McCarthy and Feldman 1987).

women's normative behavior. As Taj Hashmi (2000) makes clear, the commitment to Islam had become, by 1991 and the introduction of so-called democratic rule, a defining feature of all party platforms.

Significantly, the Awami League, initially identified with secularism, had to prove its Islamic credentials by rejecting identification with "Hindu India," a change that was accomplished by Sheikh Hasina's parliamentary proclamation, during the 1991 campaign, that she had "no quarrel with Bismillah" as part of the Constitution, and by her comportment as a "proper" Muslim woman. By the mid-1990s, following a second democratic election, she could be seen with her head covered at all public forums. Such a change parallels Menski's interpretation of Gen. Zia ul-Haq's 1985 Presidential Order no. 14 that reinforced the public and private commitment to Islam, that it "changed the chemistry of the entire Pakistani state legal system" as it became clear that being Pakistani and being a Muslim were closely aligned (2003, 3).[12] The passage of the Eighth Amendment made it increasingly difficult to draw the distinction between Bangladeshi and Muslim and thus helped to secure a regulatory regime that was legitimated by religious expectation.

Religious and Customary Law

In this section I emphasize the construction of normativity as a set of social practices constituted on the basis of moral suasion to regulate gender relations. Posed as a question, we might ask how regulatory regimes intersect so as to establish a cultural and moral system of rule, a disciplinary project. This focus differs in important ways from examining religious law and its implementation, or from exploring the continuities and contradictions that frame the coexistence of religious and state law. It differs, as well, from a focus on the important but well-rehearsed set of issues concerning the law in spirit and its execution or implementation in practice. Each of these points has been addressed elsewhere. They would be appropriate issues were we interested in institutional reform and monitoring its applicability and success (see, for example, Sobhan 1978; T. Ahmad and

---

12. Presidential Order no. 14 turned the Objectives Resolution into a substantive provision of the 1973 constitutional reform (see Article 2A).

Khan 1998; Mansoor 1999; Hashmi 2000; and S. Kamal 2001). Despite the criticality of these issues, they leave unattended the cultural construction of a system of rule in the context of specific state formations.

To be sure, in Bangladesh as elsewhere, there has been sustained reform of personal law. Relevant legislation includes the Muslim Personal Law (Shari'at) Application Act (1937), the Dissolution of Muslim Marriages Act (1961), the Muslim Family Law Ordinance (1961), the Muslim Marriages and Divorces Act (1974), the Dowry Prohibition Act (1980), the Cruelty to Women (Deterrent Punishment) Ordinance (1983), the Family Courts Act (1985), and the Repression Against Women and Children Act (2000). These reforms address marriage, dowry, divorce, maintenance and provisioning, custody and adoption, and economic and social rights, including property rights.[13] Importantly, there is clear variation in the practice of family law since it is shaped by theological and legal interpretation that differs among as well as within Muslim communities. Interpretive differences in personal law, often framed in the idiom of customary practice, reveal how legal regimes combine to shape normativity and unsettle the marked distinctions that are assumed to differentiate among such regimes.

Personal law, however, adjudicates not only Muslim women and family life but also the rights of Hindus, Christians, Buddhists, and other minorities (Menski and Rahman 1988). The Muslim Family Law Ordinance of 1961 guides personal law in contemporary Bangladesh, while Hindu law remains, as it was at the time of partition, rooted in Anglo-Hindi law and based largely in localized customary practice. Since Bangladesh inherited Pakistan's legal system through the retrospective operation of Bangladesh (Adaptation of Existing Bangladesh Law) Order 1972, which maintained the privileged status of state over religious law, it, too, privileged state law. By doing so it inherited the "conflicts of traditional *shari'at* and modern statutory reforms in the Muslim Family Law Ordinance of 1961" (Pearl and Menski 1998, 49).

Whereas changes in Muslim personal law and comparisons across different Muslim countries have been the focus of significant academic

---

13. Each of these areas has been the focus of considerable contestation, especially among feminists concerned with the implementation and interpretation of the Sharia.

and legal attention, there is considerably less written about customary law, particularly as a changing institutional and political formation. Moreover, given the absence of a codified system of rule, customary practices merit careful elaboration since they vary widely across time and place. In Bangladesh, customary law is framed in the idiom of the Sharia and is executed by village elders and prominent local leaders that often include the union council chairperson, teachers, and religious leaders. The *shalish*, or village court, mediates in civil cases of marital dispute, desertion, divorce, child custody, maintenance, and contestations over land and other property. It adjudicates, as well, in criminal offenses[14] such as rape, adultery, and dowry-related violence.[15] The *shalish*, where customary law prevails, is the institutional vehicle for informal dispute resolution where such councils resolve between 60 and 70 percent of all local disputes (A. Rahman 2002). Women, however, are less likely to seek resolution through the *shalish*, often composed of elite and conservative male elders, for fear of reprisal from those persons tasked with adjudicating any presumption of their impropriety.

Although any villager with a grievance can petition to appear before a *shalish*, which is often a person's first, and sometimes only, course of redress, among relatively poor families, too, there may be little trust in equitable representation. This situation is especially true were they to

14. Sultana Kamal (2004) points out that there is no legal basis for the *shalish* to try criminal cases as all such proceedings are regulated by the Code of Criminal Procedure or acts passed by the parliament. Such proceedings, however, recognize that the bounds of the *shalish* extend to cover a range of civil and criminal cases, leading some to argue that it is the only defense for those individuals unable to access the legal system. Others highlight the increasing power of an informal legal system whose members, because of their class and political alliances, can use their authority to elide people's constitutional rights.

15. The Village Court Act of 1976 and the Conciliation of Disputes (Municipal Areas) Ordinance of 1979 provide detailed procedures for village courts. The Local Government Ordinance of 1976 and a subsequent amendment added representation of two women and two peasant members to be nominated by the subdivisional officer. This change was largely Zia Rahman's response to the demands of the International Women's Year, with the result that the women selected represented elite families (large landowners, traders, and shopkeepers) who acted not independently but on behalf of their husbands (A. Rahman 2002).

be charged by more elite families for indiscretions, whether pertaining to land or to the women of their family. For instance, women have been brought before the *shalish* by an alleged victim as well as by local religious leaders and village elders for alleged adultery or premarital encounters with local men. These mediations include the cases of a mother of three who was burned on a stake for a charge of adultery and a married woman who worked outside the home. In the latter case, the local imams issued a fatwa asking the husband to divorce her. A fatwa also was issued against an imam because it was discovered that his wife used contraceptives (South Asia Citizens Web 2004).

In these ways, the *shalish* institutionalizes the often patriarchal interests of village elites and imposes punishment, including whipping or stoning to death, on women who are perceived to transgress normative practice. The fatwa as a regulatory instrument was declared illegal in January 2001, in anticipation of ending its extrajudicial enforcement. Perhaps not surprisingly, however, given changes in the political configuration of everyday politics, this declaration sparked violent public protest, with some Muslim groups charging an attack on their religious freedom while others continued to invoke the fatwa, particularly against women's alleged transgressions.

Today, some acknowledge this decentralized process of predominantly rural-based adjudication as neither fair nor equitable. As Blair notes, the *shalish* has been criticized for its "elite favoritism, incompetence, gender bias and corruption," and, more pointedly, "as an anachronistic patriarchal, arbitrary and legally illiterate institution" (2003, 3, 17). Customary law has also been variously defined as a "legacy of the fast-disappearing feudal system," a legacy that is sustained by the view that the *shalish* in practice operates as an Islamic court that, though "unauthorized in this moderate Muslim country, [has, in recent years, been] taken over by militant clerics as kangaroo courts to punish people, mostly women, whom they considered guilty of adultery" (Deutsche Presse-Agentur 1995, n.p.).

This cynical interpretation is offset by progressive feminist and human rights groups who view the *shalish* as a dynamic and changing institution that should be reclaimed as a way to provide needed venues for adjudication, especially for women and the poor, but also to alleviate the overburdened courts (K. Hasan 2001; Asian Development Bank 2004). Mindful that customary and religious laws "not only discriminate against women, but contradict existing legal rights," the nongovernmental organization Ain O Shalish Kendro (ASK) has sought to reform the *shalish* by extending representation to women and the poor.[16] In building village awareness and extending community participation, particularly to women, it hopes to integrate *shalish* decision-making procedures and judgments with existing law (S. Kamal 2004).

This focus on reform builds on the efforts of those persons who "believe it [the *shalish*] to be basically fair" and represents an institution that continues to retain "significant public trust," particularly against the increasing corruption of the formal court system and other government departments.[17] It thus may be useful to draw attention to the potential capacities of these village-based initiatives as vehicles for redress since the merit of doing so could enhance local control, challenge illegitimate practices, and offer an antidote to the widely recognized corruption associated with other arenas of adjudication. But where there is growing "extremist Islamist consolidation," one ought to move forward cautiously, since it is equally plausible to assume that a system of local control is a site of patriarchal domination that can directly restrain women and leave them with limited local resources for redress (Lintner 2003). This coercive rule supplements whatever forms of self-regulation women negotiate in order to make their way.

Moral Regulation in Practice

What is commonly referred to as "political Islam" is now well insinuated in the modern nation-building project of Bangladesh, where institutions, including the family, education, welfare, and religion, are incorporated

---

16. ASK, a nationally based NGO, was established in 1986 by a group of lawyers, social scientists, and development workers to provide support to women in the areas of legal counseling, mediation, and litigation through its legal aid, advocacy, and research activities.

17. Blair's (2003) interesting project, like ASK, also suggests the *shalish* as a site for improved adjudication. Following Linter, however, it is important to remain attentive to the contradictory consequences for women that may accompany reform efforts (Feldman and McCarthy 1984).

within the regulatory apparatuses of the state. This change, from religion as belief and mark of personal identity to political Islam, reflects interests and classes that vie for legitimacy through electoral politics. As Talal Asad (2003) reminds us, when religion becomes an integral part of modern politics it cannot remain indifferent to other aspects of the political economy. Importantly, Asad (1993) is careful to distinguish religion as a historical set of practices from debates on secularism and modernity. However, what remains central to his analysis is how institutionalized politics engages discourses about religion to construct relations of power and authority in a rapidly changing global political economy. For Bangladesh, such constructions cannot be separated from its history with Pakistan and from contemporary struggles in Iran, Iraq, and Afghanistan, as well as with India.

Without rehearsing the ways in which power is written on the bodies of women, it is clear that despite the democratic achievements of the Bangladeshi state, violence against women continues; it may even be on the rise. Violence there includes charges that are inappropriately and unfairly brought against women, as well as verdicts that legitimate stoning, flogging, and public humiliation as the cost of women's presumed transgressions. In most circumstances women have little or no voice or representation in court proceedings, especially where verdicts reflect a growing commitment to a fundamentalist reading of the Sharia. When this interpretation predominates, as when parents hold the right to force a child into marriage, in adultery cases, or when blame for abandonment or wife beating is assumed to be the fault of women, women often face harsher sanctions than men. In a number of these cases, and usually following public humiliation, women may commit suicide so as not to dishonor themselves and their families, even when they are falsely or unfairly blamed.

In a well-documented example, Sultana Kamal offers the following account: Nurjahan, a twenty-one-year-old woman in Chatakchara of Sylhet, was issued a fatwa

> by the self appointed religious leader Moulana Mannan. . . . [She] was buried in the ground up to her chest to be stoned publicly for allegedly having committed adultery. Nurjahan had earlier been divorced by her

husband. She was found guilty by the local *shalish* led by Moulana Mannan, for contracting an illegal second marriage when she married a fellow villager. This marriage was arranged by her parents. The *shalish* sentenced her and her second husband to death by public stoning. Her parents were also held responsible for this "un-Islamic" act and were sentenced to 50 lashes each. Nurjahan survived the stoning, but committed suicide in humiliation. (2004, 80)

This case is still pending, despite pressure from women's groups and a local police case filed against Moulana Mannan and his followers on charges of abetment of the suicide.

A parallel case is that of Zohur Akter, who committed suicide by taking poison after her cow ate the crops of a neighbor's field and a fatwa was issued that her husband was to hit her with his shoe (a common sign of disrespect). In cases where suicide is the outcome, it is worth contemplating why women might choose suicide rather than bear public humiliation. How might framing suicide as an option recognize women's agency and suggest new questions for elaboration? How might acknowledging that despite the horrific and sad outcome, women may actually negotiate the costs of public shame for themselves and their families, particularly in contexts where there is little likelihood of community support? Where morality and normative practices exact and find support in the declaration of fatwas, and in the civil response to them, women are unlikely to find social and economic security in their immediate community and, without family support, might even find migration extremely difficult.

Both these examples suggest that disciplinary power may help explain the suicides that result under these circumstances. In their invisible and diffuse presentation, disciplinary power and the broad acceptance of a normative order shape the behavior of others as well as the self to suggest that women may "choose" suicide over a life of "shame," whether for actual or presumed transgressive behavior, because of the power of a system of moral regulation. In another example:

A woman called Rokeya from [the] village Sultanpur of the Feni district was accused by the Union Parishad chairman and members of a premarital relationship with a Dulal Mia on the promise of marriage. She was physically assaulted, head shaved, she was forced to parade village streets with shoes strung around her neck. She was then tied to a tree for 8 hours and later at night raped by 4 men. Police, however, rescued her. Following investigation, the women's organizations have protested. A case has been filed but no progress has been made because of involvement of the influential family. There has not been any further government action either. The report was published in the daily *Ajker Kagoj* of 13 February 1994. ("Fatwas in Bangladesh" 1996, 76–77)

Also, as reported by Islam (1997), two schoolgirls were savagely attacked with acid in Dhaka for rejecting the advances of men (see also S. Rahman 2004). While the victims garnered the support of Sheikh Hasina and the incident was widely reported, findings from Dhaka Medical College confirm that girls are admitted every week because of acid attacks, a fact that extends the number of these incidents beyond what some refer to as the "conservative rural communities" where this threat to women was assumed to be more common. But as Islam reminds us:

Violence against women shows an alarming spiral. . . . Women are harassed and abandoned by husbands, who can legally take a second wife. There is an escalation in divorce cases and dispute over dowry. In Dhaka city alone, four cases relating to dowry are listed every day in the Dhaka chief metropolitan magistrate's court. Some cases of harassment of women have tragic endings. Take the well-publicised case of Shahina Akhter, a young housewife from Sirajnagar Village in Narsangdi district [whose husband claimed] that she had committed suicide when her body mutilated with acid was found in her home. He had killed her because she had delivered a baby girl and refused to let him marry a second time. (Inter Press Service in Islam 1997, 136)

What do these examples suggest about the interests that are served by particular regulatory regimes? According to Saira Rahman (2004), the human rights nongovernmental organization Odhikar found 186 incidents of acid throwing in the year 2000, 178 reported in 1999, and 101 in 1998. Thirty-three of the victims in 2000 were between ages six and fifteen.

Acid throwing was used as a response to jealousy, a woman's refusal of sexual advances, and revenge. These incidents, and the generalized rise in violence against women, warn women about the dangers of transgressing the expectations of men, including one's husband, and thereby contribute to fashioning women's behavior in an increasingly circumscribed way.

Forced marriage offers another window on violence against women and links the customary practices of the *shalish* with claims of moral right legitimated under Sharia. One exemplary case is that of a twenty-two-year-old teacher, Abdul Latif, who proposed marriage to a six-year-old girl, Momtaz. Momtaz's parents declined his proposal even though a fatwa was issued permitting the marriage of a minor under Sharia. Momtaz was found drowned the following month. The case has yet to be adjudicated. Forced marriages differ from arranged marriages in that they lack the free and full consent of a woman in the marriage agreement even though it is understood as a right under the Constitution. Yet abduction and forced marriages continue to be used to control female sexuality and women's autonomy, and they may be accompanied by coercion, mental abuse, blackmail, and social pressure. In the most extreme cases physical violence, abduction, false imprisonment, and rape may be used, and, as the case of Momtaz reveals, even murder is possible (Hossain and Turner 2004).

Carefully arguing on legal grounds, Sara Hossain and Suzanne Turner (2004) show how the application of personal law, based on religious and customary practice, is used in the case of forced marriages to deny women rights, particularly in situations where they lack adequate redress. As Yamani also reminds us:

> Women's rights are sometimes restricted because of social and religious norms. For example, Hanafi Sunni school, unlike the other Sunni schools, gives women the legal capacity to be her own *wali*, in other words, to marry without the consent of her . . . male guardian. But society attaches to this a taint of shamelessness despite the legal parameters. This reflects society's reluctance to equate the observance of legal rights with approved behavior. A woman's freedom is circumscribed by social conventions (such as the idea of shame) which are marginal to the legal system. (1996, 3)

Sanctions and exclusion thus mark those individuals who fail to follow religious prescriptions at a time when they have gained currency, especially in the wake of the Rushdie affair, which raised the threat of a fatwa on the international stage. In Bangladesh the introduction of the fatwa is associated with charges against Taslima Nasrin for blasphemy for her interpretation of the Koran where, it was argued, she "offended the sentiments of 90 million Muslims." As Rashiduzzaman contends, behind these confrontations was a larger cultural chasm representing the "resistance of Muslim politics and culture that did not wither away after East Pakistan became an independent and sovereign Bangladesh" (1994, 974). Rather, it continues as a tension between the secular—defined as Western development—and the religious, as expressed in the friction between NGOs, particularly the ones who support women's empowerment. This hostility reached a climax with the ransacking and bombing of the offices of BRAC and FIVDB, two large and internationally respected NGOs that provided education, training, and health resources to women (Amnesty International 1996; S. Kamal 1996; see also "Fatwas in Bangladesh" 1996). Such tensions unsettle religious sensibilities about women's place and appropriate behavior as well as state responses to women's presumed transgressions.

These incidents, and there are thousands more like them, suggest that a new cultural context is emerging in Bangladesh, with gender violence increasing in brutality (Asian Development Bank 1994, 2004; Jahan 1988a, 1988b). Although women are always under threat, today they are caught between new demands on their lives—given rising rates of abandonment, divorce, and poverty, as well as new desires for independence and autonomy—and an increasingly vocal religious elite whose political project is partially realized by their ability to control women's behavior. These contradictory demands shape the conditions of self-regulation, such as when women might choose either to forgo specific interests or desires or refuse to live under such circumstances or dishonor by committing suicide. Whatever the choice, moral regulation refers to relations of inequality and power that shape behavior but are less often recognized as forms of violence than are transgressions where direct control and physical violence take center stage.

Relevant to this argument are the tensions that incorporate contradictory valuations of individual behavior in rapidly changing contexts but also how religious prescriptions are used to frame calls for sanction. In other words, as demands for education, employment, and credit mark the needs of women, religious prescriptions help to anchor state-sanctioned regulations in ways that shape the implementation of personal law. At times, it is the threat of sanction, rather than the sanction itself, that prohibits women from using birth control, accepting credit, or securing employment. But such threats cannot be simply read from a fundamentalist reading of Islam because they are enacted through customary practices or civil corruption and incompetence in ways that link civil, religious, and customary law. The threat of sanction may also be accompanied by coercion to undermine support for alternative behaviors and beliefs, especially when police support such sanctions or argue that they are inadequately prepared to set limits on religious zealots. In these ways, synergies among different regulatory regimes shape violence against women as well as regulate women's choices in ways that may be consonant with expressions about, if not belief in, appropriate Islamic behavior.

The Powers of Moral Regulation

What I have explored in this brief chapter is the cultural space in Bangladesh against a backdrop of a dramatically changing political economy. I have suggested that women are increasingly made vulnerable to the historically specific contradictions that characterize the intersection of customary, religious, and state law in a context of the politicization of Islam. Although such laws are open to a range of interpretations and vary across and within communities, they not only operate as external measures of legitimate authority, that is, as "externally regulative," but also are "internally constitutive" since they are part of the cultural formation that women negotiate in deciding how they want to live and express themselves. As Corrigan and Sayer have emphasized, regulatory regimes are "realized through social structuring that creates social identities and subjectivities that are experienced not only as obligatory but desirable and desired" (1985, 194).

In this reading, I have also emphasized consent and normativity as relations and processes realized through negotiation and presupposing human agency, whether of women making choices from among a range of difficult alternatives or as organized political opposition to constitutional reform and customary practice. The first case suggests understanding suicide as a response to disciplinary power and the costs of normative transgression, however horrific and circumscribed, in a context where women have far too limited control of their lives and choices. The second case means viewing regulatory regimes, including civil, personal, and customary law, as an outcome of political interests distinguishable from systems of belief, identity, and patriarchy.

I have highlighted these constitutive aspects of social behavior in order to emphasize the need for and importance of broad-based interventions that do not limit discussions or practices about gender equity to constitutional reform alone. The borders between state, religious, and customary law are blurry at best and often contradictory. Thus, constitutional reform can respond to only a small part of the sociolegal and cultural environment constitutive of women's lives. Reform of customary law and the practices and representation of the *shalish* is needed as well, and the work of Ain O Shalish Kendro is to be applauded for its contribution to such efforts. By alerting readers of the changing cultural context influencing women's behavior, I have sought to show that Bangladesh is witness to a desecularization of state apparatuses in ways that promote religious morality and fundamentalist truth claims that gain legitimacy through the specific practices of religious and customary law. These relatively hidden or naturalized relations of social control narrow women's choices as well as the explanations they offer of their behavior. Perhaps our most difficult challenge ahead is to better understand the mechanisms of self-control and self-censorship as they constrain both our behavior and our political imaginations.

11. Shifting Practices and Identities

Nontraditional Relationships among
Sunni Muslim Egyptians and Emiratis

FRANCES S. HASSO

This essay is based on analysis of documents gathered and interviews undertaken during fieldwork in Egypt and the United Arab Emirates (UAE) in
2003, and focuses on the rise of especially *'urfi* (customary) and *misyar*
relationships,[1] nontraditional sexual and marital "contract" relationships
that have emerged among Sunni Muslims from various walks of life. The
nature and extent of such relationships throughout the Arab world are
unclear, although they are extensive enough to be producing some scholarly work, significant press attention in the region, fatwas (nonbinding
religious edicts) from Muslim religious authorities, and legislation and
social policy by state authorities. I argue in this paper that these marital
forms indicate the instability of gender and sexual regimes, as well as the
manner in which transnational processes such as flows of ideas, people,
products, and practices are undermining familial and national frameworks of identity and practice.

Marriage and Sexuality in Perspective

Heterosexual marriage and procreation within marriage have been and
remain fundamental to the organization of Arab societies across ethnic,
religious, and class boundaries (Hoodfar 1997, 51, 241; Sherif 1999, 619;

1. Parts of this chapter appeared in Hasso 2007.

Singerman 1995, 74). Indeed, the family, rather than the individual, is often viewed as the basic unit in Arab societies (Altorki 2000; Joseph 2000a).

In the twentieth century most Middle Eastern and North African states rationalized and formalized Sharia-based marital contracts through codification (Sonbol 1996; Charrad 2001; Amawi 2000; Ismael and Ismael 2000; Mir-Hosseini 1993), in many cases decreasing a flexibility and negotiability that previously had allowed women and men to choose among different juridical schools in making and breaking contracts (Sonbol 1996a; Mir-Hosseini 1993). Overall, however, the major juridical schools privileged men in terms of divorce, child custody, and marital rights.

The rationalization of family law has increased the power of often authoritarian states and their religious appointees, as well as male-biased lawmakers (religious and secular), over marital contracts and family law. However, research on different parts of the Middle East and North Africa demonstrates a frequent disjuncture between lived experiences and legal, religious, and cultural precepts with respect to gender and sexuality, indicating significant maneuvering and violation (Haeri 1989; Singerman 1995; Hoodfar 1997, 78–79; Longinotto and Mir-Hosseini 1998; Moors 1995, 1999).

It is important to note that the codes of personal status and the standardized marital contracts adopted and occasionally revised by most postcolonial states are themselves hybrid and plural. They are derived from and in response to the metropolitan legislation of former European colonizers, Ottoman law, religious precepts, conservative institutional and social forces (religious, tribal, and so on), postcolonial state needs, the gender interests of elite men, and pressure from women and women's organizations.

'Urfi and *Misyar* Contracts in Egypt and the Emirates

How does one explain the rise of nontraditional, often transient marital and relationship forms, such as *zawaj 'urfi* ("customary" marriage), *zawaj misyar* (ambulant or "traveler" marriage), and a range of other relationship and sexual "contracts" in parts of the Middle East and North Africa beginning in the 1990s? While the term *'urfi* implies that this practice is a traditional custom, the contracts associated with *'urfi* relationships are very much contemporary innovations. What seems to make them "customary" is that they evade registration with formal religious and state authorities. Until a controversial legal revision of personal status law narrowly passed by the parliament in late January 2000 (Arabi 2001a; Abaza 2001; A. Hasan 2003, 82), such contracts in Egypt violated a 1931 Egyptian statute "mandating registration of all marriages with a *ma'zoun* (civil marriage registrar)" (Zerrini 2000). Among other things, the revision recognized *'urfi* marriages indirectly by requiring fathers to pay child support and clarified that a woman has a unilateral right to *khul'* divorce (if she "ransoms herself" by returning some of the bridal gifts and dowry) in regular and *'urfi* marital contracts (Zerrini 2000; Zuhur 2001; Arabi 2001a, 3–4). These issues are not minor, as the man in a *'urfi* marriage frequently abandons the woman and keeps the only documentation of the marriage. His doing so creates problems for the woman who becomes pregnant or has children in this relationship, or the woman who wants to remarry but cannot do so without first being divorced.

In order to be licit, according to some Islamic legal scholars, *'urfi* marriages must follow the same basic requirements as regular marital contracts *(nikah):* both partners' consent, two men (or one man and two women) as witnesses to and signers of the contract in addition to an overseer with knowledge of Islamic law, a wedding gift to the bride, and a public announcement of the marriage, "at least to family and neighbors" (Zerrini 2000; Tadros 2000; Shahine 1999; S. Ahmed 1999). Three of the four Sunni schools of jurisprudence "also stipulate that a woman who has not been married before must be accompanied by her legitimate guardian (usually her father, brother or uncle) while signing the contract" (Shahine 1999). Indeed, in the UAE, some women contract *'urfi* relationships with men whom their fathers refused to allow them to marry, bypassing the requirement of male guardian *(wali)* permission.

Misyar marriage "is an official relationship between man and woman, but does not involve that the two live together, nor that the man is economically responsible [for the wife or household]." This type of relationship "allows the man to have a normal wife in addition to his *misyar* wife(s). The *misyar* wife is expected to live with her parents, and her husband can visit her according to a predetermined schedule" (Kjeilen 2002).

Misyar relationships have been practiced in Egypt and Saudi Arabia "for years" (they appear to have begun in significant numbers in the early 1990s), often involve a middleman or broker, and were legalized by Egyptian sheikh Mohammad Sayyed Tantawi and Saudi Arabian sheikh Abdel Aziz bin Baz in 1999 by fatwas (ibid.; Comparative Index to Islam 2002; Arabi 2001b). They were also recently recognized as legitimate by religious courts in the Emirates. According to Oussama Arabi, a scholar of Islamic law who has studied *misyar* in Saudi Arabia, the practice is "an original *bricolage*, a patchwork production of law using the flexible resources of the [Sunni] Islamic marriage contract to cater to the needs of certain Saudi middle-class segments," that post facto has been recognized by the judicial establishment as abiding by Sharia criteria (2001b, 155). Since *misyar* contracts are significantly less expensive for men in terms of responsibilities for wife and household maintenance (indeed, husbands do not live with wives), and women's obedience and sexual access to husbands have usually been premised on maintenance in marital contracts, Arabi wonders whether the "unusual economic and cohabitation arrangements of the ambulant union would accentuate a wife's autonomy or allow her a greater margin of freedom" (ibid., 159–60).

'*Urfi* marriages in Egypt, though contracted in writing, usually come to public or state attention only when legal problems arise, most often when a woman files for divorce or maintenance for herself or a child. There are about twelve to eighteen thousand ongoing paternity suits in Egypt resulting from such contracts, which were recently estimated to number about three million (al-Shibel 2004; MacFarquhar 2005). This secrecy is also the case in the Emirates, where '*urfi* marriages are reportedly less common. In most '*urfi* marriages, the publicity requirement has been transformed from the very public wedding to—as one Emirati man said—"having the girl tell seven to eight of her trusted friends and having the guy tell seven to eight of his trusted friends," calling into question definitions of secrecy and publicity.

Secrecy is one reason that '*urfi* and *misyar* marriages are considered illegitimate by some religious scholars, who view them as violating rules against fornication and adultery (Shahine 1999; Arabi 2001b, 164–65). In the Emirates, however, *misyar* marriages are now registered with the state, using a regular contract form on which all additional conditions are stated, though whether a first wife is aware of such a marriage depends on whether she researches court records. I was told apocryphal stories, functioning as morality tales, in which men's polygamous relationships were widely revealed when more than one child with the same name (customarily listed by child's first name followed by the father's full name) was registered at a school.

Although the Emirates require state registration of marriages, they did not have a unified personal status law until mid-2005, and rather relied on the rulings of local judges. Striking to me, however, was the insistence of religious scholars, men and women lawyers, and women's organizations that an increasingly complex society required a uniform federal code derived from Sharia, especially as local judges were regarded as uneducated in the finer points of the various schools of law operative in different emirates. For some, local patriarchies, which were making the situation more difficult for women, would be moderated by a unified code. For others, a uniform code was seen to be necessary because of the many foreign laborers and tourists in the country, as well as Emirati mobility between different emirates for work, pleasure, and schooling. For example, during a meeting between myself and a court official in Dubai, an Emirati man from Sharjah was allowed to enter the room to ask a question. The court official insisted that the man return to the Sharjah emirate's religious court to resolve a divorce issue with a migrant woman worker from Romania, although he worked and lived in the Dubai emirate.

The practitioners of these relationship forms are diverse, including widows, wealthy married men, older wealthy women, gay men, professional and middle-class men and women, men and women of the popular (*sha'bi*) classes, and high school and university students. The relationships occur in cultural environments that consider sexual desire and pleasure as natural and necessary, even sacred, but seek to regulate and channel them into licit (usually contractual) relationships that explicate mutual obligations (Hoodfar 1997, 251, 253; Bouhdiba 1998, 14–15, 187; Sherif 1999, 626–27).

The feasibility and spread of these relationship forms are enhanced by the proliferation of chat rooms, Listservs, and other online forms of

communication, which include discussion about and personal advertise-
ments for these types of relationships. In some cases, wealthy men, particularly from Gulf countries, use the secret contracts to legitimize brief
sexual relationships with sex workers in Egypt while on summer holiday
(al-Gawhary 1995).

Explanations and Social Responses

'Urfi and *misyar* relationships are often rationalized by lay articulations
and interpretations of cultural and Muslim religious precepts and texts
in relation to personal life. In some respects, this dynamic is similar to
the ways in which new social movements or identity movements in the
United States and Europe have worked to seek personal answers to larger
problems. One difference in Islam is *ijtihad,* which allows, and many argue
requires, continual assessment of sacred and other religious sources to
seek answers, rationalize innovations, or challenge existing practices for
the good of the community.

Mona Abaza (2001) argues that much of the press criticism of these
practices in Egypt constructs young people and women as perverse and
irresponsible for violating social norms regarding premarital and non-
marital sexual activity and evading the regulatory mechanisms of state
and religious officials. I would argue that the "woman as victim" narra-
tive is also prevalent in press accounts, ignoring how regular marital contracts and personal status laws (across religious denominations) in most
Middle Eastern and North African states fundamentally privilege men
over women.

Marriage is increasingly expensive, and young people who want to
marry often have difficulty finding the jobs and apartments necessary for
establishing themselves as a married household (Singerman and Ibrahim
2003, 96); these relationships allow them to engage in sexual relations without the economic requirements of formal marriage contracts (Tadros 2000;
Shahine 1999). Although economic problems are particularly relevant in
Egypt, such explanations for rising marital ages and new relationship
forms may be overly economic, underestimating factors such as the rise of
new sexual norms and legalized gender inequality in regular marriage. As
more than one informant in Egypt indicated, despite economic problems,

the very poor majority of Egyptians (particularly those individuals living in rural areas) and the upper middle class either have lower expectations in terms of marital support and resources or have the resources to provide for their children. Among the upper middle class, parents of the bride and groom share the costs of marriage, and among the working poor, many are foregoing the *mahr* (dower). Thus, the economic obstacles to marriage in Egypt, though present for most people, seem to be most important to the middle class.

Moreover, the scale and nature of economic barriers dramatically differ in the two countries I am examining, as Egypt is one of the poorest countries in the region and the UAE one of the wealthiest. Indeed, more than one person mentioned that Emirati men of less means will frequently marry Egyptian women (using regular and *'urfi* contracts) since the marriage costs and expectations of their families are lower. In both places "globalization" was seen as important in its impact on these forms and options, although in different ways. In Egypt the increasing gap between rich and poor as a result of neoliberal policies, high underemployment and unemployment, and increasing consumption aspirations has delayed the age of marriage, particularly of young men in the urban lower middle class.

Among the native Emirati population, a number of factors have delayed or reduced marriage rates and encouraged new sexual forms. They include high levels of consumption of expensive goods and the costly wedding "traditions" and demands made by the parents of Emirati brides. In addition, regional male migration, as well as the state's active importation of men and women laborers in an adamantly tariff- and tax-free, investment- and tourist-friendly economy facilitates the out-marriage of Emirati men, as well as their taking of non-Emirati sexual partners using various modalities (concubinage, *misyar*, or *'urfi*). Emirati women, in turn, particularly the high proportion that is college educated, were less inclined to marry young Emirati men schooled in relatively patriarchal conceptualizations of family and marriage. Their potential Emirati male partners were also likely to have attended postsecondary military or police academies, because they are guaranteed employment in these sectors, further reducing their appeal as partners for college-educated

Emirati women. Some women argued that the cultural gap produced by the two forms of postsecondary education, one dominated by women and the other by men, partly explained what Emiratis perceived was a high divorce rate among nationals.

State officials in the UAE are so concerned with out-group marriage among Emirati men, marriage delays, and high rates of singlehood among Emirati educated women that they have established the Marriage Fund (Sanduq al-Zawaj), which coordinates state-sponsored group wedding ceremonies and parties and provides large grants and free or inexpensive wedding halls for Emirati-Emirati weddings. State leaders also made an ineffective decree limiting the amount of dowry a bride's family can demand from a groom's family. There are similar programs, on a much lower scale, in Egypt. From the perspectives of women and their parents in both countries, increasing the cost of marriage for men makes the cost of divorce and remarriage higher, since men have much more institutional, cultural, and legal leverage in both cases.

The second most important concern (after what their economic future might hold) of interviewed middle-class Egyptian women students at Cairo University was whether the man they married would be oppressive, indicating the salience of gender inequality for these young women. Understandable given Egypt's archaeological riches, a term that came up quite frequently in this group interview was that Egyptian young men had "fossilized ideas" about the superiority of men in relation to women, and the "inherited culture" was strong. The women students criticized how many men distinguished between "modernity" in education and science, while at the same time protecting "tradition" in relation to family and culture (see Chatterjee 1994). Challenging historically linear understandings implied by the terms "inheritance" and "fossilization," however, they indicated that the situation had deteriorated for them in comparison to their parents' generation. As one student stated, "In my opinion, there is absolutely no justification for *'urfi* marriage because it is very reasonable and clear that almost everything about it works to the benefit of the boy. And it totally works against the girl. Amal [pseudonym] says that the girl is sometimes scared that he is her true love and he will leave— this is naïveté also—this is the type of naïveté I am talking about. Why?

Because the girl should have used her brain, not be completely derelict in this way."

This point of view was similar to the analysis of most Emirati women I interviewed. According to the fiancée of an Emirati man (they met on the Internet), "I am against it ['*urfi* and *misyar* marriage] because it does not protect women's rights. Husbands in these situations are not committed to *mahr* or living costs. And people will always think it was done for pleasure and not take such a marriage seriously." She believed that in the Emirates, "women may accept such a marriage because her parents may have refused a guy, so she accepts because a *wali* [guardian] is not required."

A male student from al-'Ain University in the UAE argued that women's employment was impacting the "constitution of a self and a mind" for Emirati women. He saw it as leading to divorce, because "when the wife has become more independent, it became easier for her to disconnect, to disconnect. Because before, a long time ago, when the wife was not educated and was tied and her destiny was with her man, if she divorced him, usually there was no way for someone to take her, and she is ruined [*tan'adim*]." Although both Emirati men's and women's expectations of marriage increase with a college education, it seems that women's expectations for marital partnership increase significantly more.

Some seek sexual relationships without the economic obligations (for men) and social constraints (for women) required of traditional marital relationships (Shahine 1999; S. Ahmed 1999; Arabi 2001b). For example, decreased resources, lack of publicity, and nonregistration can serve the purposes of divorced or widowed women who may not want a child or who have a home, custody of children, and resources (provisioned by the state, the previous husband or husband's family, or both) that they do not want to lose with the announcement and registration of marriage. There is limited evidence that some people are using them to legitimize homosexual committed or short-term relationships (Fam and McClure 2000).

These relationships may be one ironic consequence of the resurgence of different forms of Islam as a basis for personal life and imagined community (B. Anderson 1991), although one cannot take this argument too far. Although she was not addressing these emergent relationships or gender and sexuality, Andrea Rugh argued that the pursuit of an "Islamic society" for activists in late 1980s and early 1990s Egypt was "drawing upon a tendency already present in contemporary Egypt in which individuals operate more independently of their families than has been the custom in the past" (1993, 151). In a period of widespread economic, social, and political discontent, many Egyptians were looking for personal meaning, authenticity, and "cultural self-assertion," as well as political participation, within a more broadly defined community (of Muslims) that often undermined the idea of families or nations as the fundamental framework in which an individual situates himself or herself (ibid., 155, 157). These developments may be an unexpected consequence of privatization and free-market processes that are increasing poverty, the gap between rich and poor, and transborder mobility for work or pleasure. Also important are transnational social movements (religious, cultural, and others) that encourage new forms of identification and ways of life and challenge family or nation-state affiliation.

When explaining to me *'urfi, misyar,* and other nontraditional sexual and marital contracts among Sunni Muslims, for example, men and women from various walks of life in the Emirates and Egypt often evoked "Islamic" conceptualizations of sexual desire and satisfaction as natural and good, combined with discourses of "instinctive" physical needs whose fulfillment was imperative. During an interview with an Egyptian physician of middle-class background, I began to consider that the prevalence of such biologist ideas of desire might be recent and rearticulated, rather than "traditional." She mentioned that young people, even in middle and high schools, were having sexual relations using *'urfi* contracts. Contrasting the contemporary situation with her less sexualized 1960s teen and young adult years—during which political desires and work, studies, and a range of extracurricular "fun" activities with friends occupied much of her cohort's time—and reflecting on some of her hospital experiences with patients, she believed that bodily and sexual self-awareness had become more prevalent and articulated by young people. My findings corroborate her analysis in that embodied narratives of sexual desire and satisfaction, not dissimilar to the ones structuring discussion of the consumption and need for products, often permeated discussions explaining such relationship forms, whether the speaker approved or disapproved of them.

Especially in the UAE, some viewed these desires and ideas as stoked by widely available media and communication technology such as satellite television, which broadcasts popular Mexican, Egyptian, and U.S. soap operas and movies, as well as U.S. television series. On the World Wide Web, a number of (cross-national and national) Muslim chat rooms are popular in both Egypt and the UAE. In the UAE the possibilities for engaging in illicit or at least nonnormative relations were also facilitated by text messaging and the prevalence of mobile phones, which allowed unmarried girls and women to avoid family surveillance and control, as well as negotiate trysts. Parents are well aware of these possibilities and have successfully pressured the gender-segregated national universities and colleges to ban the use of cell phones on women's campuses, a requirement that faculty members (who reported this phenomenon to me) ambivalently police.

In a society where marriages arranged by parents remain the norm, younger less educated girls and women were often viewed as preferable wives since they were assumed to be less sexually knowledgeable and more malleable. Some men in the Emirates, however, argued that the two-directional migration of Emirati men and the immigration and importation of non-Emirati men and women for work, as well as television programming from places such as Egypt and Lebanon, have produced local male appetites for more expressive feminine sexualities than have been considered appropriate locally. Women, in turn, stressed the double standard of local men and cultural norms, which deem sexually expressive sartorial or bodily practices unacceptable if coming from national women and would lead to their social exclusion (as "sluts") in a society whose state and family forms are premised on benign patriarchy. Many of these women are nevertheless using new forms of communication to explore and negotiate sexual and relationship possibilities.

In both Egypt and the Emirates new bodies and desires are being articulated as people selectively draw on a range of "traditional" and contemporary discourses and practices—facilitated by cultural flows, human migration, and communication technologies and products—even as the contexts in which the articulation occurs are very much structured by socioeconomic, political, and cultural limits and opportunities. Gender inequality, of course, is constituted socially, economically, culturally, politically, and legally. My research results indicate that existing accounts of new relationships like *'urfi* and *misyar,* as well as explanations for high rates of divorce and women's singlehood (especially in Gulf states), can be overly economic, underestimating the instability and tension in existing gender regimes produced by institutional and more amorphous cultural forces. Moreover, the transnational forces and dynamics at play indicate the extent to which local, religious, "cultural," purely economic, or regionally bounded explanations are limited in the tools they provide to understand such relationships.

12. Afghan Refugee Women in Iran

Revisioning the Afghan Family

HOMA HOODFAR

Since the establishment of Afghanistan's post-Taliban regime in 2002, family law reform has been the focus of many conferences and meetings and a great deal of research.[1] However, although some female politicians are addressing family law reform, few of their male counterparts have taken up the issue. This situation stems at least in part from the history of family law reform in Afghanistan. Rulers from Amir Abdur Rahman (1880–1901) on have attempted to develop a centralized nation-state out of diverse linguistic and tribal groups.[2] Recognizing the central role of marriage and kinship dynamics in reinforcing tribal cohesion and the tribal power structure, they have sought to reform marriage practices and reengineer gender relations. However, even among the Pashtuns,

---

1. The research for this chapter was conducted under the auspices of the Women and Law Program, Columbia University, and Women Living under Muslim Laws as part of the Impact of Militarization on Women's Lives Program. It was funded by the Mellon Foundation. Several organizations such as Women Living under Muslim Laws, the Afghan Women Network, the Organization of Women Lawyers, the Organization of Women Judges, and the Women and Law Group have held workshops, meetings, and conferences, and there has also been considerable sharing of information on family law in Muslim countries by organizations such as Women Living under Muslim Laws and Sisters in Islam.

2. Ahmed Shah Durrani is generally regarded as the founder of Afghanistan in 1747, but there was no attempt to build a modern nation-state until after the second Anglo-Afghan war (1878–1880), under Amir Abdur Rahman.

223

who have otherwise supported the central government, tribal and religious leaders have vigorously resisted interference in the family and kinship system.

Tension over attempts to reform family law underlay several rebellions against the central state that toppled rulers, particularly in 1929 and 1978. State intervention in family law was concerned primarily with construction of a centralized, modern state, and not gender equity, justice, promotion of democracy, or the "liberation of women." Little effort was made to organize women and galvanize public support for family law reform beyond some limited activism among the elite. Until the late seventies there were few efforts to bring about the structural social and economic changes necessary to support change in gender roles and family structures.

Current demands for reform are, however, fundamentally different. For the first time it is women, from all walks of life, who are demanding reform, in response to major socioeconomic changes resulting from more than twenty-five years of war.[3] Aside from the internal displacement of more than one million Afghans, the exodus of more than five million people to neighboring countries such as Iran, Pakistan, Tajikistan, and India plus many Western countries has caused the breakdown of traditional social structures and institutions. New economic conditions, and the refugees' experiences of life in other Muslim contexts, have fostered new understandings and alternative visions of gender roles and of "Muslim-ness." Views on women's education, women's participation in the labor market, and women's rights in the family have shifted substantially, in part because of dire financial necessity.

In the following I argue, first, that top-down family law reform failed in the past owing to an absence of accompanying structural changes and a

---

3. The important driving force for this campaign to reform family law is the various Afghan women's organizations that were set up in Afghanistan in the 1990s. Among the activists are a notable number of young women who have undertaken law school or Islamic studies in Iran and Pakistan. Their knowledge of different histories of lawmaking and Islamic justifications has enriched the reform campaign. There is no longer a single but, rather, many different Islamic perspectives and justifications.

reluctance to mobilize women themselves. Second, I examine the realities of Afghan refugee women in Iran and how their experiences have altered their vision of their roles and rights as Muslim women. Multiplication of these significant, if diverse, changes has fueled the push for family law reform. Despite a lack of interest among Afghan politicians and international agencies, the first success came in 2007 when the powerful, conservative Legal Council ratified a modified version of the national marriage contract. It gives women the option of protecting their rights such as access to education and to labor-market participation after marriage. It also allows women to insert conditions for obtaining a divorce. Although this new marriage contract falls short of what women had demanded, it nevertheless signals the kind of reforms that may ensue.

History of Family Law Reforms

Many marriage and kinship practices are shared across Afghanistan's diverse ethnic groups (Kamali 1985) yet work to reinforce ethnic and tribal cohesion rather than creating a nation. Women rarely have a choice in mate selection and traditionally are married off young—frequently, they are betrothed as very young children. The control of women by male relatives within the tribal system is an essential aspect of social reproduction in Afghanistan. Women, through marriage and childbearing, play a central role in cementing alliances (R. Tapper 1983; L. Dupree 1973).

Traditionally, the groom pays a "bride price" to the bride's family, something not to be confused with the bridal gift, or *mahr*, he pledges to his bride. The latter is required in Sharia as part of the marriage contract; the former is a custom. However, large bride prices[4] and elaborate and expensive weddings reinforce traditional social and familial structures. Weddings are occasions for renewing social and political relationships

---

4. Other customary ways for a man to obtain a wife include inheriting the widow of a brother or another agnate kinsman and *badel* (exchange) marriage, whereby two men exchange sisters. In such cases the payment of a large bride price is usually avoided. These practices reinforce kinship ties and alliances. A man might also gain a wife as compensation from the family of someone who committed a crime against the groom's family, including murder.

and reaffirming bonds of solidarity and obligation. Since young men are hard-pressed to finance such weddings, they depend on their elders to provide for them. This largesse enables marriage, which is essential to achieve adulthood, but at the same time engenders moral and economic indebtedness, making it difficult for young people to challenge traditional, and often oppressive, structures. Thus, marriage and wedding practices have played a significant role in reproducing traditional family and social structures as well as tribal solidarity.

Recognizing the key role of marriage and kinship in political alliance making, Amir Abdur Rahman sought to strengthen the state by abolishing certain customary marriage practices, which he declared contrary to Islamic prescription.[5] The reforms included the requirement that all marriages be registered; the ability of girls betrothed in childhood, upon reaching puberty, to refuse the marriage; and the ability of women to sue for alimony (*nafagheh*) or to initiate divorce. Although in conformity with conservative Islamic law, these reforms represented an enormous change and met with great resistance. The state was unable to enforce them, and they remained largely unheeded.

The next significant reforms came during the reign of King Amanullah (1919–1929), Abdur Rahman's grandson. Inspired by Ataturk's reforms in Turkey, Amanullah opened schools for girls as well as boys and encouraged women to remove their veils. Like his grandfather, he paid special attention to marriage practices and introduced a law limiting marriage expenses (1922), on the grounds that incurring huge marriage expenses left men economically disadvantaged for life. He also encouraged men not to exceed four wives, as prescribed by Islam. His boldest reforms, however, were the abolition of forced and child marriage and the bride price and the outlawing of first-cousin marriage. In 1924 Afghan women were

---

5. Since religion was and often still is used to justify many marriage customs that conflict with Islam—such as the payment of the bride price—the early reforms were presented as reflecting *truly* Islamic practices. To this day Islam is viewed by the Afghan population (including women) as a liberating force, and our data indicate that women frequently use Islam to challenge oppressive cultural practices—a strategy adopted elsewhere as well (Hoodfar 1991, 2003).

legally given the right to choose their own husbands, consistent with the Hanafi school of Islam, to which most Sunni Afghans adhere.[6]

Although similar reforms were introduced relatively successfully in Iran, Egypt, and Turkey, in Afghanistan, despite considerable historical and intellectual communality, accompanying social transformations supportive of such reforms were absent, and thus, outside major cities, the reforms were ineffectual. Nevertheless, tribal leaders resented the state's intrusion into what they considered "family affairs," and in 1929 they formed a coalition that overthrew Amanullah. Their ideology was not unlike the Taliban's: marriage reforms were canceled, girls' schools were closed, and the veil became compulsory for women.

The coalition's short and chaotic rule was followed by the installation of King Amanullah's cousin who was shortly after succeeded by Mohammad Zahir Shah (1933–1973). Zahir Shah was unwilling to risk his throne by introducing radical changes, particularly in the area of marriage laws. However, under his rule educational opportunities for women in the cities gradually increased, and he did experiment with democracy, in 1964 setting up a national chamber with appointed and elected members and granting women the right to vote. Yet during the forty years of Zahir Shah's rule, state institutions and power outside the cities remained very limited.

Zahir Shah was overthrown in 1973. The new regime abolished the monarchy, introduced major social and economic reforms, and increased the involvement of both the Soviet Union and the United States in Afghanistan's internal politics. In 1978 the Soviet-backed People's Democratic Party of Afghanistan took power and issued a new family law known as Decree 7. Decree 7 came on the heels of the new government's policy of compulsory education for all children and land reform. Unlike earlier family law reforms Decree 7 was justified in terms of social development

---

6. However, these changes, as radical as they were at the time, did not go far enough to incorporate the views of the king or his intellectual and modernist adviser, Tazi (1866–1935), who viewed the emergence of the nuclear family model, along with education and health care, as the means for restructuring and developing the country and creating an Afghan nation from diverse tribal and ethnic communities.

rather than religion. It set the legal age of marriage at eighteen for men and sixteen for women and outlawed the betrothal of underage children. It outlawed bride price and limited the *mahr* to the nominal sum of three hundred afghani (a sum equivalent to the amount many clerics agree is in accordance with Islamic law). This change was justified on the grounds of discouraging families from treating their daughters as pawns by demanding large bride prices to maximize their financial gain (Moghadam 1993; N. Dupree 1984; N. Tapper 1984). Extravagant weddings were once again outlawed in the hope of reducing the indebtedness they generated.

Decree 7 marked the first time that bride price and large weddings were linked overtly to the oppression of women and young people in general. Though revolutionary, the decree did not address family law as a whole: it ignored the issues of divorce and custody, the inclusion of which might have made it a vehicle for improving women's status overall, rather than simply a means of transforming Afghan society from tribal to "modern."

There was general apprehension over the new laws, which were accompanied by the government's heavy-handed, top-down attempts to implement compulsory education, particularly for girls. These circumstances were ideal for tribal and religious leaders—who happened to control much of the land earmarked for redistribution—to mobilize the public against the government, which they claimed was promoting immorality with its new laws. Regardless of the government's limited ability to actually implement the law, the Afghan population saw Decree 7 as an assault on their honor and freedom. As tensions escalated and civil unrest grew, Afghans left for Iran, Pakistan, India, and the West in the hundreds of thousands. Estimated at five million, Afghans represented the largest long-term refugee population in the world between 1982 and 2002.

A Journey in Defense of Tradition

Language, religion, and geographical proximity were important factors influencing the refugees' choice of destination. The majority of Afghans who took refuge in Iran were Dari or Farsi speakers, including ethnic Tajiks, Farsis, and particularly Hazaras, who (unlike most Afghans but like Iranians) are Shiite Muslims. The majority of the Pashtu speakers left for the Pashtu-speaking areas in Quetta, Baluchistan, and the North West Frontier Province in Pakistan.

The very different policies of Iran and Pakistan toward the Afghan refugees have had a contrasting impact on the refugees themselves, Afghanistan, and the host countries, and also have implications for the formulation of international refugee policy. They merit scholarly attention in their own right but are beyond the scope of this chapter. Briefly, in Pakistan the majority of the refugees were confined to camps in the North West Frontier Province, usually organized on the basis of ethnicity and extended kinship. In Iran, however, only a very small percentage of Afghans were confined to camps (and then mostly after the 1990s). The differential consequences for the two refugee communities, particularly for women and family structure, are significant.

Afghans began arriving in Iran immediately after Iran's 1979 revolution. The new regime welcomed the refugees as Muslims in need of protection. Unlike Pakistan, which received considerable international recognition and funding for its refugees, the Islamic Republic of Iran received no significant international support to deal with its refugees. Thus, Afghan families dispersed and settled throughout rural and urban areas in search of livelihoods. At the time it was understood that Afghans, like Iranians, were entitled to education, health care, subsidized food, and, most significantly, access to the labor market. Most Afghan refugees consider this period in Iran as a "golden age" when they were treated with dignity and respect.

Things changed in 1992. It was partly because of the departure of the Russians from Afghanistan in 1989, which removed the ideological justification for hosting the Afghan refugees, and partly because Iran had grown impatient with the lack of international recognition and support for its considerable refugee burden.[7] The post-Khomeini governments were also less ideological, more pragmatic, and preoccupied with postwar reconstruction and reelection. Thus, the repatriation of Afghans became part the regime's refugee policy and has remained so since 1992, despite the continued civil

7. During this period and for many years, Iran was the largest (and still remains a top) refugee-receiving country, despite the eight-year Iran-Iraq war (1981–1988).

war and the ascendance of the Taliban and their persecution of the Hazara Shi'a, who were a majority of the Afghan refugees in Iran (Rashid 2001). Though not always enforced, this policy has created extreme financial, familial, and psychological insecurity for later refugee arrivals.

Although a considerable number of Afghan refugees moved to rural areas, the majority settled in major cities and worked as unskilled labor and in construction. While the move to Iran itself entailed major social and cultural change, the urban settlement of refugees was probably more significant, given that most came from rural areas. Afghans in Iranian cities gravitated to low-rent suburbs, living among Iranian rural-urban migrants of various ethnic backgrounds. This exposure to, as the interviewees frequently put it, "different ways of being Muslim" profoundly impacted the worldview of the Afghan community in Iran, especially for women and youth.

The Research

The data on which this chapter is based is part of a much larger study that included 450 Afghan households in Tehran and Mashhad in Iran and Peshawar and Quetta in Pakistan. The study was conducted between 1998 and 2001 in Golshar, a suburb of Mashhad, a popular point of entry and settlement for Afghans that continues to host one of the largest concentrations of Afghan refugees in Iran. In addition to in-depth interviews with eighty Afghan refugee women in Mashhad, my two research assistants and I held six informal focus-group discussions. We also interviewed several women community leaders and representatives of student organizations and consulted with charitable organizations working with the Afghan refugee population. With this sample we were able to survey a broad range of informants, from those individuals who were fairly well off to less established refugees. The interviewees' ages ranged from sixteen to seventy-four, with the majority between twenty-six and forty years old. The criteria for inclusion in the study were that women had to have been married at least one year (though they could be widowed at the time of the study) and been in Iran for more than two years.

Forty-six of the women had been in Iran with their families since the early days of the Russian invasion (1979) or since escaping the Taliban (between 1994 and 1998). Another thirteen said they first came during the Russian occupation in the 1980s but had returned home after the Russians were defeated, only to flee to Iran again because of civil war and ethnic-based killings. Others endured the hardships of the civil conflict and then fled to escape Taliban rule (1994–2001) some years later. For twenty-four households we were unable to obtain data on exactly when or how many times they came to Iran, though we know that most of them had been there more than five years. The lack of precise data is in part owing to the fact that approximately half of the two million Afghans in Iran in 2001 were nondocumented (illegal) refugees. We were careful to respect our informants' decisions on whether and how much information they provided and did not pursue matters they seemed uncomfortable discussing, even with interviewers they had known as neighbors for several years. We can state with confidence that a majority of them arrived with their households after 1992, when the Iranian policy toward Afghan refugees became stricter.

Housing and Afghan Family Structure in Iran

Residential domestic organization is a key manifestation of family ideology, and social scientists, particularly feminist and modernist theorists, have given family living arrangements particular attention. The literature asserts that the nuclear household allows for greater freedom and decision-making power for young couples, and especially for young married women, than does the extended household (Netting, Wilk, and Arnold 1984; Shorter and Zurayk 1988; Singerman 1990; S. Cole 1998). The data from our research strongly support this thesis. The household arrangements of Afghan families in Iran induced major changes in family organization and, consequently, in patterns of decision making and agency of women. It has had major consequences for family structure, ideology, and gender relations.

Ideally in Afghan society a bride moves in with her husband's family and lives as part of that extended family under the control and guidance of her mother-in-law, at least until the time that she herself becomes a mother-in-law. To some extent this system had begun to change in Afghanistan's major urban centers, particularly among poor rural migrant households.

Nonetheless, most of our interviewees said that in Afghanistan they had lived in patrilocal, extended families. The scarcity of affordable housing in Iran changed this pattern radically, even for those Afghans who had migrated as extended households. Interviewees said they had to shift to nuclear-family households because quarters sizable enough to house large family groups were not available and, when they were, were prohibitively expensive, even in the informal housing sector. Iranian landlords are also extremely reluctant to rent to large extended families or families with many children. Some interviewees said they had to place their children with relatives—at least initially—in order to rent a room; many were told to leave when the landlord realized they had more than two or three children. This situation was sobering for Afghan parents, who had never before viewed their children as a liability.

Throughout the region Afghans are known for having large families (a stereotype that is statistically supported). In Iran, following the Khomeini government's pronatalist policies of 1978–1988 and the consequent huge population increase, Iranians have seen a declining birthrate because of the state's highly successful family planning program, implemented to address population growth in the face of increasing urbanism and the high cost of living. Much of the rhetoric in support of smaller families is based on Islamic doctrine, and thus appeals to Iranians and increasingly to Afghans, who frame their lives in terms of Islamic prescriptions. According to the women we interviewed, tradition, combined with ongoing war casualties, contributed to families' desire for many children. Many were raised to believe that any attempt to limit birth was un-Islamic. During the Russian occupation women were encouraged by their communities to have many children, as a way of resisting the alleged aim of the Russians to limit the growth of the Afghan (Muslim) population.[8]

The Islamic Republic's emphasis since the late 1980s on small healthy families thus presented Afghan refugees with a different model of the Muslim family than they were accustomed to. In Iran Afghan women with three or more children, including two sons, were inclined to practice

8. Ethnic rivalry may also have affected the birthrate, as ethnic leaders urged people to ensure the growth of their own population.

birth control, usually with the agreement of their husbands. Some women believed their husbands would object and practiced birth control surreptitiously. Others viewed the issue as their own concern, preferring to avoid a possible blow to their husband's dignity as the provider by the implicit suggestion of his inability to support a large family.

Although all the women referred to housing conditions as a factor in limiting family size, they also noted that information and resources are available in Iran that were not in Afghanistan. One question we asked our interviewees aged eighteen to forty-five (N=60) was their ideal number of children. Forty percent (twenty-four women) said two children, 53.3 percent (thirty-two women) said between two and four children, and only 6.7 percent said "as many as God gives," which was the expected conventional response. Our data suggest that Afghan women in Iran increasingly accept the idea of small families and controlling fertility. The housing situation and exposure to new ideas resulted in a major departure from the traditional Afghan convention idealizing large families and tying a woman's status to the number of children she bears.

Women and Access to Education

Probably the most significant change for Afghan refugee women and the community as a whole has been the reassessment of female education, long an issue of concern in Afghanistan. As in the rest of the Middle East, successive reformists and the women's movement had viewed education as key to changing Afghan women's social and legal conditions (Centlivres-Demont 1994; Jayawardena 1986). Conservatives had argued with equal passion that educating women will lead to social upheaval and moral decay. Thus, despite great efforts by successive Afghan governments, education for girls remained limited except in the urban centers and among the small middle class. Modernists continued to view the lack of women's education as a significant factor in Afghanistan's slow economic and social development. But Zahir Shah was unwilling to risk his throne by introducing universal education. Finally, when in 1978 the Soviet-backed People's Democratic Party of Afghanistan came to power, it introduced compulsory literacy education for children and adults of both sexes (Moghadam 1993; Centlivres-Demont 1994).

Their campaign included large-scale teacher training, sending teachers to rural areas, and, with the backing of the army, forcing parents to send their daughters to school. This policy created a huge uproar in the countryside. In addition to being from other ethnic groups, many of the teachers were male. Rural families, which followed strict gender segregation, were incensed. Along with the educational initiative, the new marriage laws established under Decree 7 were unpopular. Conservative leaders urged resistance, calling the policies immoral, un-Islamic incursions into people's private matters and fanning outrage and fear. Amid growing civil unrest and believing their honor and religion were at stake, people actually left their homes for neighboring countries, primarily Iran and Pakistan. A majority of refugees surveyed in Pakistan during this period gave compulsory education and the new marriage law as important factors in their decision to leave (N. Dupree 1984). It is against this history that the present findings on Afghan refugees' attitudes toward girls' education must be understood.

The experience of living in exile in other Muslim nations, particularly the Islamic Republic of Iran, had unexpected consequences in terms of Afghan refugees' views on education and Islam. Initially, they were astonished to encounter the Islamic Republic's ongoing campaign—framed as a jihad—to eradicate illiteracy and encourage girls' education (Mehran 1991, 2002). Huge city billboards, radio and television programs, and broadcast sermons proclaimed literacy essential to being a "good Muslim." It was news to the Afghan refugees, most of whom were Hazara and shared both language and Shi'ism with Iranians and who admired the Islamic regime as the ideological opposite of the Soviet-backed regime in Afghanistan. Iranian propaganda on education, apart from its references to Islam, was not unlike the new policies of the regime they had fled. Nevertheless, within a few years Afghans in Iran came to accept the Islamic Republic's view of education as a key component of being a good Muslim. They made great efforts to send their children to school, and many adults, particularly women, joined Koranic and literacy classes "to become better Muslim mothers," as many said (Hoodfar 2004). "To educate oneself is at least as important as going to Mecca," one middle-aged woman graduate of an adult literacy program in Mashhad proudly declared.

In a reversal of reasons cited for leaving Afghanistan in the 1980s, many of our interviewees who fled after 1995 said they did so because of the closure of girls' schools and other educational institutions by the Taliban regime.[9] In a sad irony, however, by the 1990s the post-Khomeini regime had reverted to more nationalistic policies and distanced itself from pan-Islamic solidarity, refusing to issue documents to new Afghan refugees and banning undocumented refugees from attending schools. This policy reform led to the establishment by Afghan women in Iran of informal Afghan schools in all major cities, where tens of thousands of Afghan children and youth are being educated based on the Iranian curriculum (Hoodfar 2007).

Many of the interviewees had attended adult literacy classes or Koranic classes offered through a local mosque. Studying the Koran is a legitimate reason for women from even the most conservative households to go out. The adult literacy classes appear to be much more popular with women than men.[10] Achieving literacy and religious knowledge empowered the women on many levels; nearly all interviewees told us that the contacts they made through the classes helped them find work for themselves and other family members and access information on health care facilities, shopping, and other important resources. For many interviewees, especially the ones from rural Afghanistan who were unlikely to have even gone to a local market before coming to Iran, it was all very new. Some of the younger women said that living without extended family, in a community of nonkin, and interacting with refugees from various ethnic backgrounds as well as with Iranians have exposed them to the various ways Muslims understand and practice Islam. Their experience in Iran, a country where Islam is preached and practiced in all facets of

9. Clearly, the decisions of people who choose to go into exile are complex and rarely involve only one factor. However, it is a very interesting development that most refugees, and in particular the second-time refugees we interviewed in Iran (1998–2001), mentioned the closure of girls' schools and the education of their children as their reason for exile, since it is the reverse of the reason given for exile in the early 1980s.

10. Twenty of the eighty interviewees had completed adult-literacy courses, and five others had attended Koranic classes; only three of their husbands took adult-literacy classes.

daily life, has made it easier for them to examine more critically what it is to be a "Muslim woman, a Muslim wife, and Muslim mother." One elderly woman told me:

> To see Iranian women wear their scarf and *roopush* [the long, loose over-coat that Iranian women are legally required to wear over their clothes when in public] to go to university, to be on the television, to go to political demonstrations and to Friday prayer, and still attend to their homes and families made me realize I could do all these things and still be a good Muslim woman. When I was in Afghanistan I did not know this. I thought all Muslim women should stay home and if they had to go out should go with their husbands. Now when I think how much my daughter wanted to go to school and we did not let her because we thought Islam forbade women to go to school my heart aches for her. Many of our friends came to Iran and others went to Pakistan, because we thought the government forcing women to go to school will make them immoral. They also passed a law that fathers had to give their daughter in marriage free, that they couldn't ask any bride price [referring to Decree 7 of the socialist government]. Families were frightened because that would mean men could marry with no effort and then divorce and go and marry again, and it costs them nothing, but could cost our daughters' well-being. My husband and I, like many others, thought this was a major disaster and decided to leave Afghanistan. Now years later my daughters' families and many others who had returned to Afghanistan from Iran are coming back after living under the Taliban for two years. My daughter is determined that her daughters will have an education. After all, it is their Islamic *right* [*haq-e-islami*; emphasis added] and no one should deprive Muslims of their rights, especially in the name of Islam! Taliban are savage and know nothing about Islam. We have lived here in Iran, an Islamic country, and we've seen other Islamic countries on TV, and they all have schools and opportunities for women.[11]

Many Afghan refugees and former refugees now see female education not only as an Islamic right but as a requirement. Whereas in the past

---

11. This interview took place in May 2001, a few months before September 11.

conservative forces invoked Islam to block Afghan women's access to education, Afghan women now use Islam as a source of empowerment and access to education. Education, however, has other consequences. As one conventional husband put it, "You marry an educated woman and you do not get a wife that is like your mother was to your father, subservient and ready to take his commands. Rather, it is wife who wants to be your equal and more. If only I knew this before my marriage. Iran has ruined our women, and Afghans will never be the same again." The cause of his regret, however, was very often the reason for women's satisfaction.

Women in the Labor Market

According to religion, tradition, and law in Muslim societies, including Afghanistan, men are responsible for providing for their families regardless of their wives' economic situation. Afghan men take great pride in the role of breadwinner, which is a source of masculine identity and status within the household (Monsutti 2004). It has been argued that when women are entirely economically dependent on husbands and other male relatives, it is incredibly difficult for them to resist oppressive practices or question male authority over them (Hijab 1988; Hoodfar 1991, 1997). In general, when women lack the opportunity to be active in the larger public domain, they do not develop the skills and confidence to deal with the bureaucracy of the modern nation-state or to conceive of alternative social, economic, and gender roles (Hoodfar 1996a). Our data and the many tales we heard suggest that, faced with a situation where family survival depends on women's initiatives and their participation in the social and economic life of the larger society, they often do discover their potential.

Many Afghan women in Iran have now assumed economic responsibility for their families and regularly deal with demands outside of their own households. Our interviewees said that despite the hardships, they relish their new roles and responsibilities, are proud of their economic contributions, and would hesitate to give them up. Nevertheless, our informants emphasized men's obligation to provide for the family as "nature's way" and "prescribed by God," in the same way that it is solely women's responsibility to bear children. However, younger women in particular pointed out that although neither the law nor Islam dictates that women should bear financial responsibility for their families, it does not preclude them from economic activity. One literacy-program graduate who had encouraged many other women to continue their educations said:

> Men are economically responsible. . . . It is all about justice. God did not want women, the bearers of children, to be working at home and having to work outside the home. But that is not the same as saying that women *cannot* do it. Women are *capable* of doing everything that men can do. They can be doctors, engineers, teachers, and pilots. . . . The fact that men have to provide for the family does not mean that women should not work and earn a living to help and improve their lives and the lives of their families. It is their responsibility to work and help their children to be educated and well brought up, so that they do not have to suffer like so many of us did.

Other interviewees argued that women can do anything men can do, whereas there are things women can do that men have been denied by nature, such as giving birth. This public self-appraisal and self-confidence is very new among Afghan women.[12] In both group discussions and individual interviews women often referred to the Taliban's "incorrect understanding of Islam" and compared it with the perspectives and practices of Islam in Iran. Although there was certainly some criticism of the Iranian state's vision of Islam, their Iranian experience provided them with a comparative model that enabled them to reject some traditional practices.[13]

Since 1997 labor-market restrictions for non-Iranians have meant harassment in the workplace for Afghan men and a further lowering of their wages (Rajaee 2000). However, the authorities and police rarely bother Afghan women, whose paid work often takes place at home or in small-scale neighborhood industries (often managed by Iranian women). This situation has meant that more Afghan women seek employment outside their homes, while many men are forced to accept exploitative piecemeal

---

12. Some of our interviewees' husbands jested that it was a mistake to come to Iran, where their wives and daughters discovered the world.

13. In fact, they were very critical of the way the Iranian state selectively invokes Islam when it is expedient.

work that can be done at home. While only 15 percent of our interviewees were sole breadwinners, in 42 percent of households women were contributing financially. Clearly, circumstances have led women to develop abilities to navigate the public arena even in a huge city like Mashhad and perform tasks traditionally considered exclusive to men.

The women we spoke with did not underestimate the cost of this situation to their husbands. Unemployment, workplace harassment, and dependence on their wives' incomes rendered many men despondent and frustrated. The issue was often a source of great tension between husbands and wives. The women adopted various strategies to ease the situation, including an exaggerated display of respect toward their husbands, particularly in public, and turning their earnings over to them to manage. The women also pointed out to their husbands that even the prophet Muhammad was supported by his wife Khadija!

The literature indicates that earning an income does not automatically translate into more power and rights for women in the family; without other changes an income-earning woman may simply be subject to further exploitation (Beneria and Roldan 1987; Hoodfar 1997). However, control or shared management of the household budget may afford women greater decision-making power (Dwyer and Bruce 1988). To assess the household dynamic we asked women who controlled their household budgets and purchasing decisions. They told us that in Afghanistan men controlled the money and did the shopping, or, in some cases, the mother-in-law took responsibility. In Iran, however, 65 percent of interviewees (N=70) had sole responsibility for household finances and shopping, compared with 27 percent where responsibility lay with the husbands; in 4 percent of the cases the mother-in-law managed finances, and in 4 percent of cases it was sons. Fifty-four percent of the women, many raised and married in Iran, indicated over the course of conversations that they were very aware this setup represents a considerable shift in family structure and gender roles.

To assess to what degree changes in gender roles—especially regarding economic activities—resulted from living in Iran, we asked the twenty-seven women who had lived in Afghanistan as adults prior to coming to Iran to describe their economic roles in Afghanistan. Nineteen had not held paid jobs in Afghanistan but did in Iran. Six had employment in both Iran and Afghanistan, and two of the more educated interviewees had worked in Afghanistan but not in Iran. This shift is considerable, the more remarkable as the majority of interviewees originated from rural areas and had had very limited activity outside their households in Afghanistan.

Marriage Patterns: Spousal Selection and Age of Marriage

With the exception of Turkey, reform of family law in the Middle East, including Iran, has not kept pace with social and economic changes, partly because religious leaders have been unwilling to let this last bastion of influence slip away, and partly because women have had little political influence. Perhaps more important, reformist movements were deeply patriarchal and were satisfied with modernizing measures but had little desire to democratize the family (Charrad 2001; Sharabi 1988). Nonetheless, moderate reforms were introduced in Iran in 1967 and 1974, giving Iranian women some measure of protection against arbitrary divorce, polygynous marriage, and rights to child custody (Sansarian 1982; Mir-Hosseini 1996a, 1996b; Hoodfar 1999). Ayatollah Khomeini canceled these reforms and in particular celebrated the right to polygynous and temporary marriages. Fierce objections and protests, including demonstrations at the Ministry of Justice by secular women, proved futile (Paidar 1995). The new laws opened women to numerous abuses and unfair divorce practices, which were the subject of many discussions and stories published in the print media (Hoodfar 1999).

Concern over social justice for women and a just marriage law has thus been a topic of significant public debate and everyday conversation in urban Iran since the 1980s, and thus Afghans have been exposed to these debates. Islamic family law and women's rights in Islam have been the topic of many radio and television programs, films, books, newspaper articles, sermons, and in particular Friday prayers (Hoodfar 1999; Mir-Hosseini 1996a, 1996b). Given that the debates around marriage and marriage reform in Afghanistan were also topics of concern, many Afghan women (and men) followed them closely. Iranian leaders, who claim that Islam gives women greater rights than any secular law could possibly do, have consequently been obliged to address constant criticism of its gender ideology from both secular forces and Islamist women and to introduce major reforms promoting a more liberal interpretation of Sharia and other Islamic texts (Mir-Hosseini 1999). In promoting more woman-centered interpretations of religious texts and allying with more liberal-minded religious leaders to demand reform, activists continue to point to skewed family law clauses favoring men at the expense of justice and fairness (Paidar 1995; Hoodfar 1999). The most significant reform to date has been the universal marriage contract introduced in 1987, giving women the rights of continuing their studies, labor-market participation, divorce under certain conditions, and half the assets of the marriage in case of divorce (Hoodfar 2000; Kar and Hoodfar 1996). Such developments offer new perspectives through which Afghan women in Iran examine their own situations regarding marriage and family. Moreover, this public discourse has encouraged many young Afghan women and men to study law and Islamic studies in Iranian universities, including the university in Qom, the site of a major scholarly religious center in Iran. Now well versed in religious terminology and history, they are not accepting any half-baked arguments from those persons not so learned in Islam as justification for many of the cultural practices pushed on them as being Islamic.

Afghan women's exposure to procedures such as marriage registration and certificates and the existence of an active family court were revelations for many. Like most poor and rural women in Afghanistan, many of our interviewees had no birth certificates or official documentation of any sort and only heard of such documents when they were requested by Iranian landlords and authorities.

Marriages arranged by male kin and large bride prices have remained the norm in Afghanistan throughout the decades of war and upheaval, and financial hardship has only exacerbated the position of women as assets to be given to the highest bidder, as evidenced by the narratives of our interviewees about their own and others' experiences (Hoodfar forthcoming). Women were especially fearful of the common practice of *badel*, an arrangement whereby two men exchange their sisters as wives for each other and thus avoid paying bride prices. Not only do women have absolutely no say in the process, but if anything goes wrong in one marriage, it inevitably causes suffering for the women in both marriages.

Such marriages mean a smaller *mahr* and fewer gifts (usually household items and clothing), which are often the only material assets young brides receive. The banning of these practices by successive governments has had little impact on the lives of most Afghan women; none of our informants was even aware that Afghanistan has a codified family law or a family court.

Domestic problems commonly faced by Afghan women include absent husbands who fail to provide for the family yet refuse to divorce their wives and childhood fiancés who renege on the betrothal but refuse to release the bride to marry another. But by far the most common problem has been unwanted marriage arrangements, frequent among Afghan refugees in Iran, and Afghans in general. The high rate of suicide by young Afghan women facing unwanted marriage has been the subject of several research papers in recent years (United Nations Development Fund for Women 2004) and has been covered in radio programs and several highly publicized Friday prayer sermons in major cities like Kabul, Kandahar, Herat, and Mazar-i-Sharif. Such crises indicate that conventional marriage institutions and practices are no longer appropriate or in keeping with the structural and ideological changes undergone by Afghan communities. It is in this context that the widespread debates on family law, marriage, divorce, custody, and justice for women have significant resonance with Afghan refugee women in Iran as well as with the hundreds of thousands who have returned to Afghanistan since 2002.

Interviewees were convinced that marriage practices were changing partly because of changes in household organization and partly because of exposure to the variety of marriage practices by the many different Muslim ethnic groups in Iran and elsewhere in the Muslim world. Many of the refugees now have connections to other Afghans living in India, Tajikistan, Turkmenistan, Uzbekistan, and Syria and in European and North American societies. Being so focused on free trade we, as social scientists, often overlook other aspects of globalization. "Before I came to Iran I thought that marriage, work, property, and all that were concerns of men, and we just have to take care of our children and families on a day-to-day basis. Now that I've lived here for almost ten years and watched how Iranian women understand their roles and religion, it has changed my views. I am still very much an Afghani, something that I did not think about before, but I also think some of our traditions go against Islamic principles." Many interviewees believed change must be promoted by government and religious leaders and implemented through governing bodies and councils and expressed deep frustration that under the Taliban (still in power at the time of our interviews in 2001) this change would never happen in Afghanistan.

For our interviewees issues of marriage laws and practices were second only to security concerns in terms of importance, and they felt strongly that the democratization of marriage and family laws was key to improving the status of women in a reconstructed Afghanistan. They were unequivocal that after their experiences in Iran, including workforce participation and increasing religious knowledge, literacy, and educational levels, women and young people in general will refuse to accept traditional marriage practices and arrangements. However, many of the women also pointed out that kin networks and marriage continue to be the most significant institutions in every Afghan's life, especially for women in the absence of strong state institutions, and suggested that reforms in these arenas must be a priority if women are to be transformed from the property of male kin into citizens. Yet they were convinced that nobody would work to bring about the change except the women themselves—which is exactly what women have been trying to do since the fall of the Taliban, as I mentioned earlier.

Our discussions on an appropriate age of marriage also revealed significant changes. Many interviewees supported a later age of marriage, especially for women, compared to contemporary conditions in Afghanistan and refugee life. The women felt that education and maturity had to come first. Research participants also said marriage arrangements should take place only when children are old enough to be involved in spousal selection. Though most opposed the idea of their children choosing a spouse against parental wishes, they felt it equally wrong for parents to force children to marry against their will. Some of the women noted that it was un-Islamic to force an unwanted marriage on their daughters; interestingly, none of the interviewees was aware that these very issues have been at the heart of the political debate on legal reform in Afghanistan over the past one hundred years. Sixty-six out of seventy-eight responding had themselves married between the ages of nine and eighteen, and many had unhappy stories about their early years of marriage. Table 12.1 illustrates respondents' age of marriage and what they believed was the appropriate age of marriage for their own children. Thirty-eight of sixty-seven respondents considered the ideal age of marriage for daughters to be nineteen to twenty-eight, and thirty-eight out of sixty-one said men should marry between ages twenty-three and thirty-two (or older). These views indicate a considerable departure from what were considered acceptable ages of marriage in the previous generation.

In the course of open-ended interviews and group discussions the issue of age differentials between husbands and wives was raised by many of our informants. Although some felt couples of a similar age were acceptable, the ideal seemed to be a groom a few years older than a bride. Some of the women believed husbands should be older by five or six years, "because men mature more slowly than women." The perspective that a husband should be somewhat older than his wife can be read as a legitimatization of husbands' control and power within marriage. However, the women strongly condemned marriages of very young brides to men as old as their fathers, though their perception was that over the past decade marriages of this type had increased. Twenty-nine of sixty-two respondents were seven to sixteen years younger than their husbands, while four women who married between ages twelve and sixteen were twenty-three to twenty-eight years younger than their husbands. Many felt that such enormous age gaps were primarily the result of the brides' fathers seeking a large bride price from an older and richer groom. Though such marriages were not very common, the subject came up often among the women, who argued that *it must be against Islam* and should be prohibited (though there is no religious prohibition of such marriages).

Interviewees said that marriage issues are commonly discussed in their families and are a point of tension, especially between parents and children. They also said that this topic is a recent preoccupation of the community, and they feel it is linked to their experiences in Iran and to new socioeconomic realities. Some women noted that their ability to

TABLE 12.1. **Range of actual and ideal ages of marriage**

	Interviewees' age at marriage	Ideal age of marriage	
Age	*n*	*Women*	*Men*
9–11	6	0	0
12–15	27	3	0
16–18	33	15	2
19–22	8	26	17
23–25	2	9	19
26–28	2	3	13
29–30	0	4	4
32 and over	0	0	2
At mental maturity[a]	0	5	0
Later rather than sooner[a]	0	2	2
When they can afford it[a]	0	0	2
Missing data	2	13	19
Total	80	80	80

[a]Some women found the age-category criterion irrelevant and insisted on other measures.

distinguish between religion and their own cultural practices makes it easier now to reflect on possibilities for change. Many of the choice-limiting traditions the women were raised with were reinforced through references to Islam. After living in the Islamic Republic of Iran, where gender segregation and rigid gender roles coexist with relatively great freedom and opportunity for women, Afghan women can more easily and legitimately be critical of traditional Afghan practices without being accused of violating their faith, losing their religion, or becoming Westernized.[14]

◆ ◆ ◆

Afghan rulers had attempted unsuccessfully to restructure society and usher in modernity since the late 1800s by reordering kinship ties and family

14. Devout women fear such accusations and are constrained by lack of access to religious texts and information. Because religion has been a major force of cohesion and regulator of social ethics and mores, women are keen to justify their new ideas about gender roles using Islam and Islamic values.

structure. In 1978 the socialist government tried to combine new marriage laws with universal compulsory education. It helped bring the country into twenty-five years of war and destruction and spurred a mass exodus of Afghans opposed to this assault on traditional practices and values. Ironically, the refugees encountered conditions in Iran (and, the evidence indicates, in other neighboring countries like Pakistan and Tajikistan) that led to major changes in women's roles and in the conventional family structure that were previously thought unacceptable. In particular, exposure to Iranian Islamic practices, ideals, and public discourses caused the Afghan refugees to reassess some of their understandings of Islam, including the idea that girls do not need education. In Iran, particularly in the cities, education is understood as a condition of being a good Muslim. The education of girls, by itself, has brought about major changes, including changes in women's understanding of what is involved in being good Muslim women.

Now young Afghan women who have returned to Afghanistan in the hundreds of thousands from Iran and other countries are pushing for their gender vision(s) to be reflected in marriage practices, other social institutions, and the legal codes of the country. They are demanding a different status in marriage and family that corresponds to their experiences and expectations and is enshrined in the legal code of the country.

The wariness of the even more liberal-minded politicians, who do not oppose their demands, to lend them support stems from the unsuccessful past attempts to reform family law and the resulting implications for their political careers. Although legal reform can be an important tool for social change, the latter nonetheless demands many other complementary components and an appropriate social and political environment. Marriage reform in Afghanistan had not been successful because its proponents were not willing to create the necessary structural changes, including the mobilization of women and an expansion of democracy and public participation that are foundational to such changes. The new demands on the part of Afghan women to reform marriage law and practice are of a fundamentally different genre. They have been launched by a coalition of women who have little influence on the power structure but, as citizens of the country, insist that their concerns and vision be incorporated into the legal structure of the society.

The women who are mobilizing for change are frustrated that although the coalition forces were happy to use the appalling situation of women under the Taliban as a reason to justify the war, they have been reluctant to make the improvement of the social and legal status of women a priority in their support for reconstruction of Afghanistan. In many ways the returning refugee population, particularly refugees returning from other Muslim societies who are exposed to different "Muslim" social and economic organizations, can be a powerful force for social change in the Afghan family and beyond, particularly if policy makers, civil society, and women's organizations encourage women's participation in the public sphere and mobilize to articulate demands for family law reforms. Such reforms can provide greater protection for women and help democratize the Afghan family; otherwise, as long as the family structure remains undemocratic and continues to foster undemocratic, patriarchal values, Afghanistan cannot move to democracy and the inclusion of all citizens, regardless of gender or ethnicity.

Works Cited

• • •

Index

Works Cited

Abaza, Mona. 2001. "Perceptions of '*Urfi* Marriage in the Egyptian Press." *ISIM Newsletter* 7, no. 1: 20–21.

Al-Abbasi al-Mahdi al-Misri, Muhammad. 1883–1886. *The Fatwas of al-Mahdi on Egyptian Proceedings* [in Arabic]. 7 vols. Cairo: al-Matba'at al-Azhariyya.

Abdel Rahim, Muhammad. 2003. Interviewed by Frances Hasso. Dubai, UAE, Dec. 1.

Abd El Rahman, Awatef. 2003. Interviewed by Frances Hasso. Giza, Egypt, Dec. 30.

Abduh, Muhammad. 1900. *Report on the Reform of the Sharia Courts* [in Arabic]. Cairo: Matba'at al-Manar.

Abrams, Philip. 1988. "Notes on the Difficulty of Studying the State (1977)." *Journal of Historical Sociology* 1: 58–89.

Abu Zahra, Muhammad. 1950. *Personal Status: Section on Marriage* [in Arabic]. Cairo: n.p.

Acar, Feride. 1998. "Women Academics in Turkey." In *Women and Men in 75 Years*, 313–21 [in Turkish]. Istanbul: Türkiye Ekonomik ve Toplumsal Tarih Vakfı.

Acar, Feride, Ayşe Ayata, and Demet Varoğlu. 1999. *Gender-Based Discrimination: The Case of the Education Sector in Turkey* [in Turkish]. Ankara: T. C. Başbakanlık, Kadın Statüsü ve Sorunları Genel Müdürülüğü.

Afkhami, Mahnaz, and Erika Friedl, eds. 1997. *Muslim Women and the Politics of Participation: Implementing the Beijing Platform*. Syracuse: Syracuse Univ. Press.

Agence France Presse (AFP). 2004a. "Iraqi Women's Rights Imperiled." Jan. 15.

———. 2004b. "Islamic Council Members Storm Out of Crucial Iraq Constitution Talks." Feb. 28.

———. 2005. "U.S. 'Concession' Marks Turn in Iraq Constitution." *Daily Times* (Pakistan), Aug. 21. http://www.dailytimes.com.pk/default.asp?page=story_21-8-2005_pg7_42.

Agnes, Flavia. 1997. "Protecting Women Against Violence? Review of a Decade of Legislation, 1980–1989." In *State and Politics in India,* ed. Partha Chatterjee. Delhi: Oxford Univ. Press.

———. 1999. *Law and Gender Inequality: The Politics of Women's Rights in India.* New Delhi: Oxford Univ. Press.

———, ed. 2004. *Asian Age,* Mar. 23.

Ahmad, Mumtaz. 1996. "The Crescent and the Sword: Islam, the Military, and Political Legitimacy in Pakistan." *Middle East Journal* 50, no. 3: 372–87.

Ahmad, Tahmina, and Md. Maimul Ahsan Khan. 1998. *Gender in Law.* Dhaka: Adtam Publishing House.

Ahmed, Leila. 1992. *Women and Gender in Islam: Historical Roots of a Modern Debate.* New Haven: Yale Univ. Press.

Ahmed, Sarwat. 1999. "Closet Consummations." *Cairo Times Online,* Nov. 12–25. http://www.cairotimes.com/content/issues/Women/marriage.html.

Al-Ahnaf, M. 1994. "Le Code du Statut Personnel." *Maghreb-Machrek* 145: 3–26.

Akın, Ayşe, et al. 2003. *Gender and Health in Turkey* [in Turkish]. Ankara: T. C. Başbakanlık, Kadın Statüsü ve Sorunları Genel Müdürülüğü.

Alam, Anwar. 2002. "Secularism in India: A Critique of the Current Discourse." In *Competing Nationalisms in South Asia: Essays for Asghar Ali Engineer,* ed. Paul Brass and Achin Vanaik. New Delhi: Orient Longman.

Al-Ali, Nadje, and Nicola Pratt. 2006. "Women in Iraq: Beyond the Rhetoric." *Middle East Report.*

Allam, Hannah. 2004. "Iraqi Women Push for Power." Knight Ridder, Feb. 22.

Al Roken, Mohamed Abdallah Mohamed. 2003. Interviewed by Frances Hasso. Dubai, UAE, Dec. 6.

Altorki, Soraya. 2000. "The Concept and Practice of Citizenship in Saudi Arabia." In *Gender and Citizenship in the Middle East,* ed. Suad Joseph, 215–36. Syracuse: Syracuse Univ. Press.

Alvarez, Sonia E. 1990. *Engendering Democracy in Brazil: Women's Movements in Transition Politics.* Princeton: Princeton Univ. Press.

Amawi, Abla. 2000. "Gender and Citizenship in Jordan." In *Gender and Citizenship in the Middle East,* ed. Suad Joseph, 158–84. Syracuse: Syracuse Univ. Press.

Amien, Waheeda. 2006. "Overcoming the Conflict Between the Right to Freedom of Religion and Women's Rights to Equality: A South African Case Study of Muslim Marriages." *Human Rights Quarterly* 28: 729–54.

Amin, Qasim. 1899, 1902. *The Liberation of Women* (1899) and *The New Woman* (1902). Trans. Samiha Sidhom Peterson. Cairo: American Univ. in Cairo Press, 2000.

Amnesty International. 1996. "Bangladesh: Fundamental Rights of Women Violated with Virtual Impunity." In *Fatwas Against Women in Bangladesh*, 67–68. Montpellier: Women Living under Muslim Laws. Available at http://www.wluml.org/english/pubs/pdf/misc/fatwa-bangladesh-eng.pdf.

———. 2003a. *Annual Report.* Section on Pakistan. http://web.amnesty.org/report2003/Pak-summary-eng.

———. 2003b. "Turkey: End Sexual Violence Against Women in Custody!" *AI Index* EUR 44/006/2003.

———. 2004. "Turkey: Women Confronting Family Violence." *AI Index* EUR 44/013/2004.

Anderson, Benedict R. 1991. *Imagined Communities: Reflections on the Origin and Spread of Nationalism.* 2nd ed. London: Verso Books.

Anderson, J. N. D. 1951. "Recent Developments in Shari'a Law II." *Muslim World* 41: 34–48.

Anderson, Lisa. 1986. *The State and Social Transformation in Tunisia and Libya, 1830–1980.* Princeton: Princeton Univ. Press.

An-Na'im, Abddullahi A. 2002. *Islamic Family Law in a Changing World: A Global Resource Book.* London: Zed Books.

Anveshi Law Committee. 1997. "Is Gender Justice Only a Legal Issue? Political Stakes in the UCC Debate." *Political and Economic Weekly*, Mar. 1, 453–58.

Arabi, Oussama. 2001a. "The Dawning of the Third Millennium on Shari'a: Egypt's Law No. 1 of 2000, or Women May Divorce at Will." *Arab Law Quarterly* 16: 2–21.

———. 2001b. "The Itinerary of a Fatwa: Ambulant Marriage (al-Zawaj al-Misyar); or, Grass Roots Law-Making in Saudi Arabia of the 1990s." Chap. 7 in *Studies in Modern Islamic Law and Jurisprudence.* The Hague, London, and New York: Kluwer Law International.

Arabic Wikipedia. 2005. "The Iraqi Constitution" [in Arabic]. http://tinyurl.com/y6hua4.

Arat, Yeşim. 2000. "Gender and Citizenship in Turkey." In *Gender and Citizenship in the Middle East*, ed. Suad Joseph, 275–86. Syracuse: Syracuse Univ. Press.

Arat, Yeşim, and Ayşe Gül Altinay. 2007. *Türkiye'de Kadına Yönelik Şiddet* [Violence Against Women in Turkey]. Istanbul: Punto.

Arat, Zehra F. 1994a. "Kemalism and Turkish Women." *Women and Politics* 14: 57–80.

———. 1994b. "Liberation or Indoctrination: Women's Education in Turkey." *Journal of Economics and Administrative Studies* 8: 83–105.

————, ed. 1998a. *Deconstructing Images of "the Turkish Woman."* New York: St. Martin's Press.

————. 1998b. "Educating the Daughters of the Republic." In *Deconstructing Images of "the Turkish Woman,"* ed. Zehra F. Arat, 157–80. New York: St. Martin's Press.

————. 2000. "Women's Rights in Islam: Revisiting Qur'anic Rights." In *Human Rights: New Perspectives, New Realities,* ed. A. Pollis and P. Schwab, 69–93. Boulder: Lynne Rienner.

————. 2005. "Human Rights and Globalization: Is the Shrinking World Expanding Rights?" *Human Rights and Human Welfare* 5: 137–46. http://www.du.edu/gsis/hrhw/volumes/2005/arat-2005.pdf.

————, ed. Forthcoming. *Human Rights in Turkey: Policies and Prospects.* Philadelphia: Univ. of Pennsylvania Press.

Arat, Zehra F., and Thomas W. Smith. 2007. "The EU and Human Rights in Turkey: Political Freedom Without Social Welfare?" Paper presented at the annual conference of the International Studies Association, Chicago, Feb. 28–Mar. 3.

Asad, Talal. 1993. *Genealogies of Religion: Discipline and Reasons of Power in Christianity and Islam.* Baltimore: John Hopkins Univ. Press.

————. 2003. *Formations of the Secular: Christianity, Islam, Modernity.* Stanford: Stanford Univ. Press.

Asian Development Bank. 2004. "Gender and Social Justice by Ain O Shalish Kendro—ASK." http://www.adb.org/gender/working/ban001.asp.

Al-Azmeh, Aziz. 1996. *Islams and Modernities.* 2nd ed. London and New York: Verso Books.

Bachiri, Amal, and Ahmed Chahine. 2003. Jointly interviewed by Frances Hasso. Dubai, UAE, Dec. 4.

Badran, Margot. 1995. *Feminists, Islam, and Nation: Gender and the Making of Modern Egypt.* Princeton: Princeton Univ. Press.

Al-Bah, Jamal Bin Obaid. 2003. Interviewed by Frances Hasso. Dubai, UAE, Dec. 7.

Baker, Alison. 1998. *Voices of Resistance: Oral Histories of Moroccan Women.* Albany: State Univ. of New York Press.

Bangladesh Legal Profile. n.d. Emory Univ. Law School Islamic Family Law Project. http://www.law.emory.edu/IFL/legal/bangladesh.htm.

Barazangi, Nimat Hafez. 1997. "Muslim Women's Islamic Higher Learning as a Human Right." In *Muslim Women and the Politics of Participation: Implementing the Beijing Platform,* ed. Mahnaz Afkhami and Erika Friedl, 43–57. Syracuse: Syracuse Univ. Press.

Bardhan, Pranab. 1997. "The State Against Society: The Great Divide in Social Science Discourse." In *Nationalism, Democracy, and Development: State and Politics in India*, ed. Sugata Bose and Ayesha Jalal. New Delhi: Oxford Univ. Press.

Basappa v. Parvatamma. 1952. Hyderabad High Court Full Bench. *All India Reporter.* Nagpur: All India Reporter.

Basu, Monmayee. 2001. *Hindu Women and Marriage Law: From Sacrament to Contract.* New Delhi: Oxford Univ. Press.

Batatu, Hanna. 1986. "Shi'ite Organizations in Iraq: Al-Da'wah al-Islamiyah and al-Mujahidin." In *Shi'ism and Social Protest*, ed. Juan R. I. Cole and Nikki R. Keddie, 179–200. New Haven: Yale Univ. Press.

Beneria, Lourdes, and Martha Roldan. 1987. *The Crossroad of Class and Gender: Industrial Home Workers, Subcontracting, and Household Dynamics in Mexico City.* Chicago: Univ. of Chicago Press.

Bennani, Farida. 1997. "La condition de la femme au Maroc." In *Droits de citoyenneté des femmes au Maghreb*, 146–73. Casablanca: Le Fennec.

Berik, Günseli. 1984. *Women Carpet Weavers in Rural Turkey: Patterns of Employment, Earnings, and Status.* Geneva: International Labor Organization.

Bhargava, Rajeev, ed. 1998. *Secularism and Its Critics.* Delhi: Oxford Univ. Press.

Bhola Umar v. Kausilla. 1933. *Indian Law Reports, Allahabad Series.* Calcutta: Government Press.

Bin Redha, Abdul Redha Ali. 2003. Interviewed by Frances Hasso. Dubai, UAE, Dec. 11.

Blair, Harry. 2003. "Civil Society, Dispute Resolution, and Local Governance in Bangladesh: Ideas for Pro-poor Programme Support." Dhaka: Report prepared for the Department for International Development, UK High Commission.

Bose, Sugata, and Ayesha Jalal, eds. 1997. *Nationalism, Democracy, and Development: State and Politics in India.* New Delhi: Oxford Univ. Press.

Bouhdiba, Abdelwahab. 1998. *Sexuality in Islam.* Trans. Alan Sheridan. London: Saqi Books. Originally published as *La sexualité en Islam.* Paris: Presses Universitaires de France, 1975.

Brand, Laurie A. 1998. *Women, the State, and Political Liberalization: Middle Eastern and North African Experiences.* New York: Columbia Univ. Press.

Braude, Joseph. 2005. "American Soft Power and the Women of the Middle East: Gender Gap." *New Republic,* TNR Online, Mar. 18. https://ssl.tnr.com/p/docsub .mhtml?i=w050314&s=braude031805.

Bremer, L. Paul, III, with Malcolm McConnell. 2006. *My Year in Iraq: The Struggle to Build a Future of Hope.* New York: Simon and Schuster.

Brown, Nathan J. 2002. *Constitutions in a Nonconstitutional World: Arab Basic Laws and the Prospects for Accountable Government.* Albany: State Univ. of New York Press.

Buncombe, Andrew. 2005. "Iraqi Activist Taken Up by Bush Recants Her Views." *The Independent,* Aug. 28. http://news.independent.co.uk/world/middle_east/article308604.ece.

Burton, Antoinette. 1999. Review of *Contentious Traditions: The Debate on Sati in Colonial India,* by Lata Mani. *American Historical Review* 104: 1281–82.

Butalia, Urvashi. 1998. *The Other Side of Silence: Voices from the Partition of India.* New Delhi: Viking, Penguin Books, India.

Çağlayan, Handan. 2007. *Analar, Yoldaşlar, Tanrıçalar: Kürt Harekentinde Kadınlar ve Kadın Kimliğinin Oluşumu* [Mothers, Comrades, and Goddesses: Women and the Formation of Gender Identity in the Kurdish Movement]. Istanbul: İletişim.

Çalışmaya Hazır İşgücü Olarak Kentli Kadın ve Değişimi [Urban Women as a Potential Workforce and Its Transformation]. 1999. Ankara: T. C. Başbakanlık, Kadın Statüsü ve Sorunları Genel Müdürülüğü.

Carroll, Lucy. 1989. "Law Custom and Statutory Social Reform: The Hindu Widows Remarriage Act, 1856." In *Women in Colonial India: Essays on Survival, Work, and the State,* ed. J. Krishnamurty, 1–26. Delhi: Oxford Univ. Press.

Carroll, Rory. 2005. "Women Fear Iraqi Constitution." *The Guardian,* Aug. 16.

Census of India, 1921. 1924. Calcutta: Superintendent Government Printing.

Centlivres-Demont, Micheline. 1994. "Afghan Women in Peace, War, and Exile." In *The Politics of Transformation in Afghanistan, Iran, and Pakistan,* ed. Myron Weiner and Ali Banuazizi. Syracuse: Syracuse Univ. Press.

Chakravarthy, U. 1989. "Whatever Happened to the Vedic Dasi? Orientalism, Nationalism, and a Script for the Past." In *Recasting Women: Essays in Colonial History,* ed. K. Sangari and S. Vaid, 27–87. New Delhi: Kali for Women.

Chandra, Bipan. 1989. *Communalism in Modern India.* New Delhi: Vikas.

Chandra, Sudhir. 1998. *Enslaved Daughters: Colonialism, Law, and Women's Rights.* New Delhi: Oxford Univ. Press.

Charrad, Mounira M. 1996. "State and Gender in the Maghrib." In *Arab Women: Between Defiance and Restraint,* ed. Suha Sabbagh, 221–28. New York: Olive Branch Press.

———. 1997. "Policy Shifts: State, Islam, and Gender in Tunisia, 1930s–1990s." *Social Politics* 4, no. 2: 285–319.

———. 1998. "Cultural Diversity Within Islam: Veils and Laws in Tunisia." In *Women in Muslim Societies: Diversity Within Unity,* ed. Herbert L. Bodman and Nayereh Tohidi, 63–79. Boulder: Lynne Rienner.

————. 2001. *States and Women's Rights: The Making of Postcolonial Tunisia, Algeria, and Morocco*. Berkeley and Los Angeles: Univ. of California Press.

Chatterjee, Partha. 1994. *The Nation and Its Fragments: Colonial and Postcolonial Histories*. Delhi and New York: Oxford Univ. Press.

————. 1998. "Secularism and Tolerance." In *Secularism and Its Critics*, ed. Rajeev Bhargava. Delhi: Oxford Univ. Press.

Chhachi, Amrita. 1994. "Identity Politics, Secularism, and Women: A South Asian Perspective." In *Forging Identities: Gender, Communities, and the State in India*, ed. Zoya Hasan. New Delhi: Kali for Women.

Chhachi, Amrita, Farida Khan, Gautam Navlakha, Kumkum Sangari, Neera Malik, Ritu Menon, Tanika Sarkar, Uma Chakravarty, Urvashi Butalia, and Zoya Hasan. 1998. "UCC and Women's Movement." *Economic and Political Weekly*, Feb. 28, 487–88.

Choudhury, G. W. 1969. *Constitutional Development in Pakistan*. Vancouver: Univ. of British Columbia Press.

Chowdhry, Prem. 1989. "Customs in a Peasant Economy: Women in Colonial Haryana." In *Recasting Women*, ed. Kumkum Sangari and Sudesh Vaid, 302–36. New Delhi: Kali for Women.

————. 1994. *The Veiled Women: Shifting Gender Equations in Rural Haryana, 1880–1990*. New Delhi: Oxford Univ. Press.

Christensen, Hanne. 1990. *The Reconstruction of Afghanistan: A Chance for Rural Afghan Women*. Geneva: United Nations Research Institute for Social Development.

Christensen, Hanne, and Scott Wolf. 1988. *Survey of Social and Economic Conditions of Afghan Refugees in Pakistan*. Geneva: United Nations Research Institute for Social Development.

Chukri, Farid. 2000. "The Code of Personal Status." In *Women's Rights Between Crisis and Alternative*, ed. Khadija Mufid, 15–31 [in Arabic]. Casablanca: Dar al-Furqan.

CIEDS Collective and EKTA. 1990. *Beyond Darkness: Some Reflections on Communalism*. Bangalore, India: CIEDS Collective and EKTA.

Coalition Provisional Authority (CPA). 2004. "Bush Calls Women's Rights and Liberty 'Inseparable.'" Coalition Provisional Authority, Mar. 12. http://www.iraqcoalition.org/transcripts/20040312_bush_women.html.

Cobban, Helena. 2003. "Oxford Survey on Iraqi Opinion." Dec. 2. http://just worldnews.org/archives/000374.html.

Cole, Juan, ed. 1992. *Comparing Muslim Societies*. Ann Arbor: Univ. of Michigan Press.

———. 2003. "The United States and Shi'ite Religious Factions in Post-Ba'thist Iraq." *Middle East Journal* 57, no. 4: 543–66.

———. 2006. *The Ayatollahs and Democracy in Iraq.* Institute for the Study of Islam in the Modern World Annual Lecture. Amsterdam: Amsterdam Univ. Press.

Cole, Sally. 1998. "Reconstituting Households, Retelling Culture: Emigration and Portuguese Fisheries Workers in Canada." In *Transgressing Borders: Critical Perspectives on Gender, Household, and Culture,* ed. Suzan Ilcan and Lynne Phillips, 13–32. Westport, Conn.: Bergin and Garvey.

Coleman, Isobel. 2006. "Women, Islam, and the New Iraq." *Foreign Affairs* 85, no. 1. http://www.foreignaffairs.org/20060101faessay85104/isobel-coleman/women-islam-and-the-new-iraq.html.

Collectif 95 Maghreb Égalité. 1995. *One Hundred Measures and Provisions for a Maghrebian Egalitarian Codification of the Personal Statute and Family Law.* Rabat: Friedrich Ebert Stiftung.

Comparative Index to Islam. 2002. "Misyar Marriage." http://www.answering-islam.org/Index/M/misyar.html.

Constable, Pamela. 2004. "Iraqi Women Decry Move to Cut Rights." *Washington Post,* Jan. 16.

Corrigan, Philip Richard D. 1981. "On Moral Regulation: Some Preliminary Remarks." *Sociological Review* 29: 313–37.

———. 1990. "State Formation (Entry for a Dictionary) (1986)." In *Social Forms/Human Capacities: Essays in Authority and Difference,* by Philip Richard D. Corrigan, 264–68. London and New York: Routledge.

———. 1994a. "Commentary and Debate/*Commentaire et debat*: Undoing the Overdone State." *Canadian Journal of Sociology/Cahiers Canadiens de Sociologie* 19: 249–55.

———. 1994b. "State Formation." In *Everyday Forms of State Formation: Revolution and Negotiation of Rule in Modern Mexico,* ed. Joseph M. Gilbert and Daniel Nugent, xvii–xix. Durham: Duke Univ. Press.

———. 2002. "Some Further Notes on the Difficulty of Studying the State, England, and the First Empire, 1975 Onwards." *Journal of Historical Sociology* 15: 120–65.

Corrigan, Philip Richard D., and Derek Sayer. 1985. *The Great Arch: English State Formation as Cultural Revolution.* London: Basil Blackwell.

Cuno, Kenneth M. 1992. *The Pasha's Peasants: Land, Society, and Economy in Lower Egypt, 1740–1858.* Cambridge: Cambridge Univ. Press.

————. 2008. "Divorce and the Fate of the Family in Modern Egypt." In *Family in the Middle East: Ideational Change in Egypt, Iran, and Tunisia,* ed. Kathryn Yount and Hoda Rashad, 196–216. London: Routledge.

Dadaji Bhikaji v. Rukhmabai. 1885. Bombay High Court.

Dadaji Bhikaji v. Rukhmabai. 1886. 10 Bombay High Court.

Dainik Sangbad. 1994. Dhaka, Aug. 12.

Damietta Divorce Register. 1897–1898. Egyptian National Archives. Sharia Court of Damietta. Divorce Registers. *Ma'dhun* Muhammad al-Nahhas, old no. 52, new no. 1, 9 Dhu al-Qa'da 1314–12 Sha'ban 1315 (Apr. 11, 1897–Jan. 6, 1898) [in Arabic].

Daoud, Zakya. 1993. *Feminism et politique au Magreb, soixante ans de lutte.* Maison-neuve and Larose. Casablanca: Eddif.

————. 1998. "Femmes, movements feminists, et changement social au Maghreb." In *Islam et changement social,* 249–59. Lausanne: Payot.

Daqahliyya Legal Proceedings. 1899, 1909. Egyptian National Archives. Court of the Province of al-Daqahliyya. Legal Proceedings *(murafa'at)* registers. No. 44, Jan.–Dec. 1899, and no. 65. Jan.–Dec. 1909 [in Arabic].

Daragahi, Borzou. 2005. "Draft Constitution Covers Diverse Interests." *Global News Wire: Asia Africa Intelligence Wire,* Aug. 30.

Darwiche, Nawla. 2003. Interviewed by Frances Hasso. Mohandeseen, Cairo, Egypt, Dec. 22.

"Debate Flares Up over the Decision of the Iraqi Governing Council to Apply the Sharia to Cases of Personal Status" [in Arabic]. 2004. *Al-Sharq al-Awsat,* Jan. 27.

Deeb, Sarah El. 2004. "Iraqi Women Deal with a Mixed Legacy." Associated Press, Jan. 26.

Denoeux, G., and L. Gateau. 1995. "L'essor des associations au Maroc: A la recher-che de la citoyenneté." *Magreb-Machrek* 150: 19–39.

Dergham, Raghidah. 2004. *Al-Hayat,* Feb. 28.

Deringil, Selim. 1998. *The Well-Protected Domains: Ideology and the Legitimation of Power in the Ottoman Empire, 1876–1909.* London: I. B. Tauris.

Derrett, J. D. M. 1957. *Hindu Law Past and Present: Being an Account of the Controversy Which Preceded the Enactment of the Hindu Code, the Text of the Code as Enacted, and Some Comments Thereon.* Calcutta: A. Mukherjee.

Derrida, Jacques. 1978. "From Restricted to General Economy: A Hegelianism With-out Reserve." Chap. 9 in *Writing and Difference.* Chicago: Univ. of Chicago Press.

Desai, Manisha. 1997. "Constructing/Deconstructing 'Women': Reflections from the Contemporary Women's Movement in India." In *Feminism and the New Democracies: Resiting the Political,* ed. Jodi Dean. New York: Sage.

———. 2001. "India: Women's Rights from Nationalism to Sustainable Development." In *Women's Rights: A Global Perspective*, ed. Lynn Walters. Westport, Conn.: Greenwood.

Deutsche Presse-Agentur. 1995. "101 Lashes for Women Who Refused to Wed." *Seattle Times*, Oct. 22. http://www/corpur.com/bdju9510.htm.

Al-Dhahabi, al-Sayyid Mustafa b. Hanafi. 1997. *The Report of al-Sayyid Mustafa . . . al-Dahabi on the Commentary of al-Sharqawi on* [Zakariya al-Ansari's] *The Gift to the Students on* [Ansari's] *Explication of the Emancipating of the Reexamination of the Quintessence* [in Arabic]. 4 vols. Beirut: Dar al-Kutub al-Ilmiyya.

Dhavan, Rajeev. 1997. *Law and Society in Modern India*. New Delhi: Oxford Univ. Press.

Diamond, Larry. 2005. *Squandered Victory: The American Occupation and the Bungled Effort to Bring Democracy to Iraq*. New York: Times Books.

Al-Diqqi, Hisa. 2003. Interviewed by Frances Hasso. Dubai, UAE, Dec. 8.

Directory of Women's Organizations in Turkey, 2003. 2003. http://supurge.dincsa.com/index.php?lang=eng.

Diyarbakır Barosu. 2006. *Law No. 4320 on the Protection of Family* [in Turkish]. Diyarbakır Araştırma Raporu. Diyarbakır: Diyarbakır Barosu.

Douie, J. M. 1931. *The Punjab Land Administration Manual*. Chandigarh: Government of Punjab.

Dupree, Louis. 1973. *Afghanistan*. Princeton: Princeton Univ. Press.

Dupree, Nancy Hatch. 1984. "Women and Emancipation Before the Saur Revolution." In *Revolution and Rebellion in Afghanistan*, ed. Nazif Shahrani and Robert Canfield. Berkeley: Institute for International Studies.

Durakbaşa, Ayşe. 1998. "Kemalism as Identity Politics in Turkey." In *Deconstructing Images of "the Turkish Woman,"* ed. Zehra F. Arat, 139–56. New York: St. Martin's Press.

Dwyer, Daisy Hilse, and Judith Bruce, eds. 1988. *A Home Divided: Women and Income in the Third World*. Stanford: Stanford Univ. Press.

Ecevit, Yıldız. 1991. "Shop Floor Control: The Ideological Construction of Turkish Women Factory Workers." In *Working Women: International Perspectives on Labour and Gender Ideology*, ed. N. Redclift and M. T. Sinclair, 59–69. New York: Routledge.

———. 1998. "A Gender Analysis of Women's Wage-Labor in Turkey." In *Women and Men in 75 Years*, 267–84 [in Turkish]. Istanbul: Türkiye Ekonomik ve Toplumsal Tarih Vakfı.

————. 2007. "Women's Rights, Women's Organizations, and the State." In *Human Rights in Turkey: Policies and Prospects,* ed. Zehra F. Kabasakal Arat, 197–201. Philadelphia: Univ. of Pennsylvania Press.

Efrati, Noga. 2005. "Negotiating Rights in Iraq: Women and the Personal Status Law." *Middle East Journal* 59, no. 4: 577–95.

Egypt. 1898. *Inventory of High Orders and Decrees Issued in the Year 1897* [in Arabic]. Bulaq, Egypt: Government Press.

El Afify, Nadia Abdel Wahab. 2003. Interviewed by Frances Hasso. Cairo, Egypt, Dec. 28.

Engineer, Asghar Ali. 1992. *The Rights of Women in Islam.* New York: St. Martin's Press.

Englard, Itzhak. 1987. "Law and Religion in the State of Israel." *American Journal of Comparative Law* 35.

Enloe, Cynthia. 1989. *Bananas, Beaches, and Bases: Making Feminist Sense of International Politics.* Berkeley and Los Angeles: Univ. of California Press.

————. 2004. *The Curious Feminist: Searching for Women in a New Age of Empire.* Berkeley and Los Angeles: Univ. of California Press.

Ertürk, Yakın, and Nüket Kardam. 1999. "Expanding Gender Accountability? Women's Organizations and the State in Turkey." *International Journal of Organization Theory and Behavior* 2: 167–97.

Esposito, John L., and Natana J. DeLong-Bas. 2001. *Women in Muslim Family Law.* 2nd ed. New York: Syracuse Univ. Press.

"Ev İşi Kimin İşi" [Whose Work Is Housework?]. 2006. BİA Haber Merkezi. http://www.bianet.org/2006/01/20/73566.htm.

Fam, Mariam, and Mandy McClure. 2000. "Gay Marriage Results in Prosecution." *Cairo Times Online,* Apr. 20–26. http://www.sodomylaws.org/world/egypt/egnews01.htm.

"Fatwas in Bangladesh." 1996. In *Fatwas Against Women in Bangladesh,* 76–79. Montpellier: Women Living under Muslim Laws. Available at http://www.wluml.org/english/pubs/pdf/misc/fatwa-bangladesh-eng.pdf.

Fawaz, Leila Tarazi, and C. A. Bayly, eds. 2002. *Modernity and Culture: From the Mediterranean to the Indian Ocean.* New York: Columbia Univ. Press.

Fayyad, Ma'd. 2004. "Iraqi Governing Council Repeals Decree 137" [in Arabic]. *Al-Sharq al-Awsat,* Feb. 28.

————. 2005. "Iraqi MP Reveals Details of the Longest Night in the National Assembly" [in Arabic]. *Al-Sharq al-Awsat,* Aug. 17.

———. 2006. "Mariam Areyyes to al-Sharq al-Awsat" [in Arabic]. *Al-Sharq al-Awsat,* Oct. 29.

Feldman, Shelley. 1988. Field notes.

———. 1990. Field notes.

———. 1996. Field notes.

———. 1997. "NGOs and Civil Society: (Un)stated Contradictions." *Annals of the American Academy of Political and Social Science* 55: 46–65.

———. 2001. "Exploring Theories of Patriarchy: A Perspective from Contemporary Bangladesh." *Signs* 26: 1097–1127.

Feldman, Shelley, and Florence McCarthy. 1983. "*Purdah* and Changing Patterns of Social Control among Rural Women in Bangladesh." *Journal of Marriage and the Family* 45: 949–59.

———. 1984. *Rural Women and Development in Bangladesh: Selected Issues.* Oslo: NORAD, Ministry of Development Cooperation.

Feyzioğlu, Feyzi Necmeddin. 1986. *Family Law* [in Turkish]. 3rd ed. Istanbul: Filiz Kitabevi.

Filkin, Dexter. 2005. "Secular Iraqis Say New Charter May Curb Rights." *New York Times,* Aug. 24.

Gandhi, Nandita, and Nandita Shah. 1991. *Issues at Stake: Theory and Practice in the Contemporary Women's Movement in India.* New Delhi: Kali for Women.

Gargash, Samira Abdulla. 2003. Interviewed by Frances Hasso. Dubai, UAE, Dec. 8.

Al-Gawhary, Karim. 1995. "Sex Tourism in Cairo." *Middle East Report* 25, no. 196: 26–27.

Ghabish, Saleha Obaid. 2003. Interviewed by Frances Hasso. Sharjah, UAE, Dec. 16.

Glenn, Evelyn N. 1999. "The Social Construction and Institutionalization of Gender and Race." In *Revisioning Gender,* ed. Myra Marx Ferree, Judith Lorber, and Beth B. Hess, 3–43. New Delhi and London: Sage.

Gök, Fatma, and Deniz Ilgaz. 2007. "The Right to Education: The Turkish Case." In *Human Rights in Turkey: Policies and Prospects,* ed. Zehra F. Arat. Philadelphia: Univ. of Pennsylvania Press.

Goldberg, Ellis. 1992. "Smashing Idols and the State: The Protestant Ethic and Egyptian Sunni Radicalism." In *Comparing Muslim Societies,* ed. Juan R. I. Cole, 195–236. Ann Arbor: Univ. of Michigan Press.

Granzer, Sieglinde. 1999. "Changing Discourse: Transnational Advocacy Network in Tunisia and Morocco." In *The Power of Human Rights: International Norms and Domestic Changes,* ed. Thomas Rissa, Stephen C. Ropp, and Kathryn Sik-kink. Cambridge: Cambridge Univ. Press.

Griffiths, John C. 1967. *Afghanistan.* New York: Fredrick A. Praeger.

Group interview with three women faculty (Mona al-Bahr, Maryam Sultan Lou-tah, and Najat Muhammad Rida) by Frances Hasso. 2003. United Arab Emirates National Univ., Dec. 9.

Group interview with six men students by Frances Hasso. 2003. United Arab Emirates National Univ., al-Ain, Abu Dhabi, Dec. 9.

Group interview with seven women students by Frances Hasso. 2003. Sharjah Univ., women's campus, Sharjah, UAE, Dec. 14.

Group interview with nine women students by Frances Hasso. 2003. Cairo Univ., Cairo, Egypt, Dec. 27.

Gümüşoğlu, Firdevs. 1998. "Gender Roles in Textbooks of the Republican Era." In *Women and Men in 75 Years,* 101–28 [in Turkish]. Istanbul: Türkiye Ekonomik ve Toplumsal Tarih Vakfı.

Güneş-Ayata, Ayşe. 2001. "The Politics of Implementing Women's Rights in Turkey." In *Globalization, Gender, and Religion: The Politics of Women's Rights in Catholic and Muslim Contexts,* ed. J. Bayes and N. Tohidi, 157–77. New York: Palgrave.

Haeri, Shahla. 1989. *Law of Desire: Temporary Marriage in Shi'i Iran.* Syracuse: Syracuse Univ. Press.

Haider, Iqbal. 2005. "Life under the Hasba Law." *Dawn,* July 30. http://www.dawn.com/2005/07/30/op,htm#3.

Hammami, Rema. 2004. "Attitudes Toward Legal Reform of Personal Status Law in Palestine." In *Women's Rights and Islamic Family Law: Perspectives on Reform,* ed. Lynn Welchman, 125–43. London: Zed Press.

Hammami, Rema, and Penny Johnson. 1999. "Equality with a Difference: Gender and Citizenship in Transitional Palestine." *Social Politics* 6, no. 3: 314–43.

Hamzawi, Riad Amin. 2003. Interviewed by Frances Hasso. Al-Ain, Abu Dhabi, UAE, Dec. 9.

Haris, Ziad. 2004. "Sharia Religious Law Takes on a Secular Past in Iraq." *Deutsche Presse-Agentur,* Jan. 21.

Hasan, Aznan. 2003. "Granting Khul' for a Non-Muslim Couple in Egyptian Personal Status Law: Generosity or Laxity?" *Arab Law Quarterly:* 81–89.

Hasan, K. M. Justice. 2001. "A Report on Mediation in the Family Courts: Bangladesh Experience." In *Conference of the Family Courts of Australia.* Sydney.

Hashmi, Taj I. 2000. *Women and Islam in Bangladesh: Beyond Subjection and Tyranny.* London: Macmillan.

Hasso, Frances. 2007. "Comparing Emirati and Egyptian Narratives on Marriage, Sexuality, and the Body." In *Global Migration, Social Change, and Cultural Transformation,* ed. Emory Elliott, Jasmine Payne, and Patricia Ploesch, 59–76. New York: Palgrave/Macmillan.

Hauftman, Z. 1995. "Rape: The Basis of Consent and the Laws of Evidence" [in Hebrew]. In *Woman's Status in Israeli Law and Society,* ed. Frances Raday, Carmel Shalev, and Michal Liban-Kobi, 189–234. Tel Aviv: Shocken.

Hijab, Nadia. 1988. *Womanpower: The Arab Debate on Women at Work.* Cambridge: Cambridge Univ. Press.

Hill, Enid. 1979. *Mahkama! Studies in the Egyptian Legal System.* London: Ithaca Press.

Hobsbawm, Eric, and Terence Ranger, eds. 1983. *The Invention of Tradition.* New York: Cambridge Univ. Press.

Hoodfar, Homa. 1991. "Return to the Veil: Personal Strategies and Public Participation in Egypt." In *Working Women: International Perspectives on Labour and Gender Ideology,* ed. Nanneke Redclift and M. Thea Sinclair. London: Routledge.

———. 1996a. "The Impact of Egyptian Male Migration on Urban Families: Feminization of Egyptian Families or Reaffirmation of Traditional Gender Roles?" In *Development, Change, and Gender in Cairo: A View from the Household,* ed. Diane Singerman and Homa Hoodfar. Bloomington: Indiana Univ. Press.

———, ed. 1996b. *Shifting Boundaries of Marriage and Divorce in Muslim Communities.* Montpellier: Women Living under Muslim Laws.

———. 1997. *Between Marriage and the Market: Intimate Politics and Survival in Cairo.* Berkeley and Los Angeles: Univ. of California Press.

———. 1999. *The Women's Movement in Iran: Women at the Crossroad of Secularization and Islamization.* Montpellier: Women Living under Muslim Laws.

———. 2000. "Culture and Religion: Assets or Hindrance to Advancing Iranian Women's Economic and Property Rights." In *Securing Women's Rights to Land, Property, and Housing: Country Strategies.* Montreal: Rights and Democracy.

———. 2001. "Iranian Women at the Intersection of Citizenship and the Family Code: The Perils of Islamic Criteria." In *Women and Citizenship in the Middle East,* ed. Suad Joseph. Syracuse: Syracuse Univ. Press.

———. 2003. "The Impact of Egyptian Male Migration on Urban Families: Feminization of the Egyptian Families or Reaffirmation of Traditional Gender Roles?" In *Sociology of Gender: The Challenge of Feminist Sociological Knowledge,* edited by Sharmila Rege. New Delhi: Sage.

————. 2004. "Families on the Move: The Changing Role of Afghan Refugee Women in Iran." *Hawwa: Journal of Women of the Middle East and the Islamic World* 2, no. 2: 141–71.

————. 2007. "Women, Religion, and the Afghan Education Movement in Iran." *Journal of Development Studies* 43, no. 2: 265–93.

————. Forthcoming. "Trials and Tribulations of Repatriation: Afghan Refugee Youth in Iran." In *Children and Armed Conflict,* ed. Jason Hart. Basingstoke: Falmer Press.

Horowitz, Richard S. 2004. "International Law and State Transformation in China, Siam, and the Ottoman Empire During the Nineteenth Century." *Journal of World History* 15: 445–86.

Hossain, Sara, and Suzanne Turner. 2004. "Abduction for Forced Marriage: Rights and Remedies in Bangladesh and Pakistan." International Centre for the Legal Protection of Human Rights (INTERIGHTS). http://www.soas.ac.uk/honourcrimes/FMarticleHossain.pdf.

Howard, Rhoda E. 1995. "Women's Rights and the Right to Development." In *Women's Rights, Human Rights, International Feminist Perspectives,* ed. Julie Peters and Andrea Wolper, 301–13. London: Routledge.

Human Development Report, 1999. 1999. United Nations Development Programme. New York: Oxford Univ. Press.

Human Development Report, 2007/2008. 2007. United Nations Development Programme. New York: Oxford Univ. Press.

Human Rights Watch. 2003. "Background on Women's Status in Iraq Prior to the Fall of the Saddam Hussein Government." Nov. http://www.hrw.org/backgrounder/wrd/iraq-women.htm.

Human Rights Watch/Asia. 1994. "Bangladesh: Violence and Discrimination in the Name of Religion." 1–8.

Hunt, Swanee, and Cristina Posa. 2004. "Where Are the Women in the New Iraq?" *Boston Globe,* June 22. http://www.ksg.harvard.edu/news/opeds/2004/hunt_iraqwomen_bg_062204.htm.

Ibn Abidin, Shaykh Muhammad Amin. 1905–1908. *The Response of the Discussant to the Selected Pearls, a Commentary on the Illumination of Vision, on the Jurisprudence of the School of the Great Imam Abu Hanifa the Blessed* [in Arabic]. 5 vols. Bulaq, Egypt: Government Press.

İlkkaracan, İpek. 1998. "Urban Women and Work Life." In *Women and Men in 75 Years,* 285–303 [in Turkish]. Istanbul: Türkiye Ekonomik ve Toplumsal Tarih Vakfı.

İlyasoğlu, Aynur. 1998. "Islamist Women in Turkey: Their Identity and Self-Image." In *Deconstructing Images of "the Turkish Woman,"* ed. Zehra F. Arat, 241–62. New York: St. Martin's Press.

İnsan Hakları Açısından Kadının Durumu, Sorunları ve Çözüm Önerileri [Women's Status, Problems, and Proposed Solutions from a Human Rights Perspective]. 1999. Ankara: İnsan Hakları Koordinator Üst Kurulu.

"Iraqi Women Demand 40% Share of Political Power." 2004. Middle East Online, Feb. 18. http://www.middle-east-online.com/english/?id=8943.

Iraq Press. 2004. "Civil Status Courts Must Apply Islamic Shariah, IGC Says." Jan. 3. http://www.theworldpress.com/press/iraqpress.htm.

Islam, Tabibul. 1997. "Bangladesh: Rising Wave of Violence Against Women." *Dossier* 18: 134–36. Montpellier: Women Living under Muslim Laws.

Ismael, Jacqueline S., and Shereen T. Ismael. 2000. "Gender and State in Iraq." In *Gender and Citizenship in the Middle East,* ed. Suad Joseph, 185–211. Syracuse: Syracuse Univ. Press.

Jaffrelot, Christophe, ed. 2002. *Pakistan: Nationalism Without a Nation?* London: Zed Books.

Jahan, Roushan. 1988a. *Hidden Danger: Women and Family Violence in Bangladesh.* Dhaka: Women for Women.

———. 1988b. "Hidden Wounds, Visible Scars: Violence Against Women in Bangladesh." In *Structures of Patriarchy,* ed. B. Agarwal, 199–227. London: Zed Books.

Jallad, Filib. 1890–1892. *Dictionary of Administration and the Judiciary* [in Arabic]. 4 vols. Alexandria: Matba'at Yani Laghudaki.

Al-Jamil, Sayyar. 2004. "The Personal Status Law in Iraq: Not an Everyday Document" [in Arabic]. *Al-Zaman,* Jan. 19. http://www.azzaman.com/azz/articles/2004/01/01-18/698.htm.

Jayal, Niraja Gopal. 1999. *Democracy and the State: Welfare, Secularism, and Development in Contemporary India.* Delhi: Oxford Univ. Press.

Jayawardena, Kumari. 1986. *Feminism and Nationalism in the Third World.* London: Zed Books.

Johnson, Penny. 2004. "Agents for Reform: The Women's Movement, Social Politics, and Family Law Reform." In *Women's Rights and Islamic Family Law: Perspectives on Reform,* ed. Lynn Welchman, 144–63. London: Zed Press.

Joseph, Suad. 1991. "Elite Strategies for State-Building: Women, Family, Religion, and State in Iraq and Lebanon." In *Women, Islam, and the State,* ed. Deniz Kandiyoti, 176–200. Philadelphia: Temple Univ. Press.

————, ed. 2000a. *Gender and Citizenship in the Middle East.* Syracuse: Syracuse Univ. Press.

————. 2000b. "Theoretical Introduction." In *Gender and Citizenship in the Middle East,* ed. Suad Joseph, 3–30. Syracuse: Syracuse Univ. Press.

————. 2001. *Women and Citizenship in the Middle East.* Syracuse: Syracuse Univ. Press.

Kabasakal, Hayat. 1998. "A Profile of Top Women Managers in Turkey." In *Deconstructing Images of "the Turkish Woman,"* ed. Zehra F. Arat, 225–40. New York: St. Martin's Press.

Kabeer, Naila. 1991. "The Quest for National Identity: Women, Islam, and the State in Bangladesh." *Feminist Review* 37: 38–58.

Kabir, Sandra M. 1996. "An Experience of Religious Extremism in Bangladesh." *Reproductive Health Matters* 8: 104–9.

Kaduthi v. Madu. 1884. *Indian Law Reports, Madras Series.* Madras: Government Press.

Kalaycıoğlu, Ersin, and Binnaz Toprak. 2004. *Women in Work Life, Top Management, and Politics* [in Turkish]. Istanbul: TESEV Yayınları.

Kalaycıoğlu, Sibel, and Helga Rittersberger. "Examining Work-Relations from a Women's Perspective." In *Women and Men in 75 Years,* 225–35 [in Turkish]. Istanbul: Türkiye Ekonomik ve Toplumsal Tarih Vakfı.

Kamal, Ahmad Husain. 1997. *Tarikh-i Jam'iyyat-I 'Ulama'-i Islam.* Lahore: Makki Darulkutub.

Kamal, Sultana. 1996. "Undermining Women's Rights." In *Fatwas Against Women in Bangladesh,* 69–74. Montpellier: Women Living under Muslim Laws. Available at http://www.wluml.org/english/pubs/pdf/misc/fatwa-bangladesh-eng.pdf.

————. 2001. *Her Unfearing Mind: Women and Muslim Laws in Bangladesh.* Dhaka: Ain O Salish Kendra (ASK).

————. 2004. "The Fate of 'Nurjahans' and the Constitution of Bangladesh." Dhaka: Ain O Salish Kendra (ASK). http://www/sacw/net/i_aii/Noorjehan .html.

Kamali, Mohammad Hashim. 1985. *Law in Afghanistan: A Study of the Constitutions, Matrimonial Law, and the Judiciary.* Leiden: E. Brill.

KA-MER 2003 Report. 2004. *Alışmayacağız! "Namus" Adına İşlenen Cinayetler 2003 Raporu* [We Will Not Get Used to It! 2003 Report on Killings in the Name of "Honor"] [in Turkish]. Diyarbakır: KA-MER.

Kandiyoti, Deniz. 1988. "Bargaining with Patriarchy." *Gender and Society* 2: 274–90.

———. 1991a. Introduction to *Women, Islam, and the State*, ed. Deniz Kandiyoti, 1–21. Philadelphia: Temple Univ. Press.

———, ed. 1991b. *Women, Islam, and the State*. Philadelphia: Temple Univ. Press.

———. 1992. "Women, Islam, and the State." In *Comparing Muslim Societies*, ed. Juan Cole, 237–60. Ann Arbor: Univ. of Michigan Press.

———. 1997. "Beyond Beijing: Obstacles and Prospects for the Middle East." In *Muslim Women and the Politics of Participation: Implementing the Beijing Platform*, ed. Mahnaz Afkhami and Erika Friedl, 3–10. Syracuse: Syracuse Univ. Press.

Kaplan, Caren, Norma Alarcón, and Minoo Moallem, eds. 1999. *Between Woman and Nation: Nationalisms, Transnational Feminisms, and the State*. Durham: Duke Univ. Press.

Kapur, Ratna, and Brenda Crossman. 1996. *Subversive Sites: Feminist Engagements with Law in India*. New Delhi: Sage.

Kar, Mehranguiz, and Homa Hoodfar. 1996. "Personal Status Law as Defined by the Islamic Republic of Iran: An Appraisal." In *Special Dossier: Shifting Boundaries in Marriage and Divorce in Muslim Communities*, 1:7–36. Montpellier: Women Living under Muslim Laws.

Kardam, Nuket. 2004. "The Emerging Global Gender Equality Regime from Neoliberal and Constructivist Perspectives." *International Feminist Journal of Politics* 6, no. 1: 95–109.

Kazgan, Gülten. 1979. "Women's Participation in the Workforce, Occupational Distribution, Educational Level, and Socioeconomic Status Within the Turkish Economy." In *Women in Turkish Society*, ed. Nermin Abadan-Unat, 137–70 [in Turkish]. Istanbul: Araştırma, Eğitim, Ekin Yayınları.

Keck, Margaret, and Kathryn Sikkink. 1998. *Activists Beyond Borders: Advocacy Networks in International Politics*. Ithaca: Cornell Univ. Press.

Kepel, Gilles. 1997. *Allah in the West: Islamic Movements in America and Europe*. Stanford: Stanford Univ. Press.

Khadr, Asma. 1998. *Law and the Future of Palestinian Women* [in Arabic]. Jerusalem: Women's Centre for Legal Aid and Counselling.

Khalil, Ashraf. 2004. "Women Call for Equal Representation in Iraq." *Women's Enews*, Inter Press Service, Feb. 5.

Al-Kitbi, Ebtisam Suheil. 2003. Interviewed by Frances Hasso. Dubai, UAE, Dec. 11.

Kjeilen, Tore. 2002. "Misyar Marriage." In *Encyclopaedia of the Orient*. Oslo. http://lexicorient.com/cgi-bin/eo-direct.pl?misyar.htm.

The Koran. 1974. Trans. M. J. Dawood. 4th ed. London: Penguin.

The Koran Interpreted. 1955. Trans. Arthur J. Arberry. New York: Macmillan.

Krane, Jim. 2004a. "Top Iraqi's Islamic Law Proposal Could Lead to Major Changes in Iraqi Life." Associated Press, Feb. 11.

———. 2004b. "U.S. Administrator Threatens Veto of Iraqi Islamic Law Measure." Associated Press, Feb. 16.

Al-Kubaisi, Ahmed. 2003. Interviewed by Frances Hasso. Dubai, UAE, Dec. 10.

Kumar, Radha. 1993. *The History of Doing: An Illustrated Account of Movements for Women's Rights and Feminism in India, 1800–1990.* New Delhi: Kali for Women.

Labadi, Fadwa. 2004. "The Making of a Fatwa: Muftis, Early Marriage, and Islamic Law." *Birzeit University Review of Women's Studies* 2: 72–84.

Lacoste-Dujardin, Camille, and Yves Lacoste. 1991. *L'état du Maghreb.* Casablanca: Le Fennec.

Lalit Mohan v. Shyamapada Das. 1952. Calcutta High Court. *All India Reporter.* Nagpur: All India Reporter.

Lintner, Bertil. 2003. "Bangladesh Extremist Islamist Consolidation." *Faultlines* 14. New Delhi: Institute of Conflict Management. http://www.satp.org/satporgtp/publication/faultlines/volume14/Article1.htm.

Lobe, Jim. 2004. "U.S. Lawmakers Warn of Brewing Crisis over Women's Rights in Iraq." CommonDreams.org News Center, Feb. 3. http://www.commondreams.org/headlines04/0203-06.htm.

Longinotto, Kim, and Ziba Mir-Hosseini. 1998. *Divorce Iranian Style* [videotape]. New York: Women Make Movies.

Lootah, Wedad Naser. 2003. Interviewed by Frances Hasso. Dubai, UAE, Dec. 6.

Lucas, Marie-Aimee Helie, and Harsh Kapoor, eds. 1996. *Fatwas Against Women in Bangladesh.* Montpellier: Women Living under Muslim Laws. http://www.wluml.org/english/pubs/pdf/misc/fatwa-bangladesh-eng.pdf.

MacFarquhar, Neil. 2005. "Paternity Suit Against TV Star Scandalizes Egyptians." *New York Times,* Jan. 26.

Mahmud, Arshad. 1987. "The Popular Justice of a Bangladesh Village Court." *The Guardian,* June 13.

Maley, William, ed. 1998. *Fundamentalism Reborn? Afghanistan and the Taliban.* Lahore: Vanguard Books.

Malti v. State of Uttar Pradesh I. 2001. Divorce and Matrimonial Court, Allahabad High Court.

Mani, Lata. 1989. "Contentious Traditions: The Debate on *Sati* in Colonial India." In *Recasting Women: Essays in India Colonial History,* ed. Kum Kum Sangari and Sudesh Vaid, 88–126. Delhi: Kali for Women.

Mansoor, Taslima. 1999. *From Patriarchy to Gender Equity: Family Law and Its Impact on Women in Bangladesh.* Dhaka: Univ. Press.

Mansura Legal Proceedings. 1857. Egyptian National Archives. Sharia Court of al-Mansura of First Instance. Legal Proceedings *(murafa'at)* register no. 281, 1 Shawwal 1273–13 Jumada I 1274 (May 25–Dec. 18, 1857) [in Arabic].

McCarthy, Florence, and Shelley Feldman. 1987. "Administrative Reforms in Bangladesh: Incorporation or Democratization?" *International Journal of Contemporary Sociology* 24: 99–111.

McMichael, Philip. 2000. *Development and Social Change: A Global Perspective.* 2nd ed. Thousand Oaks, Calif.: Pine Forge Press.

Mehran, Golnar. 1991. "The Creation of the New Muslim Women: Female Education in the Islamic Republic of Iran." *Convergence* 23, no. 4: 42–52.

———. 2002. "The Presentation of Self and Other in Post- Revolutionary Iranian School Textbooks." In *Iran and the Surrounding World,* edited by Nikki R. Kiddie and Rudi Matthee. Seattle: Univ. of Washington Press.

Menon, Nivedita. 1998. "State/Gender/Community: Citizenship in Contemporary India." *Economic and Political Weekly,* Jan. 31, 3–10.

Menon, Ritu, and Kamla Bhasin. 1998. *Borders and Boundaries: Women in India's Partition.* New Delhi: Kali for Women.

Menski, Werner F. 2003. *South Asian Muslim Law Today: An Overview.* Center for Applied South Asian Studies, Univ. of Manchester. http://www.art.man.ac.uk/CASAS/pdfpapers/southasianlaw.pdf.

Menski, Werner F., and Tahmina Rahman. 1988. "Hindus and the Law in Bangladesh." *South Asia Research* 8: 111–31.

Mernissi, Fatima. 1989. *Doing Daily Battle: Interviews with Moroccan Women.* Trans. Mary Jo Lakeland. New Brunswick: Rutgers Univ. Press.

Miadi, Zineb. 1997. "Le status de la femme Marocaine dans l'institution familiale." In *Droits de citoyenneté des femmes au Maghreb,* ed. Aïcha Belarbi, 210–23. Casablanca: Le Fennec.

Mies, Maria. 1986. *Patriarchy and Accumulation on a World Scale: Women in the International Division of Labor.* 2nd ed. New York: St. Martin's Press.

Mir-Hosseini, Ziba. 1993. *Marriage on Trial: A Study of Islamic Family Law, Iran, and Morocco Compared.* London and New York: I. B. Tauris.

———. 1996a. "Stretching the Limits: A Feminist Reading of the Sharia in Post-Khomeini Iran." In *Feminism and Islam: Legal and Literary Perspectives,* ed. Mai Yamani, 285–319. Reading: Ithaca Press.

———. 1996b. "Women and Politics in Post-Khomeini Iran: Divorce, Veiling, and the Merging of Feminist Voice." In *Women in Politics in the Third World,* ed. Haleh Afshar. London: Routledge.

———. 1999. *Islam and Gender: The Religious Debate in Contemporary Iran.* Princeton: Princeton Univ. Press.

Moghadam, Valentine M. 1993. *Modernizing Women: Gender and Social Change in the Middle East.* Boulder: Lynne Rienner.

———. 2000. "Gender, National Identity, and Citizenship: Reflections on the Middle East and North Africa." *Hagar* 1: 41–70.

———. 2005. *Globalizing Women: Transnational Feminist Networks.* Baltimore: Johns Hopkins Univ. Press.

Mohanty, Chandra T. 1995. "Women Workers and Capitalist Scripts: Ideologies of Domination, Common Interests, and the Politics of Solidarity." In *Feminist Genealogies, Colonial Legacies, Democratic Futures,* ed. M. Jacqui Alexander and Chandra T. Mohanty, 3–29. New York and London: Routledge.

Monsutti, Alessandro. 2004. *Guerres et migrations: Réseaux sociaux et stratégies économiques des hazaras d'Afghanistan.* Neuchâtel and Paris: Éditions de l'Institut d'Ethnologie/Éditions de la Maison des Sciences de l'Homme.

Moors, Annelies. 1995. *Women, Property, and Islam: Palestinian Experiences, 1920–1990.* New York: Cambridge Univ. Press.

———. 1999. "Debating Islamic Family Law: Legal Texts and Social Practices." In *A Social History of Women and Gender in the Modern Middle East,* ed. Margaret L. Meriwether and Judith E. Tucker, 141–75. Boulder: Westview Press.

Morocco. 1994. *Les caractéristiques socio-économiques et socio-démographiques de la population.* Rabat: Direction of Statistics.

———. 1995. *Research for the Setting of a Female Development Action Strategy.* Ministry of Employment and Social Affairs. Rabat: EDESA.

———. 1997. *Répertoire des ONGs oeuvrant dans le domaine de l'intégration des femmes au dévelopment.* Rabat: Ministry of Foreign Affairs and Cooperation.

———. 1998a. *Genre et développement: Aspects socio-demographiques et culturels de la differenciation sexuelle.* Ministry of Economic Prevision and Plan. Rabat: Centre d'Études et de Recherches Démographiques.

———. 1998b. *Secretary of State in Charge of Social Protection, the Family, and Childhood.* Rabat: Socio-demographics and Socio-economics.

———. 1999. *Le plan national pour l'intégration des femmes au développement.* Rabat: Secretary of State in Charge of Social Protection, the Family, and Childhood.

Morvaridi, Behrooz. 1992. "Gender Relations in Agriculture: Women in Turkey." *Economic Development and Cultural Change* 40, no. 3: 567–86.

Mostafa, Magdy. 2003. Interviewed by Frances Hasso. Al-Ain, Abu Dhabi, UAE, Dec. 9.

Moulay R'chid, Abderrazak. 1991. *La femme et la loi au Maroc.* Casablanca: Le Fennec.

Mufid, Khadija. 2000. "Women's Rights Between Crisis and Alternative." In *Women's Rights Between Crisis and Alternative,* ed. Khadija Mufid, 32–47 [in Arabic]. Casablanca: Dar al-Furqan.

Müftüler-Bac, Meltem. 1999. "Turkish Women's Predicament." *Women's Studies International Forum* 22: 305–15.

Mullally, Siobhan. 2004. "Feminism and Multicultural Dilemmas in India: Revisiting the Shah Bano Case." *Oxford Journal of Legal Studies* 24, no. 4: 671–92.

Murshid, Tazeen Mahnaz. "Women, Islam, and the State: Subordination and Resistance." http://www.lib.uchicago.edu/e/su/southasia/Tazeen.html.

Murugayi v. Viramakali. 1877. *Indian Law Reports, Madras Series.* Madras: Government Press.

Muttahida Majlis-e-Amal (MMA). 2002. "Constitution of the Muttahida Majlis-e-Amal" [in Urdu]. Unpublished photocopy. Peshawar.

———. 2003. "Islamization in NWFP: Draft Document." Unpublished photocopy. Peshawar.

———. 2005. "Hasba Act (Amended)." Unpublished photocopy. Peshawar.

Nair, J. 1996. *Women and Law in Colonial India.* New Delhi: Kali for Women.

Nandy, Ashis. 1998. "The Politics of Secularism and the Recovery of Religious Toleration." In *Secularism and Its Critics,* ed. Rajeev Bhargava. Delhi: Oxford Univ. Press.

Narayan, Uma. 1997. *Dislocating Cultures: Identities, Traditions, and Third World Feminism.* New York: Routledge.

Nashwan, Karem. 1998. "Draft Requirements for a Unified Law of Personal Status" [in Arabic]. Unpublished paper prepared for the Model Parliament in Gaza.

Nasr, Seyyed Vali Reza. 1994. *The Vanguard of the Islamic Revolution: The Jama'at-i Islami of Pakistan.* Berkeley and Los Angeles: Univ. of California Press.

———. 2001. *Islamic Leviathan: Islam and the Making of State Power.* Oxford and New York: Oxford Univ. Press.

———. 2002. "Islam, the State, and the Rise of Sectarian Militancy in Pakistan." In *Pakistan: Nationalism Without a Nation?* ed. Christophe Jaffrelot, 85–114. London: Zed Books.

Nayyer, A. H. 2003. "Pakistan: Islamisation of Curricula." *South Asian Journal* 2: 71–87.

Nederveen Pieterse, Jan. 2004. *Globalization and Culture: Global Mélange*. Lanham, Md.: Rowman and Littlefield.

Nelson, Fraser. 2003. "Iraq Aftermath: Analysis—the Coalition Removed Saddam, but Inept Planning Has Delayed the Reconstruction of Iraq." *The Scotsman*, Dec. 24.

Netting, Robert McC., Richard R. Wilk, and Eric J. Arnold, eds. 1984. *Households: Comparative and Historical Studies of the Domestic Group*. Berkeley and Los Angeles: Univ. of California Press.

New Production Processes and Women's Labor [in Turkish]. 1999. Ankara: T. C. Başbakanlık, Kadın Statüsü ve Sorunları Genel Müdürülüğü.

"Notice of Fees Established for the Sharia Courts" [in Arabic]. 1880. In *Dictionary of Administration and the Judiciary*, ed. Filib Jallad, 4:159. Alexandria: Matba'at Yani Laghudaki.

Al-Nowaihi, Mohamed. 1979. "Changing the Law on Personal Status in Egypt Within a Liberal Interpretation of the Shari'a." In *Religion and Politics in the Middle East*, ed. Michael Curtis. Boulder: Westview Press.

"NWFP Government Vows to Defend Hasba Bill at All Fora." 2005. *Dawn*, July 16. http://www.dawn.com/2005/07/16/nat25.htm.

Oldenburg, Veena Talwar. 2002. *Dowry Murder: The Imperial Origins of a Cultural Crime*. New Delhi: Oxford Univ. Press.

Omvedt, Gail. 1994. *Reinventing Revolution: New Social Movements and the Socialist Tradition in India*. New York: M. E. Sharpe.

"Ordinance of Judges" [in Arabic]. 1856. 28 Rabi' II 1273 (Dec. 26, 1856). In *Dictionary of Administration and the Judiciary*, ed. Filib Jallad, 4:129–32. Alexandria: Matba'at Yani Laghudaki.

"Ordinance of the Sharia Courts" [in Arabic]. 1880. 9 Rajab 1297 (June 17, 1880). In *Dictionary of Administration and the Judiciary*, ed. Filib Jallad, 4:145–56. Alexandria: Matba'at Yani Laghudaki.

"Ordinance Organizing the Sharia Courts and the Proceedings Pertaining to Them" [in Arabic]. 1897. May 27. In *Inventory of High Orders and Decrees Issued in the Year 1896*, 155–75. Bulaq, Egypt: Government Press.

Owen, Roger. 1992. *State, Power, and Politics in the Making of the Modern Middle East*. London: Routledge.

Paidar, Parvin. 1995. *Women and the Political Process in Twentieth-Century Iran*. Cambridge: Cambridge Univ. Press.

Pakistan. 2002. *National Policy for Development and Empowerment of Women.* Islamabad: Ministry for Women's Development.

———. 2004. "Hisba Judgement" [in Urdu]. Trans. Juan Cole. Unpublished judgment by the Council of Islamic Ideology, Sept.

Pakistan Institute of Legislative Development and Transparency. 2003. "State of Democracy: Revival of Democracy in Pakistan Report, 3rd Quarter of Democracy, May 16, 2003, to August 15, 2003." Lahore: Pakistan Institute of Legislative Development and Transparency.

Panikkar, K. N., ed. 1991. *Communalism in India: History, Politics, and Culture.* New Delhi: Manohar.

Parasher, Archana. 1992. *Women and Family Law Reform in India: Uniform Civil Code and Gender Equality.* New Delhi: Sage.

Paris, Mirelle. 1989. "Mouvement de femmes et feminism au Maghreb." In *Annuaire de l'Afrique du Nord,* 28:430–44. Paris: Centre National de la Recherche Scientifique.

Parla, Ayşe. 2001. "The 'Honor' of the State: Virginity Examinations in Turkey." *Feminist Studies* 27.

"Parliament of the Iraqi Kurds Rejects the Decision of the Iraqi Governing Council Amending the Law of Personal Status" [in Arabic]. 2004. *Al-Sharq al-Awsat,* Feb. 6.

Pearl, David, and Werner F. Menski. 1998. *Muslim Family Law.* 3rd ed. London: Sweet and Maxwell.

Pervizat, Leylâ. 2003. "In the Name of Honor." In *Human Rights Dialogue: An International Forum for Debating Human Rights,* 2:30–31. http://www.carnegie council.org/viewMedia.php/prmID/1061.

Phillips, Joshua E. S. 2005. "Unveiling Iraq's Teenage Prostitutes." Salon.com, June 24.

Pirzada, Sayyid A. S. 2000. *The Politics of the Jamiat Ulema-i-Islam Pakistan, 1971–77.* Karachi: Oxford Univ. Press.

Poster, Winifred, and Zakia Salime. 2002. "Micro-Credit and the Limits of Transnational Feminism: USAID Activities in the United States and Morocco." In *Women's Activism and Globalization: Linking Local Struggles and Transnational Politics,* ed. Nancy A. Naples and Manisha Desai, 191–219. New York: Routledge.

Punjab District Gazetteer, Rohtak District, 1910. 1911. Lahore: Civil and Military Gazette Press.

Raday, Frances. 1983. "Equality of Women under Israeli Law?" *Jerusalem Quarterly* 27.

———. 2000. "Religion and Equality as Reflected in the Case Law." In *Sepher Berenson*, ed. Aharon Barak and Haim Berenson, 2:341 [in Hebrew]. Jerusalem: Nevo.

———. 2003a. "Culture, Religion, and Gender." *International Constitutional Law Journal* 1, no. 4.

———. 2003b. "The Fight Against Silencing." In *Women of the Wall: Anthology*, ed. Phyllis Deutsch. Lebanon, N.H.: Univ. Press of New England.

———. 2003c. "On Equality: Judicial Profiles." *Israel Law Review* 35.

———. 2003d. "Self-Determination and Minority Rights." *Fordham International Law Journal* 26.

Raday, Frances, Carmel Shalev, and Michal Liban-Kobi, eds. 1995. *Woman's Status in Israeli Law and Society* [in Hebrew]. Tel Aviv: Shocken.

Rahman, Abu Tayeb Rafiqur. 2002. *Human Security in Bangladesh: In Search of Justice and Dignity.* Dhaka: United Nations Development Programme.

Rahman, Saira. 2004. "Reflections on Women and Violence in Bangladesh." Asia-Pacific Human Rights Information Center (HURIGHTS OSAKA). http://www/hurights.or.jp/asia-pacific/no_24/05Saira.htm.

Rajaee, Bahram. 2000. "The Politics of Refugee Policy in Post-Revolutionary Iran." *Middle East Journal* 54, no. 1: 44–63.

Rakover, Nachum. 1980. *Yearbook of Jewish Law,* 6–7 [in Hebrew].

Rama Appa v. Sakhu Dattu. 1954. Bombay High Court. *All India Reporter.* Nagpur: All India Reporter.

Ranchod Nilsson, Sita, and Mary Anne Tétreault, eds. 2000. *Women, States, and Nationalism: At Home in the Nation?* London: Routledge.

Rashid, Ahmad. 2001. *Taliban: Islam, Oil, and the New Great Game in Central Asia.* London: I. B. Tauris.

Rashiduzzaman, M. 1994. "The Liberals and the Religious Right in Bangladesh." *Asian Survey* 34: 974–90.

———. 1997. "The Dichotomy of Islam and Development: NGOs, Women's Development, and Fatawa in Bangladesh." *Contemporary South Asia* 6: 239–46.

Riesebrodt, Martin. 1993. *Pious Passion: The Emergence of Modern Fundamentalism in the United States and Iran.* Trans. Don Reneau. Berkeley and Los Angeles: Univ. of California Press.

Rubinstein, Amnon. 1991. *Constitutional Law of the State of Israel* [in Hebrew]. Tel Aviv: Shocken.

Rugh, Andrea B. 1993. "Reshaping Personal Relations in Egypt." In *Fundamentalisms and Society: Reclaiming the Sciences, the Family, and Education,* ed. Martin E. Marty and R. Scott Appleby, 151–80. Chicago: Univ. of Chicago Press.

Sağlık Sektöründe Kadın [Women in the Health Sector]. 2000. Ankara: T. C. Başbakanlık, Kadın Statüsü ve Sorunları Genel Müdürülüğü.

Said, Atef Shahat. 2003. Interviewed by Frances Hasso. Zamalek, Cairo, Egypt, Dec. 22.

Salime, Zakia. 1997. "Frauen in der Marokkanischen Ôkonomie: Veränderungen und Strukturanpassung." *Informationsprojekt Naher und Mittlrer Osten* (INAMO) 9: 11–17.

———. 1998. "L'entreprise feminine à Fès, une tradition." In *Initiatives féminines,* ed. Aïcha Belarbi, 31–46. Casablanca: Le Fennec.

———. 2001. "Femmes-politique-alliance difficile: Parole de jeunes." In *Femmes et democratie: La grande question,* ed. Aïcha Belarbi, 37–66. Casablanca: Le Fennec.

———. 2007. "The War on Terrorism: Appropriation and Subversion by Moroccan Women." *Signs: Journal for Women in Culture and Society* 33, no. 1: 1–24.

———. Forthcoming. "Between Feminism and Islam: New Political Transformations and Movements in Morocco." Working title. Minneapolis: Univ. of Minnesota Press.

Sandler, Lauren. 2003. "So This Is Liberation?" *Nation,* Dec. 17.

Sangari, K., and S. Vaid, eds. 1989. *Recasting Women: Essays in Colonial History.* New Delhi: Kali for Women.

Sansarian, Eliz. 1982. *The Women's Rights Movement in Iran: Mutiny, Appeasement, and Repression from 1900 to Khomeini.* New York: Praeger.

Santos, Boaventura de Sousa. 1995. *Toward a New Legal Common Sense.* New York: Routledge.

Sarker, Abu Elias. 2003. "The Illusion of Decentralization: Evidence from Bangladesh." *International Journal of Public Sector Management* 16: 523–48.

Al-Sawi, Ahmad b. Muhammad. 1995. *Sufficiency for the Traveller for the Nearest Path on the Short Explication of . . . Ahmad al-Dardir* [on al-Dardir's *Nearest Path*]. 4 vols. Beirut: Dar al-Kutub al-'Ilmiyya.

Al-Sayegh, Ma'sooma, and 'Uday al-Qazweeni. 2003. Interviewed by Frances Hasso. Dubai, UAE, Dec. 4.

Shafqat, Saeed. 2002. "From Official Islam to Islamism: The Rise of Dawat-ul-Irshad and Lashkar-e-Taiba." In *Pakistan: Nationalism Without a Nation?* ed. Christophe Jaffrelot, 131–47. London: Zed Books.

Shaham, Ron. 1997. *Family and the Courts in Modern Egypt: A Study Based on Decisions by the Shari'a Courts, 1900–1955.* Leiden: Brill.

Shahine, Gihan. 1999. "Illegitimate, Illegal, or Just Ill-Advised?" *Al-Ahram Weekly Online*, Feb. 18–24. http://www.ahram.org.eg/weekly/1999/417/li1.htm.

Sharabi, Hisham. 1988. *Neopatriarchy: A Theory of Distorted Change in Arab Society.* New York: Oxford Univ. Press.

Al-Sharif, Anisa. 2003. Interviewed by Frances Hasso. Dubai, UAE, Dec. 8.

Shawa, Menashe. 1991. *The Personal Law in Israel* [in Hebrew]. 3rd ed. Tel Aviv: Massada.

Sherif, Bahira. 1999. "The Prayer of a Married Man Is Equal to Seventy Prayers of a Single Man: The Central Role of Marriage among Upper-Middle-Class Muslim Egyptians." *Journal of Family Issues* 20, no. 5: 617–32.

Sheth, D. L. 1990. "Nation-Building in Multi-ethnic Societies: The Experience of South Asia." In *Beyond Darkness: Some Reflections on Communalism*, 17–24. Bangalore, India: CIEDS Collective and EKTA.

Sh'hada, Nahda. 1999. "Gender and Politics in Palestine: Discourse Analysis of the Palestinian Authority and Islamists." ISS Working Paper no. 307. The Hague: Institute of Social Studies.

———. 2005. "Justice Without Drama: Enacting Family Law in Gaza City Shari'a Court." Ph.D. thesis, Institute of Social Sciences.

Al-Shibel, Luna. 2004. "The Secret Marriage in Our Arab World: Its Reasons and Precariousness." Episode of the weekly program *For Women Only*, al-Jazeera Arabic satellite station, Dec. 27. Trans. Suha al-Qattan.

Shochatman, Eliav. 1995. *Woman's Status in Israeli Law and Society.* Ed. Frances Raday et al. [in Hebrew]. Tel Aviv: Shocken.

Shorter, Fredric C., and Huda Zurayk. 1988. *The Social Composition of the Household in Arab Cities: Cairo, Beirut, Amman.* Regional Papers no. 31. Cairo: Population Council.

Singerman, Diane. 1990. "Politics at the Household Level in a Popular Quarter of Cairo." *Journal of South Asian and Middle Eastern Studies* 12, no. 4: 3–21.

———. 1995. *Avenues of Participation: Family, Politics, and Networks in Urban Quarters of Cairo.* Princeton: Princeton Univ. Press.

———. 2005. "Rewriting Divorce in Egypt: Reclaiming Islam, Legal Activism, and Coalition Politics." In *Remaking Muslim Politics: Pluralism, Contestation, Democratization*, ed. Robert W. Hefner, 161–88. Princeton: Princeton Univ. Press.

Singerman, Diane, and Homa Hoodfar, eds. 1996. *Development, Change, and Gender in Cairo: A View from the Household.* Bloomington: Indiana Univ. Press.

Singerman, Diane, and Barbara Ibrahim. 2003. "The Cost of Marriage in Egypt: A Hidden Variable in the New Arab Demography." In *The New Arab Family,* ed. Nicholas S. Hopkins. *Cairo Papers in Social Science* 24, nos. 1–2: 80–116. Cairo: American Univ. in Cairo Press.

Sirman, Nükhet. 1989. "Feminism in Turkey: A Short History." *New Perspectives on Turkey* 3: 1–34.

Smith, Dorothy E. 1987. *The Everyday World as Problematic: A Feminist Sociology.* Boston: Northeastern Univ. Press.

Sonbol, Amira El Azhary. 1996a. "Adults and Minors in Ottoman *Shari'a* Courts and Modern Law." In *Women, the Family, and Divorce Laws,* ed. Amira El Azhary Sonbol, 236–56. Syracuse: Syracuse Univ. Press.

———, ed. 1996b. *Women, the Family, and Divorce Laws.* Syracuse: Syracuse Univ. Press.

South Asia Citizens Web. 2004. "Threats of Violence and Violations of Human Rights by Imams of Mosques and the Religious Right in Bangladesh." http://www.sacw.net/FreeExpAndFundos/threats.html.

State Institute of Statistics, Türkiye'de Kadın Bilgi Ağı. 2004. http://www.die.gov.tr/tkba/istatistikler.htm.

Statistical Indicators, 1923–2002. 2003. Ankara: State Institute of Statistics.

Steele, Arthur. 1827. *The Hindu Castes, Their Law, Religion, and Customs.* Bombay: Courier Press; Delhi: Mittal.

Stowasser, Barbara. 1994. *Women in the Qur'an, Traditions, and Interpretations.* New York: Oxford Univ. Press.

———. 1998. "Gender Issues and Contemporary Qur'an Interpretation." In *Islam, Gender, and Social Change,* ed. John Esposito and Yvonne Haddad, 30–44. Oxford: Oxford Univ. Press.

Sultan Al Olama, Shaikh Mohammad Abdul Rahim. 2003. Interviewed by Frances Hasso. Al-Ain, Abu Dhabi, UAE, Dec. 9.

Sunder Rajan, Rajeswari. 2003. *The Scandal of the State: Women, Law, and Citizenship in Postcolonial India.* Durham: Duke Univ. Press.

Supporting Women's Enterprises in Turkey [in Turkish]. 2000. Ankara: T. C. Başbakanlık, Kadın Statüsü ve Sorunları Genel Müdürülüğü.

Tadros, Mariz. 2000. "One Step Forward, a Hundred to Go." *Al-Ahram Weekly Online,* Jan. 13–19. http://www.ahram.org.eg/weekly/2000/464/spec1.htm.

Tapper, Nancy. 1984. "Causes and Consequences of the Abolition of Bride-Price in Afghanistan." In *Revolution and Rebellion in Afghanistan,* ed. Nazif Shahrani and Robert Canfield. Berkeley: Institute for International Studies.

Tapper, Richard, ed. 1983. *The Conflict of Tribe and State in Iran and Afghanistan.* New York: St. Martin's Press.

Tekeli, Şirin, ed. 1982. *Women, Political Life, and Public Domain* [in Turkish]. Ankara: Birikim Yayınları.

Tilly, Charles, ed. 1975. *The Formation of the Nation State in Western Europe.* Princeton: Princeton Univ. Press.

Tripp, Charles. 2000. *A History of Iraq.* Cambridge: Cambridge Univ. Press.

Tucker, Judith. 1985. *Women in Nineteenth-Century Egypt.* Cambridge: Cambridge Univ. Press.

————. 1998. *In the House of the Law: Gender and Islamic Law in Ottoman Syria and Palestine.* Berkeley and Los Angeles: Univ. of California Press.

Türkiye'de Kadınlara Ait Girişimlerin Desteklenmesi [Supporting Women's Enterprises in Turkey]. 2000. Ankara: T. C. Başbakanlık, Kadın Statüsü ve Sorunları Genel Müdürülüğü.

United Nations Development Fund for Women (UNIFEM). 2004. *Report of Mission to Herat (17–21 Feb).* Afghanistan: Gender and Law Working Group.

United Nations Development Programme (UNDP). 1990. *Human Development Report, 1990.* New York: Oxford Univ. Press.

————. 1998. *Human Development Report, 1999.* New York: Oxford Univ. Press.

————. 1999. *Human Development Report, 1999.* New York: Oxford Univ. Press.

————. 2004. *Human Development Report, 2004.* New York: Oxford Univ. Press.

United Nations Division for the Advancement of Women. 1979. "Convention on the Elimination of All Forms of Discrimination Against Women (CEDAW)." http://www.un.org/womenwatch/daw/cedaw/.

————. 1995. "Fourth World Conference on Women." Platform for Action, Beijing. http://www.un.org/womenwatch/daw/beijing/platform/.

————. 2002. "Optional Protocol to the Convention on the Elimination of All Forms of Discrimination Against Women (A/RES/54/4)." http://www.un.org/womenwatch/daw/cedaw/protocol/text.htm.

————. 2005. "Review and Appraisal of the Beijing Declaration and Platform for Action and the Outcome Document of the Twenty-third Special Session of the General Assembly." Feb 28–Mar. 11. http://www.un.org/womenwatch/daw/Review/english/49sess.htm.

————. 2007. "Consideration of Reports Submitted by States Parties under Article 18 of the Convention on the Elimination of All Forms of Discrimination Against Women." Pakistan. http://daccessdds.un.org/doc/UNDOC/GEN/N05/454/37/PDF/N0545437.pdf?OpenElement.

United Nations General Assembly (UNGA). 1994. Resolution Adopted on the Report of the Third Committee (A/48/629). "Implementation of the Nairobi Forward-Looking Strategies for the Advancement of Women." 48/108. Feb. 28. http://www.un.org/esa/gopher-data/conf/fwcw/nfls/ar48-108.en.

United Nations High Commissioner of Human Rights (UNHCHR). 1952. *Convention on the Political Rights of Women.* http://www.unhchr.ch/html/menu3/b/22.htm.

———. 1989. *Convention on the Rights of the Child.* http://www.ohchr.org/english/law/crc.htm.

———. 1993. *Vienna Declaration and Programme of Action.* http://www.ohchr.org/english/law/vienna.htm.

United Nations International Conference on Population and Development (UNICPD). 1994. *Programme of Action.* Cairo. http://www.iisd.ca/Cairo/program/p00000.html.

Urban Women as a Potential Workforce and Its Transformation [in Turkish]. 1999. Ankara: T. C. Başbakanlık, Kadın Statüsü ve Sorunları Genel Müdürülüğü.

Vanaik, Achin. 1997. *Communalism Contested: Religion, Modernity, and Secularization.* New Delhi: Vistaar.

Visvanathan, Nalini, Lynn Duggan, Laurie Nisonoff, and Nan Wiegersma, eds. 1997. *Gender and Development Reader.* London: Zed Books.

Vithu v. Govind. 1898. *Indian Law Reports, Bombay Series.* Bombay: Government Press.

Wadud, Amina. 1999. *Qur'an and Woman: Rereading the Sacred Text from a Woman's Perspective.* New York: Oxford Univ. Press.

Weisband, Edward, and Sera Öner. 2007. "So Near, yet So Far: Freedom of Association and Workers' Rights." In *Human Rights in Turkey,* ed. Z. F. Kabasakal Arat, 105–22. Philadelphia: Univ. of Pennsylvania Press.

Weiss, Anita M., ed. 1986. *Islamic Reassertion in Pakistan: The Application of Islamic Laws in a Modern State.* Syracuse: Syracuse Univ. Press.

———. 1999. "Women, Civil Society, and Politics in Pakistan." *Citizenship Studies* 3, no. 1: 141–50.

———. 2003. "Interpreting Women's Rights: The Dilemma over Eliminating Discrimination Against Women in Pakistan." *International Sociology* 18, no. 3: 581–601.

Weiss, Anita M., and S. Zulfiqar Gilani, eds. 2001. *Power and Civil Society in Pakistan.* Oxford: Oxford Univ. Press.

Welchman, Lynn. 2000. *Beyond the Code: Muslim Family Law and the Shar'i Judiciary in the Palestinian West Bank.* The Hague: Kluwer Law International.

————. 2003. "In the Interim: Civil Society, the *Shar'i* Judiciary, and Palestinian Personal Status Law in the Transitional Period." *Islamic Law and Society* 10, no. 1: 34–69.

————, ed. 2004. *Women's Rights and Islamic Family Law: Perspectives on Reform.* London: Zed Press.

West, Lois, ed. 1997. *Feminist Nationalism.* London: Routledge.

"We Will Not Get Used to It! Killings in the Name of 'Honor'" [in Turkish]. 2003. In *KA-MER 2003 Report.* Diyarbakır: KA-MER.

"Whose Work Is Housework?" [in Turkish]. 2006. BİA Haber Merkezi. http://www.bianet.org/2006/01/20/73566.htm.

Wiley, Joyce N. 1992. *The Islamic Movement of Iraqi Shi'ites.* Boulder: Lynne Rienner.

Wolfowitz, Paul. 2004. "Women in the New Iraq." *Washington Post,* Feb. 1.

Women in the Health Sector [in Turkish]. 2000. Ankara: T. C. Başbakanlık, Kadın Statüsü ve Sorunları Genel Müdürülüğü.

"Women on Iraqi Council, United in Gender, Have Divergent Views." 2003. Knight Ridder, Nov. 20.

Women's Status, Problems, and Proposed Solutions from a Human Rights Perspective [in Turkish]. 1999. Ankara: İnsan Hakları Koordinator Üst Kurulu.

Wong, Ed. 2005. "Iraqi Constitution May Curb Women's Rights." *New York Times,* Aug. 20.

World Organization Against Torture (OMCT). 2003. "Press Release: OMCT Observes the International Day for the Elimination of Violence Against Women." Nov. 25. http://www.omct.org/base.cfm?_page=article&num=3823&consol=close&kwrd=EQL.

Yamani, Mai. 1996. Introduction to *Feminism and Islam: Legal and Literary Perspectives,* ed. Mai Yamani, 1–29. New York: New York Univ. Press.

Yeni Üretim Süreçleri ve Kadın Emeği [New Production Processes and Women's Labor]. 1999. Ankara: T. C. Başbakanlık, Kadın Statüsü ve Sorunları Genel Müdürülüğü.

Yıldırak, Nurettin, et al. 2003. *The Work and Living Conditions and Problems of Migrant and Temporary Female Farm Workers in Turkey* [in Turkish]. Ankara: Tarım-İş.

Yüksel, Şahika. 1990. "Battering by Spouses and the Solidarity Campaign Against Battering." In *Turkey in the 1980s from Women's Perspective,* ed. Şirin Tekeli, 315–24 [in Turkish]. Istanbul: İletişim Yayınları.

Yunis, Feisal Abd al-Qadir. 2003. Interviewed by Frances Hasso. Cairo, Egypt, Dec. 20.

Zerrini, Caroline. 2000. "Triumphant Milestone for Urfi Marriages." http://www
.arabia.com/life/article/print/english/0,4973,37528,00.html.

Zeytinoğlu, Işık Urla. 1998. "Constructing Images as Employment Restrictions:
Determinants of Female Labor in Turkey." In *Deconstructing Images of "the
Turkish Woman,"* ed. Zehra F. Arat, 183–98. New York: St. Martin's Press.

Ziai, Fati. 1997. "Personal Status Codes and Women's Rights in the Maghreb." In
*Muslim Women and the Politics of Participation: Implementing the Beijing Plat-
form,* ed. Mahnaz Afkhami and Erika Friedl, 72–82. Syracuse: Syracuse Univ.
Press.

Zoughlami, Neila. 1989. "Quel feminisme dans les groupes-femmes." *Annuaire de
l'Afrique du Nord* 28: 443–53. Paris: CNRS.

Zuhur, Sherifa. 2001. "The Mixed Impact of Feminist Struggles in Egypt During
the 1990s." *Middle East Review of International Affairs Journal* 5, no. 1. http://
meria.idc.ac.il/journal/2001/issue1/jv5n1a6.html.

Index

Italic page numbers denote tables.